PARODY//META-FICTION

PARODY//
META-FICTION

AN ANALYSIS OF PARODY AS
A CRITICAL MIRROR TO THE WRITING AND
RECEPTION OF FICTION

MARGARET A. ROSE

CROOM HELM LONDON

© 1979 Margaret A. Rose
Croom Helm Ltd, 2–10 St John's Road, London SW11

British Library Cataloguing in Publication Data

Rose, Margaret, b. 1947
    Parody / meta-fiction
    1. Parody
    I. Title
    809.3   PN6149.P3

    ISBN 0-85664-883-3

Printed in Great Britain by
REDWOOD BURN LIMITED
Trowbridge & Esher

CONTENTS

ILLUSTRATIONS

ACKNOWLEDGEMENTS

I would like to take this opportunity to thank Professor Leslie Bodi and Dr David Roberts of the German Department, Monash University, Victoria, for their initial encouragement of this study, Professor Ian Donaldson, Director of the Humanities Research Centre, Canberra, for the opportunity to hold a three-day seminar on the subject of literary parody in June 1976 and the speakers and participants who attended the seminar. Part of Chapter 1 of this study is based on a paper given at that seminar, which, with other papers, will be published in a special number on Parody of *Southern Review* (Adelaide) in 1980, while part of Chapter 4.1 was read at the XIVth FILLM congress in Aix-en-Provence in August 1978 and will appear in abstract in its proceedings. I should also like to thank Dr George Davie, Edinburgh, for the opportunity to discuss some of the work with him and colleagues and for his perseverence in encouraging it. Special thanks go to Dr Gunther Witting (Konstanz) for permission to reproduce his original photo-montage and for the opportunity to read a proof copy of the study of parody in modern German literature which he and Professor Theodor Verweyen have recently completed. My thanks go also to the Alexander von Humboldt Stiftung for the opportunity to complete my research in Düsseldorf and Konstanz and, not least, to my publishers for their assistance in preparing the manuscript.

Our parodies are ended. These our authors,
As we foretold you, were all Spirits, and
Are settled into air, into thin air.
And, like the baseless fabric of these verses,
The Critic's puff, the Trade's advertisement,
The patron's promise, and the World's applause, —
Yes, all the hopes of poets — shall dissolve,
And, like this unsubstantial fable fated,
Leave not a groat behind!

> Horace Twiss — after Shakespeare,
> whose own comedies proved, however,
> that parody could leave many literary
> riches in its wake

INTRODUCTION

It is little wonder that, following the Russian Formalists' use of literary parodies such as *Don Quixote* and *Tristram Shandy* in their influential theories, present structuralist and post astructuralist criticism should not only be debating questions raised by those parodies — such as the role of discontinuity in literary history and the structural problems of 'intertextuality' and 'interiority' — but that it should have begun to apply meta-literary questions to itself, and to see itself (like most other forms of 'strong reading') as 'parody'. A discussion of these phenomena, and of the history of the usage and definition of parody will be linked in this study to an analysis of the role of parody as a meta-fictional mirror to fiction, and as an 'archaeology' of the text in modern Western literature.

As a form of meta-fiction, parody has often been used as a basis for general literary theory, and to study such parody is to study the analysis of fiction made from within fiction itself. Recently Michel Foucault has also implicitly suggested a role for parody in the transformation of the epistemes and discourses of an age, on the basis of his analysis of *Don Quixote* in *Les Mots et les Choses*, and in this study parody will also be considered as a reflexive 'archaeology' of the text, in which epistemological, historical and social conditions affecting the composition and reception of fictional texts are foregrounded and analysed.

Though critics of today have — like the Structuralists and Formalists before them — based general theories on the analysis of specific parody texts, the parodist's intimate understanding of the complex nature of communication between author and reader, of the problematic character of the writer's representation of reality, and of the importance of the roles played by publishers, censors and other such figures of authority in the production and distribution of the book has not always been given its due. It is now time to return to a study of literary parody itself, and to works which — by analysing the act of communication between author and reader from within fiction — have set up meta-fictional 'mirrors' to the processes of writing which tell us much about the aims and character of fiction, while also challenging the use of art to 'mirror' the outer world.

As a form of meta-fiction parody has also served to expand the corpus of fiction, contributing to progress in literary history, while also presenting critiques of the epistemological processes, structural problems, and social assumptions involved in the writing and reception of literary texts. The present study — while exploring the possibilities and limits to meta-fictional analysis — thus also seeks to establish a basis for further exploration of the multiplicity of literary, philosophical and social problems relating to the presentation of the reader and the book within fiction which literary criticism now explores over a broad range of literary forms, but which parody has always, in comic or ironic manner, attempted to carry out from within literature itself, as an archaeology of its own medium.

Finally, following a survey of the use and definition of the term in earlier periods of literary history, and a theoretical analysis of parody as a reflexive form of meta-fiction which 'lays bare' the devices of fiction to refunction them for new purposes, this study seeks to suggest how parody could become both a symptom and a critical tool of the modernist episteme. Here the sceptical analysis of language, the criticism of the concept of art as a reflection and reproduction of its subject, and the Formalists' and Structuralists' interest in discontinuity in discourse, and in its place in the history of their episteme, are all seen to be expressed in the modern use of parody as a self-reflexive and self-critical, as well as satirical, form of discourse.

PART ONE: DEFINING PARODY

1 WAYS OF DEFINING PARODY

Definitions have the function of setting limits to the meaning of words, limits which also serve as signposts to the analysis of texts, but which are themselves defined and limited by historical, social and linguistic factors. Thus they both reflect the interests of certain historical ages, and influence the historian's selection and canonisation of certain texts. These two aspects of the historicity of literary terms should be borne in mind in tracing the history of the usage of the term 'parody', and in formulating new limits to its meaning. Even seeming historical approaches to the definition of the term have concealed a lack of historical thinking. So, for example, the OED definition of parody as παρῳδια as meaning 'a burlesque poem or song' has been based on an eighteenth-century view of parody, while the word 'burlesque', which it uses as a synonym for parody and the ancient Hellenistic concept of παρῳδια it seeks to define, is only traceable to the seventeenth century. Many misunderstandings are, and have been, generated by such 'definitions', and a more critical approach seems necessary.

Traditionally, parody has been defined in the terms of either

1. its etymology;
2. its usage as comedy in literary texts or in speeches as a rhetorical device ('specific parody');
3. the attitude of the parodist to the work parodied and to the reader;
4. the effect of parody on the reader;
5. the structure of texts in which parody is not just a specific technique but the mode of the work itself ('general parody' as in Cervantes' *Don Quixote*).

Several attempts have been made to clarify the concept of parody, by limiting or expanding such typologies, but the complexity of great parody, as found in the works of Aristophanes, or Cervantes, has rarely been acknowledged as implying the necessity of investigating *all* of the above categories at once in a theory of parody. Before such a task can be undertaken, some of the older problems relating to the definition of the term must be tackled, and in the following sections of this chapter various aspects of parody, and its definition, will be discussed in the sequence suggested above.

1.1 Etymology

Dispute and uncertainty have prevailed for some time in the definition of the etymological root of the word parody. Of all terms used to describe comic quotation or imitation (such as burlesque, pastiche, persiflage) parody alone has its roots in the classical literature and poetics of the Greeks, and has gained some importance in the Western tradition from this fact. But it is also due to this long history that the meaning of the term has become the subject of so much argument. This is so not just because time has allowed dispute to propagate itself, but because, in time, records of its earliest usage have been lost. Some interpreters of the ancient meaning of 'parodia' ($\pi\alpha\rho\omega\delta\iota\alpha$) have described it as a song sung in opposition to another on the basis of evidence about the 'parodes' sung by the Homeric rhapsodists of the 5th century BC. Even this evidence is, however, not complete enough, and critics have had to resort to supposition. Whereas some commentators attribute the parodes to the rhapsodists, others claim that 'parodoi' improvised imitations of the Homeric hexameters to create variety for the audience of the rhapsodists. The word 'paradoi' (singular 'parodos'), meaning 'singing in imitation' or an 'imitating singer',[1] is in fact thought to be older than the word 'parodia' ('imitative song'),which is not found before Aristotle, who applies it in his *Poetics*[2] to Hegemon's 'Gigantomachia', thought by some to be a mock-heroic satyr play similar in form to Euripides' 'Cyclops'.

The earliest complete example of an epic 'parode' extant is the mock-heroic epic of the 'Battle of the Frogs and the Mice', the *Batrachomyomachia*.[3] Athenäus had named Hipponax as the founder of the genre, but our knowledge of the Ancients' usage of the word 'parodia' is obviously sketchy. Other fragments of information are that one non-Homeric parodist from that period mentioned by Athenäus (following Polemo) was Sopater, the phlyakographer, a writer of comic dramatic sketches. Other forms of parody were the cento (a string of quotations, termed a 'quodlibet' after the Baroque), and the 'silloi', epic poems used to attack philosophical arguments. Dryden's dedication to *Juvenal* of 1697 speaks of them as 'satyric poems, full of parodies; that is verses patch'd up from great poets and turned into another sense than their author intended them'.[4]

Other critics have looked to the Athenian satyr plays and to the 'paratragoedia' rather than to the mock Homeric epics to describe the meaning of 'parodia' for the Greeks. They have described 'parodia' as a song sung next to that sung by the chorus of the drama, and the word 'paratragoedia' has been applied by some critics[5] to Aristophanes' comedies, in which examples of parodic choruses can be found. In *The Frogs* the eponymous creatures indeed appear to be used to ironically 'foreground'[6] this convention of the comedy. While Dionysus attempts to row Charon's barge, expecting to take his rhythm from that of the frogs' singing, the frogs (who are also used to parody the verses of Euripides) begin singing in an 'opposite' metre (trochaic against iambic), winning the battle when Dionysus naively proclaims his victory over them in their metre! This combination of chorus and battle demonstrates, moreover, how Aristophanes did not restrict parody to the chorus in the 'paratragoedia'. The old Attic comedy, as we see it in his works, consisted of an introduction of a humorous nature by the chorus (which was called the 'parodos'), the 'agon' (or contest), and the 'Parabasis', the chorus' address to the audience. Ironic remarks about the audience were often made from the stage in parts of the play other than the parabasis, as in *The Frogs*:[7]

> *Dionysus.* Any sign of those murderers and perjurers he told us about?
> *Xanthius.* Use your eyes, sir.
> *Dionysus.* (Seeing the audience): By Jove, yes, I see them now. Well, what are we going to do?
> *Xanthius.* We'd better be pushing on guvnor. The place is full of 'orrible monsters, or so the gentleman said.

Parodies were also to be found in the 'agon' as well as in the chorus. An example of the latter may be found in Aeschylus' parody of Euripides in the 'agon' of *The Frogs*, which is followed by Aristophanes' ironic imitation of Aeschylus' own style in the latter's example of his 'superior' verse.[8] The word 'parodos' was also used in the time of Aristophanes to describe the side entrance to the right of the stage in the ancient theatre.

1.2 The Comic Effect in Parody

Here we shall also briefly discuss definitions of parody as a technique of stylistic 'imitation' and distortion, and definitions of the techniques used by the parodist to achieve these ends. More detailed analyses of these techniques will be given in Part Two.

Assuming that Aristotle was speaking of a mock-epic, and not of a satyr play when using the term 'parodia', Fred J. Householder, Jnr. defines 'parodia'[9] as a 'narrative poem of moderate length, in epic metre, using epic vocabulary, and treating a light, satirical, or mock-heroic subject', and borrowing its words and phrases from Homer. But Householder also points out that scholiasts had defined parody as a technique, and not used it to describe a specific genre. In view of this argument the application of the word to two apparently different genres — the drama and the mock-epic — can be seen as an extension of the term rather than as 'misuse'. The scholiasts had spoken of parody as a 'device for comic quotation',[10] and, in commenting on Aristophanes, had described its main characteristics as the juxtaposition of the comic and the tragic, the substitution of words, and paraphrase. Thus, when Quintilian, in his *Institutia Oratoria*, speaks of parody as 'a name drawn from songs sung in imitation of others, but employed by an abuse of language to designate imitation in verse or prose' (Book 9, 2, 35) he may be speaking of an 'abuse' which is in fact reversing an earlier abuse of the term. Householder's interpretation of the scholiasts' definition implies that the restriction of the term parody (as either $\pi\alpha\rho\omega\delta\iota\alpha$ or $\pi\alpha\rho\omega\delta\eta$) to 'songs' was itself, that is, an abuse of a term formerly used to describe comic quotation in any genre or speech. Many problems with the term are resolved by this interpretation of its use by the scholiasts. For them, as again for Quintilian, parody was, moreover, a device for *comic* quotation, an important qualification, which has served to distinguish parody from other literary forms of imitation or criticism. One form of parody recognised by both the scholiasts and the rhetoricians was the pun, a figure found in several genres. Quintilian approaches the definition of the scholiasts in speaking of 'prosopopoeia' ('impersonation'), the portrayal of character by appropriate speeches, when he calls the imitation of the style of written documents 'a figure close to $\pi\alpha\rho\omega\delta\eta$', but the comic effect of parody must not be omitted from its definition if it is to serve a useful, distinct purpose as a literary term.

Householder has pointed out that the scholiasts attributed a comic effect to parody, and that often an adjective designating humour was attached to the term. Quintilian, like the scholiasts, discusses the pun as a form of parody, and in Book 6 speaks of it when discussing wit, and writes that: 'Apt quotation of verse may add to the effect of wit.' Speaking more specifically, he adds that wit may also be created by the 'invention of verses resembling well-known lines, a trick styled parody by the Greeks'. The attribution of a comic effect of parody also, however, introduces into its definition the question of the role played by the reader in the reception of the parodist's text, and in the parodist's evocation of certain expectations in his readers by the quotation of a text.

One recent criticism of the definition of parody as comic has been offered by Sander L. Gilman, in his work, *The Parodic Sermon*.[11]

Gilman accuses Erwin Rotermund of having made a typical mistake in defining parody as comic, in not distinguishing the description of a mode — that is, structural discrepancy between texts in the parody — from the evaluation of the comic effect of this mode on the reader. Gilman is particularly concerned to avoid the intentional fallacy of ascribing a particular intention to an author from the effect of his text. But this does not mean we must exclude the comic 'effect' from our definition of parody. The comic element is clearly described as an effect in classical criticism and only in modern times has the effect become confused with the structure of the work itself. Granting this distinction, the effect of parody on the reader (be it comic, surprising, or shocking) need not be excluded from a description of the work as a whole — particularly when many parodists (such as Cervantes) have put a reader, as the recipient of the comic effect produced by the contrast between texts, into their parody in the figure of fictional readers. These readers may be easily recognised in caricature, or only implied.

It is, however, the case, that the attribution of the comic effect to parody has misled many literary historians into seeing the parodist as merely a mocker of other texts, and to condemning parody on moral grounds. Yet the complicated structure of the parody — in which the target text may not only be satirised but also 'refunctioned'[12] — often conceals a more subtle use of other literary works than is implied by the term 'mock' when it is used in the sense of 'mockery' or 'spoof'. The ambiguity of the word 'mock' is terms such as 'mock-epic' is often over-looked, moreover, for there it means both spoof and counterfeit, as in 'mock-disbelief'. One of the chief sources of the comic effect in parody has, moreover, been the incongruous juxtaposition of texts, in which counterfeit may play a preparatory role in evoking the reader's expectations for imitation.

1.3 Imitation and Incongruity

In his *Institutio Oratoria* (Book 6, 3, 85) Quintilian had described 'simulatio' and 'dissimulatio' as methods used in some forms of wit, and other rhetoricians following Quintilian have attributed these functions to both irony and parody. Though the terms assume a reflec-tive function to be the aim of the ironist or parodist, the 'simulation' of other styles has been a technique used by many parodists to elicit the expectations of their audience for a text, before presenting another in which the parodist may also use the text of his target as a 'word-mask' behind which to conceal the meaning of his own. Thus parody may also use dissimulation to achieve its critical ends, but in such parody the target text may either be the object of satire or a mask used primarily to allow other targets to be attacked in a covert manner, where direct criticism might run the danger of bringing down censorship (or a libel suit) onto the parodist, or where the parodist may in fact wish to defend the parodied text as having been reduced to parody by its imitation by other writers or poetasters, or by the misreadings of readers or critics.

Alfred Liede has argued in his article on Parody,[13] that parody is only a special form of conscious imitation (which he sees as an age-old human activity), and that it is 'above all' an exercise in learning or perfecting a technique or style. This very basic stylistic approach to parody runs into the danger, however, of reducing it to several different aesthetic types (Liede lists for example 'artistische', 'agitatorische', 'kritische' parody), and of restricting it to a form of imitation while ignoring its wider meta-fictional and historical functions. According to Liede (in what becomes a somewhat circular argument) the most popular form of parody is 'artistic parody', the ultimate goal of which is 'complete imitation', in which it is the success of the similarity of the parody to its model which determines its level of artistic quality. The conclusion of this argument is, therefore, that complete artistry in the writing of parody exists when 'it is not able to be distinguished from the original'. Both Liede's argument and his conclusion must be viewed critically, as also his extension of his criterion of imitation to other types of parody, as when, for example, he claims that the aim of polemical parody to 'destroy' its original means that the successful polemical parody will consist in making itself look as little like the original as possible. In all cases Liede's central criterion for the parody is its imitative relationship to its model. A history of parody will show, however, that parody has served to bring the concept of imitation itself into question, and that while imitation may be used as a technique in the parody it is the use of incongruity which distinguishes the parody from other forms of quotation and literary imitation, and shows its function to be more than imitation alone. The criticism of imitation implicit in much meta-fictional parody will be returned to in considering the role of parody in the critical refunctioning of the functions of literary language in the 'modernist episteme', in Part Two of this study.

Incongruity or discrepancy will be taken as a significant distinguishing factor in parody in our definition. But rather than restrict ourselves to the older distinction between ideal and reality, high and low, in explaining the factors involved in the creation of discrepancy in the parody, we will attribute a comic effect in parody to the perception of any type of incongruity, be it dissimilarity or anachronistic similarity

between texts. This approach may bring us closer to the classical understanding of parody as a device for comic quotation, without obscuring
the changing historical nature of both the subject-matter of the parody
and its form itself. In specific satirical attacks on other texts discrepancy between the parodied text and its new context is one of the
chief sources of the comic effect which distinguishes the parody from
other types of literary criticism.

So for Kant, for example, the essence of humour lay in raising the
expectation for X and giving Y. This simple dictum has been accepted
by most analysts of comedy and is particularly well suited to describing
the mechanism at work in parody, when a text is quoted and the
quotation then distorted or changed into something else. But in the
case of parody more than one element may, of course, be the subject of
reader expectations. Because both the text of the parodist and the
parodied work are the subject of the reader's attention, the latter may
be surprised to see the parodied text offered in its new distorted form
(X as Y), but he may also be surprised by a change of style in the work
of the parodist (Y as X).

The shock destruction of expectations has long been recognised as a
basic ingredient of the comic effect. In Book 6, 3 of his *Institutio
Oratoria*, Quintilian wrote:

> There remains the prettiest of all forms of humor, namely the jest
> which depends for success on deceiving anticipations or taking
> another's words in a sense other than he intended. The unexpected
> element may be employed by the attacking party, as in the example
> cited by Cicero, 'What does this man lack save wealth and — virtue?'[14]

Quintilian's designation of the deception of anticipation as characteristic of jest might also be kept in mind in reading Henry Fielding's 'The
Tragedy of Tragedies; or the Life and Death of Tom Thumb the Great'
with 'the Annotations of H. Scriblerus Secundus'[15] of 1731. Here
Fielding used the device to present not only a parody of heroic tragedy
but, in the annotations of H. Scriblerus Secundus, a parody of commen-
taries on tragedy, which also served to explain (though through a veil
of irony) details of parody in which Fielding was indulging on the stage.
So, for example, Doodle's opening conceit, in which nature is said to
wear 'one universal grin' is explained by Scriblerus as a beautiful 'version'
of phrases such as Lee's poetic lines concluding 'All nature smiles'.
Fielding's ironic mockery of the cliches of classical English tragedy is
achieved through the voice of the foolish wise man, so that (in the

manner of the topsy-turvy world of parody) his own 'foolish' irony is presented as wisdom. But when 'Scriblerus Secundus' also writes in a comment to Tom Thumb's announcement of a secret in Act II/1, that 'this method of surprising an audience by raising their expectations to the highest pitch, and then balking it, hath been practised with great success by most of our tragical authors', he is not only ironically exaggerating the sense of surprise in the passage, but juxtaposing Quintilian's description of a method of comedy with the methods of tragedy. Ironically he thus also describes his own function in Fielding's play as a tool of parody, and a function of the play in turning the conventions of the tragedies under attack upside down.

The evocation and destruction of audience expectations is also basic to the parody in which quotation or imitation evokes other texts, and places them in conflict with the reality of the audience's world. Act I/1 of Aristophanes' comedy *The Frogs* begins with preparations being made for the Dionysiac festival, a potential play-within-the-play. The slave Xanthias is arguing with Dionysus about the script:

> *Xanthias.* Do you mean to say I've been lugging all these props
> around and now I'm not even allowed to get a laugh out of them?
> It's the regular thing I tell you. Phrynichus, Lysis, Ameipsias, all
> the popular writers do it. Comic Porter Scene. There's one in every
> comedy.
> *Dionysus.* Well there's not going to be one in this comedy.

Ironically, 'this comedy'[16] (if no objection is made to the analysis being made through this English translation — with due regard for Aristophanes' original text) refers both to the Dionysiac festival, the play-in-the-play, and to the Aristophanic comedy of which the characters are shown to be naively and ironically unaware. Thus, while Dionysus sees his statement as being true for his play, it is ironically not true for Aristophanes', in which we do now derive humour from the parody of the popular comic porter scene spoken of by Xanthias as his authority. Xanthias has unwittingly already played out a comic porter scene, while speaking of not being able to, and a comic effect has, therefore, ironically already been created. It might also be suggested that the verification of the truth of Xanthias' words — 'There's one in every comedy' — is made possible by reference to the reality of the fictional world as received by the audience — that is, by its perception of the 'play-outside-the-play', the play on stage. But verification other than by reference to the dramatist's work appears not to be explicitly called for, and this verification is based in an ironically satiric attack on the literary conventions similar to those used by the parodist: parody is in this case reflexive and playful, and distinct from the satire in which the author's statements are only directed outwards to the world of the reader. The problem of verifying literary statements by adjusting or matching them to the world of the reader will be returned to in Part Two, Section 4.1.

In the comedy of Aristophanes, parody is both satiric and specific, and general and ironic in 'laying bare' the devices of fiction, and in complicating the communication between the stage and the audience by the device of the play within the play, or by other such meta-fictional reflections on the fiction on the stage.

Further techniques of parody will be discussed when distinguishing it from satire and irony. Some techniques, however, also have the specific function of signalling the parody, and it is from a consideration of these signals that we shall also come to a consideration of the role of reader in the composition and reception of the parody.

1.4 Signalling Parody

The signals by which the reader recognises parody in the above Aristophanic play are to be found within the text or its performance. As a basic premise it will be maintained, that a prime distinguishing feature between the imitation (or the non-ironic, non-critical reproduction of the whole or a part of another literary work in a text) and the literary parody is the effect of comic discrepancy between the original work and its 'imitation'. Types of discrepancy, or the signals of parody in a text most frequently to be found by the reader, can be broadly listed under the following categories.

I. *Changes to the coherency of the text quoted*
    1. Semantic change
       a) apparently meaningless, absurd change
       b) change meaningful for the reader's world (often satiric).
    2. Changes in literal and metaphoric functions of words.
    3. Syntactic change (which may affect the semantic level).
    4. Changes in tense, persons, or other sentence grammatical features.
    5. Changes to the associations of the imitated text by the new context and other co-textual (and 'beyond the sentence') changes.
    6. Changes in sociolect, idiolect, or in other elements of the lexicon.
II. *Direct statement*
    1. Comments on the parodied text or on the author of the parody.
    2. Comments on the world of the reader.

     3. Comments on the parody as a whole text.

III. *Effect on the reader*
     1. Shock or humour from conflict with reader expectations about
        the text parodied.
     2. Change effected in the world of the reader of the parodied text.

Discrepancy may thus be created within the text quoted and between
that text and its new context. But — as suggested earlier — the reader
may also recognise the ironic use of quotation by finding a significant
contrast between the familiar style of the author of the parody and his
style in the parody in which he is writing (Y as X). That James Joyce
did not normally write in the style of Dickens is but one indication of
the parodistic nature of the 'Dickens passage' in the 'Oxen of the sun'
parodies of *Ulysses*.

1.5 The Reader

The reception of the parody, and the possibilities for its reception by
the reader, are thus of particular importance to a theory of parody. The
parody may be said to contain at least two (connected) models of
communication — that between parodist and the author of the parodied
text, and that between parodist and reader. In brief, the work to be
parodied is decoded by the parodist and offered again (encoded) in a
'distorted' form to another decoder, the reader, who — knowing and
having previously decoded the original — is in a position to compare it to
its new form in the parody.

The Reader's Reception of the Parody

Phenomenological analyses, but also 'text-linguistic' studies such as
those by S.J. Schmidt,[17] have concentrated on the analysis of the
reception of texts by the reader, on the expectations of the reader, and
on the author's awareness of the factors involved in reader reception in
encoding his work. In S.J. Schmidt's terminology the reception of a
text would be described as the reception of a text-world, TW, in a
reader's world, RW, at x time and place. If we apply these categories to
the description of the reception of parody, we would, however, have
to speak of the parody as consisting of *two* text-worlds — those of the
parodist and his target or TW_1 and TW_2 — received by the reader at x
time and place. The advantage of using such a terminology is that the
distinctive role of parody within literature, of offering two texts within
one work, can be clearly depicted.[18]

Recognition of Parody

The reception of the parody by the reader will depend on his reading of the 'signals' in the text for the parodistic relationship between the parodist's imitation and the original text. We have listed some of the most common signals for parody. Some general possibilities of the reader's reception of the parody, or some of the most common reactions of modern readers to the signals for parody may be listed as the following:

1. The reader does not recognise the presence of parody, because he does not recognise TW_2, the parodied text, as a quotation from another work but reads it as part of TW_1. The inability to recognise the existence of two text-worlds inhibits a reader's ability to recognise the parody in a work. (The modern reader unacquainted with mythology or the Bible may be put in this position when confronted with a parody of those works.) In this case the reader could be described as the naive victim of an irony from the viewpoint of the author or a second reader.

2. The reader recognises the quotation, and the presence of two text-worlds, but does not comprehend the intention of the author or the relationship (usually one of discrepancy) between the two texts. He may, e.g., believe the author is unintentionally misquoting. But one other reason for this reaction may be that he does not feel the discrepancy because his sympathy for the parodied text is so strong that his assumptions about it have not been affected by the parody. As a friend to the parodied author such a reader might be seen as both the victim of irony and the target of satire.

3. The friend to the parodied text recognises the parodistic effect of the work and feels both himself and the parodied text and its author to be the targets of satire.

4. The reader recognises the parodistic effect from the discrepancy between TW_1 and TW_2 and also enjoys the recognition of the hidden irony and satire against the parodied text and the reader sympathetic to it. This might also be regarded as the 'ideal' reader reaction.

In this last case, however, the perspicacious reader may be unsure as to whether he has read the discrepancy and its signals in the text correctly and is in fact seeing a parody where there is not one and placing himself in the position of victim of a general irony. In this case the 'ideal' reader reaction also exhibits the reader's sensitivity to the ambiguity, and subtlety, of great parody.

In describing the signals for parodistic discrepancy, I have tried to

avoid distinctions between form and content made in most lexical
definitions of parody. Except in cases of comic imitation of particular
genres, the definition of parody as the 'imitation of the form of a work
with a change to its content' is no longer very useful or meaningful. An
example from Heinrich Heine's 1824 prose piece *Ideen. Das Buch le
Grand*, from Chapter 14, may illustrate this. When speaking of a
physically and financially well-endowed 'Millionarr' (millionaire fool)
Heine parodies the biblical parable of the camel who could not pass
through the eye of the needle (which served to illustrate the position
of the man who could not pass into Heaven) by juxtaposing elements
from within the parable. It will be argued that these elements can better
be described in terms of semantic and syntactic components than in
terms of form and content, which (except in the case of strongly
identifiable stylistic features) are often not clearly separable in the
recognition of biblical passages by the reader. Bringing the metaphysical
lesson of the Bible down to realities of the nineteenth century, Heine
wrote (my translation): 'A camel will find it easier to enter the kingdom
of heaven, than this man to pass through the eye of a needle.' Here
lexical elements within a single story are rearranged – technically without the addition of new 'content' and with a change to the 'form' of
the story (and we would still call it parody – though used to satirise
modern reality) – to bring about semantic change and the effect of
comic discrepancy through syntactical restructuring. As in most cases of
form and content relationships, semantic-syntactic dependency here
means that a change to one aspect is accompanied by a change to the
other, and because the terms semantic and syntactic rather imply this
interdependency than preclude it as have the terms 'form' and 'content',
they are preferred here. The foregrounding of the role of the reader's
interpretation of the parody and its target in the parody itself will be
returned to in Chapter 4.

1.6 Attitudes of the Parodist

There are in brief, two main theories about the nature of the attitude of
the parodist to the text quoted. The first maintains that the imitation
by the parodist of his chosen text has the purpose of mocking it, and
that his motivation in parodying it is contempt. The second holds that
the parodist imitates a text in order to write in the style of that text,
and is motivated by sympathy with text. The first view sees parody as
an unambivalent form of comic imitation, while the second acknowledges
that the parodist has both a critical and an admiring attitude to his
'target' or 'model'. The roots of this second theory may be found in

interpretations given the meaning of the word 'Parodia' as both 'Gegengesang' and 'Beigesang' by classical rhetoricians (such as Quintilian). In Book 9, 2, 35, of the *Institutio Oratoria* (translated in Section 1.2) Quintilian wrote:

> Incipit esse quodammodo παρωδη, quod nomen ductum a canticis ad aliorum similitudinem modulatis abusive etiam in versificationis ac sermonum imitatione servatur.[19]

To the concept of parody as an abusive song sung in imitation of another, Quintilian added (as we have seen earlier) that the 'parody' had come to describe the imitation of any literary work. But he had himself enlarged this concept by describing some parody as using ambiguity in the comic and critical imitation of another work (in Book 6, section 3) as where he speaks of Ovid's lost 'cento' parody:

> Adiuvant urbanitatem et versus commode positi, seu toti ut sunt (quod adeo facile est, ut Ovidius ex testrastichon Macri carmine librum in malos poetas composuerit), quod fit gratius, si qua etiam ambiguitate conditur . . .[20]

Quintilian also speaks of ironic ambiguity, of substitution, and of the simulation of a work in parodic quotation: ' . . . seu ficti motis versibus similes, παρωδια quae dicitur.' Here the imitation of a text is described as a trick, a technique of comedy, and 'Imitation' is used to describe the ironic simulation of conventional quotation, Quintilian giving the example of the absurd connection of quotations as a trick of the parodist. Yet Quintilian also classes parody with the aphorism, the epigram, and other examples of the brief, compressed literary phrase as a form of 'urbane' literature:[21] wit is not denigrated as an unpoetic form, but described as a sophisticated rhetorical device. Here Quintilian's description of parody and the attitude of the parodist is representative of a sympathetic approach to parody which is, for example, hardly found in post-Reformation Germany before the writings of Friedrich Schlegel and the revival of interest in the work of Cervantes.

Lutz Röhrich also indicates that there exist two major concepts of the nature of the attitude of the parodist to the parodied work. The second which Röhrich mentions describes parody as mockery born of the poet's realisation that his age is 'epigonal'.[22] The first sees parody as the desire to imitate a favourite style. Röhrich writes that the second opinion is more widely held:

Die weitverbreitete Meinung, man könne nur parodieren, was man liebe gilt doch wohl nur bedingt. Viel häufiger ist Parodie das Zeichen eines Überdrusses. Parodien werden bestimmt durch eine negative Tendenz gegenüber der Überlieferung. Sie haben eine Tendenz zum Widerspruch. Es wird protestiert gegen das Überlieferte. Langeweile, Überdruss oder mangelnder Glaube entladen sich im Scherz.[23]

The view that the parodist's attitude is sympathetic (as expressed, for example, by Thomas Mann in his novel *Doktor Faustus*) is dismissed by Röhrich as being a minority opinion. As Röhrich himself points out, however, parody is not only destructive (as the second, more popular opinion would have it), but it is also reconstructive:

Parodistische Veränderungen vorgegebenen Traditionsmaterials dürfen nicht nur negativ als Zersungenes oder Zersagtes angesehen werden. Sie offenbaren zugleich auch einen Prozess sprachlicher Umbildung und Neubildung . . .

As an extension of this argument it might also be maintained that the love of the parodist for the object of his parody[24] can often not be separated from his desire to change and modernise it. It is also often argued that history proves that only parodies of well-known and also powerfully poetic works survive. The parody must also, however, have something new to say about these works for it to survive independently as a parody. The parodist need not, moreover, be attracted only to the style of the work, for, as argued previously, parody is not necessarily restricted to the imitation of 'form'. Moreover, it might be suggested that when such definitions were most popular, and applied to the parody of genres, or other easily recognisable literary forms, parody was also defined as a form of 'imitation' of other texts. As will be argued in Part Two, Section 4.4, however, parody has also been used for the 'deconstruction' of imitation, and for many other specific purposes than the imitation of formal characteristics in literary works.

   The Formalist Jurij Tynjanov has emphasised the ambivalent attitude of the parodist to his target in his paper on Dostoevsky and Gogol and the Theory of Parody, arguing that this also explains the liberal parodistic use of such sacred texts as the Bible. Yet here the different canons of different orthodoxies, and the different interpretations of these canons, and of parody, have led to varying attitudes to the parody of the Bible, and the broader sociological issues involved

here can also not be overlooked. Though the ambivalence of parody
may sometimes allow it to be used against a canonised text, or for its
refunctioning, or its ambiguity allow it some defence when charged
with blasphemy, the subtleties of its ambiguity have, moreover, often
also been overlooked by the authorities involved in evaluating it.

To some extent, the ambivalent nature of ironic parody, described
by Tynjanov, is operative in the acceptance of biblical parody by some
groups of readers, but the large amount of difference amongst readers
in the reception of one parodic text may also be dependent on the
degree of orthodoxy of a public, and on the degree of psychological
acceptance created in the reader by the relative strictness of the
canonisation of the Bible. In medieval literature, for instance, biblical
parody as a means of comic criticism is said by Paul Lehmann to have
been acceptable. What is later regarded as mockery, was then 'condoned'
– or legalised – by authority. Sociological investigations of the context
of the literary work are, thus, not only necessary for an understanding
of the character of the parodist's audience, and the conditions for the
reception of his work, but for an awareness of the 'preconditions' of its
publication, of, for example, censorship and publication controls.

An archetype of parody, the medieval carnival, has, for example,
offered many examples of the changing relationship between parodist
and censor, and our understanding of this relationship is also changing.
This subject will be returned to in Part Two – one example of the
relationship given above, which might be given here, is the example of
the 'Lords of Misrule' festival. The master of ceremonies of this festival
is now thought to have played the role of 'censor' on the parodistic
activities in the carnival allowed by the medieval Church to 'overturn'
the existing order of things – in play – for the short time of the
festival. Like the Subdeacon's festival, the 'Lords of Misrule' was
banned in the sixteenth century. The Subdeacon's festival had begun
with the revolutionary biblical prophecy: 'The first shall be last and the
last first.' Once the world had actually been turned on its head by the
Puritan revolution (and the biblical prophecy secularised) the metaphoric
inversion of the status quo by the fool was frowned upon. (An interesting parallel might also be found in the Saint-Simonians' call for a new
'holy censorship' to stabilise the 'organic period' which was to follow
the July Revolution of 1830 in France. Though this parallel is only to
be made in the broadest terms, their contemporary Heine also com-
mented several years later on the banning of the carnival under the July
monarchy as an attempt to quell the revolutionary spirit of its past.)
Like Heine (whose works he knew well) Freud was also to equate

revolution, carnival, parody and sensualism, as temporary liberations from external and internal censorship. His theories have been further developed by the Formalist Michail Bachtin in his studies of parody and the 'carnivalistic' in Rabelais, which will be discussed further in 4.6.

Regarding the parodistic use of the Bible in the carnival, history shows it to have had a history of both official patronage and official and unofficial repression. On 16 May 1559, Queen Mary's decree banning the use of religious and political themes for the theatre was published; while in 1605 King James' 'copyright' of the English Bible was finalised by the first piece of English legislation against blasphemy. (To put this another way, it could be said that the first law against blasphemy had the function of protecting the copyright of that Bible.) In the post-Reformation period when satire and biblical parody were regarded as lower forms of wit, the interconnection between political censorship and the denigration of parody must also be kept in mind. In Germany Gottsched's diatribe against satire and parody as 'immoral' forms of literature, and his banning of the Hanswurst from the stage had a lingering effect (as suggested earlier) on the evaluation of parody as a form of 'serious' literature. The imprisonment of Voltaire for his satire, and the trials for blasphemy against William Hone (at the beginning of the nineteenth century in England) demonstrate how the Church and the state, the original 'masters' of the topsy-turvy parodistic world of the carnival, saw themselves threatened by these metaphoric forms of revolution. Once revolution had been realised and secularised, and taken out of the hands of those who had controlled it, its metaphoric forms were also censored. The trials of William Hone also demonstrate the confusion of law regarding blasphemy (and parody) which arises with the separation of Church law from that of the state. For Hone was able to win his case against the charge of blasphemy by arguing he had used biblical parody in the older tradition of the Reformation for the purpose of political satire. The decision of the court in freeing him from the charge against him, of blasphemy, illustrated a distinction between Church and state law, as well as uncertainty as to whether his ambiguous parody had as its target the state or the book on which it had been based, the Bible.

Parodies have been differentiated by means of stylistic and politically-oriented criteria as playful, or frivolous, critical or agitatory, engagé or propagandistic, secularising or blasphemous, imitative or plagiaristic, imitative or counter-imitative.

In works of different authors parody has also been used for different purposes in different texts and at different times. So, for

example, Heine used his parodistic refunctioning of the Bible in
satirical polemics against the reunion of the Church and state in the
Restoration of the 1820s, in secularising the New Testament for the
'Third Testament' philosophy of sensualism of the Saint-Simonians in
the early 1830s, and in the works of his late period in a 'blasphemously-
religious' return to the stories of the Old Testament – to use masks
such as those of Job and Lazarus to interpret political and social
issues of the day.[25]

Because parody is often a symptom not only of external but internal
censorship, an understanding of its function in discourses other than
fictional work is also important, but can only be briefly alluded to here.
Theodor Verweyen's study of Peter Rühmkorf's satirical parodies has
raised some questions about contemporary agitatory parody in
journalism and other mediums of public communication, but as these
are not meta-fictional parodies they are not included in this study of
parody as meta-fiction, as an ambivalent, self-reflexive form of discourse
analysis.

1.7 Ambivalence and the Concept of General Parody

Although accompanied by a comic effect, it has been seen that parody
need not necessarily ridicule the work of its target.[26] Householder cites
Aristophanes' admiration for Euripides to make this point. Parody used
in prosopopoeia often mocks the poetaster, or 'unwitting parodist',
and his distortion of a text, without necessarily attacking the text
itself. But, more significantly perhaps, an ambiguity exists in the word
'parodia' – in that 'para' can be translated to mean both nearness and
opposition.[27] The ambivalence of great parody – from Aristophanes to
today – of apparent empathy with and distance from the text imitated
– can thus be said to be implied in the classical term itself. Yet the root
word 'para' was rarely translated as meaning both opposition to its
object and nearness by post-Renaissance critics: more usually it became
either opposition *or* consonance – in German, for example, either
'Gegengesang' or 'Beigesang'. In the nineteenth century, after Gottsched's
attack on satires which served no moral purpose, and after the demise in
popularity of classical parody in Germany, August and Friedrich
Schlegel revived the use of the word 'Parodie' and called for a more
serious study of Cervantes.[28] August Wilhelm Schlegel emphasised the
ambivalence of parody as a form of literary criticism containing
elements of respect for its target, and spoke of it (when commenting
on Aristophanes) as being both dependent on and independent from
its object:[29]

> Parodie setzt immer eine Beziehung auf das Parodierte und
> Abhängigkeit davon voraus.
> (Parody always implies a dependent and an independent relationship
> to its object.)

In the nineteenth century this ambiguous relationship of parody to its
target of dependence and independence was also interpreted dialectically
as the 'Aufhebung' (supersession) and transformation of the subject. In
works such as *Don Quixote*, in which parody has had the function of
both destroying a specific target and refunctioning that target for a new
audience (or for a similar audience whose expectations for the old
text are to be revised) parody has been described as the transformation
of one genre into another, and has been seen both as a form of literary
satire and as offering a general aesthetic of the text and its reception.

That concept of general parody need not, of course, exclude that of
specific parody, for the techniques of the latter also serve to create the
ambivalent dependence of general parody on its target as we find it in
Don Quixote. Parody, unlike some other forms of satire which do not
make their target a part of their text, is not only ambivalently dependent
on the object of its criticism, but may satirically unmask and deflate
other writers by using their works ironically as a temporary 'word-mask'
for the parodist. It has been said that imitation of another writer can in
itself be interpreted as an attack on that writer, rather than as flattery,
but again parody need not be seen as embodying only one of these
alternatives. Explicit parody can make the discrepancy between the
parodist's style and that of his target text into a weapon against the
latter, while (at the same time) refunctioning the target's work for a
new purpose. Both by definition and structurally, parody is ambivalently
critical and sympathetic towards its target. In parody, familiar literary
structures are deliberately made more complex and even confusing – or
so it would appear to the reader, and the structural role assumed by
the parodied text in the parody is ambivalent, in that it not only
functions as the target of satire but contributes to the structure and
effect of the parody by lending it its 'preformed'[30] linguistic material.
Luis Borges alludes to this in writing of Cervantes:

> Cervantes has created for us the poetry of seventeenth century Spain,
> but neither the century nor that Spain were poetic for him . . . The
> plan of his book precluded the marvellous; the latter, however, had
> to figure in the novel at least indirectly, just as crimes and a mystery
> in a parody of a detective story . . . [31]

Hence unlike other forms of satire, literary parody — which we shall at this point define as the critical refunctioning of preformed literary material with comic effect — makes the object of attack part of its own structure, and thus also depends in part on the reader's conditioned reaction to this object of attack for the response to itself. The parodies which demonstrated this ambivalence to Schlegel, the parodies of Aristophanes and Cervantes, are also the works which have survived both the danger of redundancy built into the parody by its 'destruction' of the author or his text it mockingly imitates, and the demise of the public familiar with the target of satire. By incorporating parts of the target text into the parody in a way which preserves the balance of dependence and independence between the texts, the parodist can both ensure the closeness to his target necessary for an accurate firing of his arrows of satire, and preserve the essential features of the target which will make the parody outlive the demise of the target's readership. In this parody differs from satire, travesty, persiflage, and other forms of literary criticism in fiction. The balance between close imitation or quotation and the 'supersession' of the target text, which distinguishes parody from other forms of literary satire (and literary criticism), must also, as suggested earlier, be seen as being accompanied by a comic effect, resulting from the establishment of discrepancy between texts.

In this section, where we are restricting our discussion of parody to its definition and to the definition, in particular, of its specific techniques, the significance of its definition as 'Gegengesang' or 'counter-song', as a symptom of the defensiveness of poetics against attacks on the concept of imitation can only be hinted at. The role of parody in undermining belief in the function of fiction is imitation, and representation, will be returned to be discussed in more detail in Part Two.

Notes

1. Fred Householder, Jnr., 'Parodia', in *Journal of Classical Philology*, 39 (January 1944), p.2.
2. Aristotle, *Poetics* 2–3 (144 8a 12–13).
3. F. Wild has discussed the use of 'Batrachomyomachia' in his thesis (Vienna, 1918) *Die Batrachomyomachia in England.*
4. 'A discourse Concerning the Original and Progress of Satire' in Dryden's *Of Dramatic Poesy and Other Critical Essays*, George Watson (ed.) (London and New York, 1962), vol. 2, p. 103.
5. Peter Rau, *Paratragödia. Untersuchungen einer komischen Form des Aristophanes* (München, 1967).
6. The term 'to foreground' is a translation of the Prague linguist Mukarovsky's

concept of the 'actualisation' of dead metaphor. It is used here to describe a function of punning, where the latter has the poetic and 'creative' function of giving a word new meaning, or returning to it an older 'dead' sense.

7. *The Frogs*, transl. David Barrett (Middlesex, 1971), p. 167.

8. Ibid., p. 263.

9. Householder, 'Parodia', pp. 3, 4.

10. Ibid., p. 5.

11. Sander L. Gilman, *The Parodic Sermon in European Perspective* (Wiesbaden, 1974), p. 2.

12. The term 'to refunction' is a translation from German 'Umfunktionierung'. It was used by Brecht to describe the modern re-use of older literary texts. As literature is seen by Brecht as being,'produced' in answer to certain social needs, Brecht also sees it as being, like any other product, capable of being 'refunctioned' for new purposes. Here the term is used to describe the *new functions* gained by a text in a new context such as parody.

13. Alfred Liede, 'Parodie' in *Reallexikon*, 1966, vol. 3, p. 14, etc.

14. Quintilian, *Institutio Oratoria*, transl. H.E. Butler (Harvard, 1960), pp. 484, 485.

15. The play first appeared in 1730 without the 'Annotations'.

16. Aristophanes, *The Frogs*, pp. 156f.

17. See Siegfried J. Schmidt, *Texttheorie* (München, 1973), and *Literaturwissenschaft als argumentierende Wissenschaft* (München, 1975).

18. I have discussed the possibilities of applying S.J. Schmidt's analysis of text-reception to the analysis of parody in the concluding chapter of *Die Parodie. Eine Funktion der biblischen Sprache in Heines Lyrik*, Anton Hain (Meisenheim/ Glan, 1976).

19. Quintilian, *Institutio Oratoria*, transl. H.E. Butler, Harvard, 1960, vol. 3, p. 394.

20. Ibid., vol. 2, p. 490.

21. Ibid., pp. 495 and 497.

22. Also see A. Liede, 'Die Parodie' in *Reallexikon* (Berlin, 1966), vol. 3, p. 41.

23. See L. Röhrich, *Gebärde – Metapher – Parodie* (Düsseldorf, 1967), p. 215.

24. Ibid., p. 221.

25. I have discussed the development of Heine's use of biblical parody in *Die Parodie. Eine Funktion der biblischen Sprache in Heines Lyrik* (Meisenheim/ Glan, 1976), and the development in Marx' and Engels' use of parody in their work (up to the *Eighteenth Brumaire*) in *Reading the Young Marx and Engels: Poetry, Parody, and the Censor* (Croom Helm, London, 1978).

26. The German term for the parodied author is 'parodant', the English 'parodee'. These terms are given as information. It is not necessarily implied by this that they must be used!

27. F.J. Lelièvre, 'The Basis of Ancient Parody', in *Greece and Rome* (1954), p. 66.

28. Even before Schlegel, Lessing had described Cervantes' art as 'serious manner of joking'. Later the Romantics were accused of overemphasising the tragic aspects of Don Quixote.

29. A.W. Schlegel, 8th Lecture on Aristophanes, in 'Vorlesungen uber dramatische Kunst and Literatur', in *Kritische Schriften und Briefe*, 1809–11, New edn. (Edgar Lohner, Mainz (1966), p. 132.

30. The term 'preformed' linguistic material is used to distinguish the subject-matter of literary parody from that of other forms of caricature and mimicry. As it can be argued that the distinction between form and content used in many dictionary definitions of parody may only be relevant to the parody of genres, and can be misleading in other cases, a new word must be found to define the

material parodied as belonging to a recognisable work of literature. The word 'preformed' is chosen to express the concept of the writer as 'producer' who uses given materials to develop new literary forms and who may also thereby — or by means of satire — offer criticism of the past use of these materials. These terms may sound mechanical, but a theory of parody must now try to describe essential structural characteristics of parodistic texts as well as their 'spirit'.

31. 'Partial Magic in *Quixote*', in *Labyrinths* (Harmondsworth, 1976), p. 228.

2 DISTINGUISHING PARODY FROM RELATED FORMS

In defining parody[1] critics have spent some time in distinguishing parody from other forms of quotation and literary satire, and it is these distinctions which will be discussed in the following sections.

2.1 Limits of the Term 'Burlesque'

The eighteenth-century division of parody into high and low burlesque limited the broader meaning of the scholiasts' term, and reflected a philosophical dualism which is not necessarily applicable to all texts or authors. John Jump chose to discuss parody under the title of 'Burlesque' in his *Critical Idiom* series[2] yet, as he himself pointed out, the word burlesque is — unlike the term parody — not classical, but comes from the Italian 'burla' (to ridicule), and has, as we have already mentioned in our opening discussion of defining parody, a comparatively short history. Henryk Markiewicz[3] states moreover that the word was only imported from Italy (where it had been in use in the sixteenth century) to France in the seventeenth century, where it 'acquired more diverse meanings', sometimes of a pejorative colouring. 'Le burlesque', according to Markiewicz, could mean 'grotesque, rank or flat comicality, extravagence of imagination or style (especially using vulgar or extraordinary language), no matter to what literary genre the work belonged; in its more narrow sense, the word was applied to travesty or to the mock-heroic poem, or as the name for a category including these last two'. The original breadth of the term appears to have been narrowed in the course of history, through the development of many different and sometimes contradictory definitions.

Addison's distinction between 'high' and 'low burlesque', made in No. 249 of the *Spectator* in 1711, has enjoyed relative permanency and been imitated by critics from the eighteenth century on. Yet the continued use of this definition to describe works of the modern period anachronistically preserves its eighteenth-century distinction between heroism and baseness, the high and the low — the very dualism attacked by satirists who use parody to 'level' society:[4]

Burlesque is . . . of two kinds: the first represents mean persons in the accoutrements of heroes; the other describes great persons acting

and speaking like the basest among the people. Don Quixote is an
instance of the first, and Lucian's gods of the second.

Parody has been defined by critics maintaining this eighteenth-century
distinction between the high and the low as 'high burlesque' in which
the low is compared to the high ideal. David Worcester[5] follows this
tradition in defining the high burlesque as placing a standard above the
victim to spotlight his faults (giving the example of a fishwife compared
to Dido), and low burlesque as placing the standard below, to bring the
high down from its pedestal, so that Dido would, for example, be
brought low by being compared to a fishwife. But though this may be
true of some parody or, in the latter case, travesty, it cannot be made a
rule. Works such as Seneca's 'Apokolokyntosis' ('Pumpkinification') –
a model for Byron's 'Vision of Judgement' – which is both a parody of
Seneca's own 'laudatio Funebris' to Claudius and a travesty of the
ensuing deification (or, ambiguously, 'pumpkinification') of the
Emperor, also show that parody and travesty can be used in the same
text.
     Most critics now overlook the philosophical implications of dividing
burlesque into high and low, and use them, without question, in the
traditional manner for any work. So John Jump classes travesty and
hudibrastic together as forms of low burlesque, distinguishing them in
terms of the particular or general nature of their subject-matter, though
hudibrastic might be better distinguished by the specific nature of its
form, the octosyllabic verse of *Hudibras*. In Jump's teminology parody
is described as 'high burlesque of a particular work (or author) achieved
by applying the style of that work (or author) to a less worthy subject',
while the mock heroic 'lavishes the style characteristic of the class
upon a trifling subject'. From these descriptions it remains unclear,
however, if the target of satire in the high burlesque is the 'less worthy
subject', or the style used to throw it into an unflattering light.
Confusion is compounded by the critics who do not class parody as a
sub-category of the burlesque, but the burlesque as a form of parody.
When burlesque came under attack from the Lord Chamberlain in the
1730s in England, no distinction was made between its high and low
forms, and, ironically (as Fielding tells us in his Preface to *Joseph
Andrews*), it was claimed that there was 'no such thing to be found in
the writings of the Ancients'. Hence the use of the term burlesque
might also be said to have made it easier for parody (of both ancient
and modern kinds) to be banished from the canon of 'serious' and
'acceptable' literature at that time.[6]

2.2 Persiflage, Plagiarism and 'Pekoral'

Persiflage implies a light satirical mocking of another's work and comes close to the English use of the word burlesque for 'mimicry', where no distinction between high and low burlesque is made. It is important to note that 'persiflage' is more descriptive of the attitude of the parodist than of the structure or techniques of the work, and that, while it may describe mimicry, it is not necessarily concerned with literary quotation, as is parody.

The term 'Plagiat' or 'plagiarism' has sometimes been used against the parodist, to characterise his close imitation (or quotation) of other literary texts as a literary theft, and to bring him before the law.[7]

In his article 'Was parodiert die Parodie?',[8] Hans Kuhn has introduced the term 'pekoral' from the Swedish (where it designates 'Geschreibsel', 'Machwerk', 'Unsinn') to describe those unwitting parodies written by authors or poetasters ('Dichterlinge', 'Schreiberlinge') imitating another style of work. The 'pekoral' has itself often become the subject of more sophisticated parodies. The play of Snug the Joiner in Shakespeare's *Midsummer Night's Dream* may be taken as an example of the parody of a fictional pekoral, a parody within a parody, by means of which the lack of consciousness in the first parody is brought to consciousness by the second. Yet the effect of an actual pekoral may not always be comic, while that of the parody will be, granting the ideal condition for its reception — the existence of a reader conversant with the work being parodied, and sensitive to the function of the discrepancy between it and the parodist's text.

2.3 The Literary Hoax and Pastiche

The literary hoax may be distinguished from the pekoral as being an ironic simulation of another work, in which techniques of imitation, and sometimes parody can be distinguished, Quintilian speaks in Book 9, 2, 35 of fictional letters (used in a law court) as parody, where, perhaps, the comic effect of the hoax resulted from the revelation of the deception. Ulrich von Hutten's 'Letters to the Obscuranti', of the Reformation, parodistically imitated the style of the authors under attack, and the gullibility of their readers. Such hoaxes usually established for themselves at least two audiences, of those who would be deceived by the imitation of another work, and of those who would understand its satiric purpose: in doing this they were both ironic and satiric. Counterfeited letters such as the *Letters of the Obscuranti* have also been popular amongst parodists seeking to insinuate themselves into the camp (and style) of their enemy while using that enemy's style as their disguise. Wearing the mask of their targets has, however, often led to confusion amongst their readers and critics as to their intentions, and, occasionally, to a misfiring of the hoax. In the case of Ern Malley, a fictitious Australian poet invented by James McAuley and Harold Stewart to trick the modernists of their literary world into accepting a parody of their ideals as the work of a great modern poet, the acclaim given the parody as a great modern work of art might be seen as an irony produced by the success of the hoax. For while the modernists' acceptance of Ern Malley — a previously unknown Australian poet and motor mechanic — proved the success of the hoax, it not only showed that the modernists had 'naively' accepted a parody of their programme to be proof of its truth, but that the creators of Ern Malley had created some independently excellent poems in writing parodies of the modernists, and that parody was, moreover, a form to be favoured by the modernists themselves. One of the parodistic methods used by McAuley — of taking passages from a military manual on swamp disease to create new literary characters, such as the Greek hero Anopheles (the Malley root is also found in such swamps) — was not unlike a method being used by James Joyce at that time.

Joyce's *Ulysses* was a modern Homeric parody, which, like *Don Quixote*, has created a new literary form from the parodistic imitation of its models, and a model for the modernist use of parody. A different kind of parody, but one ironically very similar to the kind used in the Ern Malley hoax, is to be found in Joyce's work of the 1920s in the 'Litter to Mr James Joyce', thought to have been written by the same writer,[9] but bearing the macaronic signature of Vladimir Dixon. In the tradition of von Hutten's 'Letters to the Obscuranti', this letter sets out to parody the ignorance of Joyce's critics, and while the level of its humour is as high as in other Joycean works, its aim is lower. But the parody here is also cleverly ambivalent — not only as a hoax which must deceive but at the same time signal its deception to the reader, but as the means to creating a language which may be seen as being either subnormal or extremely clever. Thus, while Vladimir Dixon's misspellings, malapropisms, and slips of the tongue condemn him to the former, Mr Joyce's expertise in punning in creating Vladimir's mistakes reveal him to be the latter:

Dear Mister Germ's Choice,
in gutter dispear I am taking my pen toilet you know that being Leyde up in bad with the prewailent distemper (I opened the

window and in flew Enza), I have been reading one half ter one other the numboars of 'transition' in witch are printed the severeall instorments of your 'Work in Progress'

Vladimir — who is apparently only capable of accuracy in quoting other texts — continues:

> You must not stink I am attempting to ridicul (de sac!) you or to be smart, but I am so disturd by my inhumility to onthorstand most of the impslocations constrained in your work that (although I am by nominals dump and in fact I consider myself not so brilliantly ejewcatered but still above Averroëge men's tality and having maid the most of the oporto unities I kismet) I am writing you, dear mysterre Shame's Voice to let you no how bed I feeloxerab out it all . . .

But here the double-meanings of 'Vladimir's' criticisms are too comically self-condemning to be innocent and, as in von Hutten's letters, signal to us that he himself is the target of the actual author behind his text, who is using parody as both an ironic 'imitation' of his target and a higher form of meta-comment to the same.

Not all literary hoaxes are comic, but those using parody not only hoist their victim with his own petard, but create the ambiguity necessary to the evocation and destruction of credibility in the false text.

Pastiche has also been described as a type of literary forgery, though not necessarily as having the intention to 'hoax'. The term is taken from the painting term 'pasticcio analogen', and means the compilation of motives from several works. There is little inference of the discrepancy typical of parody in the etymology of the term, or of the critical refunctioning of texts found in parodistic works, yet it has often been used as a synonym for parody, and especially in French literature, where it was, for example, used by Proust to describe both conscious and unconscious parody. Greater space than will be given here to the consideration of pastiche has been given by Wolfgang Karrer in an overview of modern definitions of parody.[10] Karrer also refers to L. Albertsen's article 'Der Begriff Pastiche',[11] in which Albertsen suggests that the concept of pastiche should be separated from that of the counterfeit with which it has often (outside of French criticism especially) been associated.

2.4 Satire and Parody

One major factor distinguishing literary parody from satire is its meta-linguistic use of preformed language as the vehicle of its criticism, and the meta-fictional context given this criticism. Satire, on the other hand, need not be restricted, to the imitation, distortion, or quotation of other literary texts.

Tuvia Shlonsky writes in his article, 'Literary Parody, Remarks on its Method and Function', that 'to subordinate parody to satire is to undermine its literary exclusiveness in which resides its particular power, function and effect'.[12] His claim, however, that while parody is not indifferent to the extra-literary model, social, religious, or philosophical norms essential to satire, 'the norms with which it deals are strictly literary', does not perhaps explain sufficiently the dialectical relationship between the fiction and its social context which has often been of importance in the parodist's use of other literary works. In refunctioning the preformed language material of other texts and discourses parody not only creates allusions to another author, another reader, and another system of communication, but to the relationship between the text, or discourse, and its social context. Thus while parody may be distinguished from other forms of satire as a form dealing with the refunctioning, or criticism, of other preformed literary and linguistic material, such a definition need not imply that parody is therefore only concerned with literary norms. And while the satirist may concern himself with attacking that which is considered normative, the parodist may also recreate his norms in order to attack them – internalising and foregrounding both his target and the process by which it has become canonised, the process of the quotation itself. While the perspective of the parodist may be anti-normative and distortive, as Shlonsky's following statement suggests, it might also be argued that the parody has also served to renew these norms, recreating them in a new context, and creating a contrast with their older form, before making them the subject of a new 'deconstruction'. Shlonsky writes:

> In so far as parody is an imitation, it simply takes its generic
> characteristics from a specific original and since each parody may
> have a different genre for a model, in itself is generically neutral.
> In so far as it is not a simple imitation but a distortion of the
> original the method of parody is to disrealize the norms which the
> original tries to realize, that is to say, to reduce what is of normative
> status in the original to a convention or a mere device.

This may not necessarily be true of all parody, but it is in the type of parody described here that the maximum shock effect is obtained, and it is here too that parody critically attacks established, popular literary works and brings into question their relevance to present literary and social conditions in the manner of satire.

Shlonsky also discusses the analysis made by the parodist of the fictional nature of literature:

> Non-parodic works which attempt to convince the reader of their truth and reality strive to blur the awareness of the reader as to the presence of a medium by the employment of various devices while effacing them as far as possible. Parody, on the other hand, can operate only when awareness of the reader is at its peak. Moreover, since it aims at sharpening the reader's awareness of the literary medium, parody employs the devices of its original while laying them bare, to use the term coined by the Russian Formalists. In general the parodic method is the extension, in various directions and to various degrees, of the device of laying bare the device. In its attempt to expose that illusion which it originally tries to conceal, parody has a close affinity with irony.[13]

The relationship between parody and irony will be returned to presently. To describe the mechanics of specific parody which distinguish it from satire first — it can be said that such parody works by juxtaposition, omission, addition condensation, and by discontinuance of the semantic and metaphoric logic of the original context which it quotes or alludes to in order to refunction it. Simple forms of parody, such as are found, for example, in Arno Holz's montage of literary quotations and 'geflügelte Worte' (already cliched texts) in his *Blechschmiede* and in other works using the cento form, do not juxtapose or contrast perspectives, by commenting on the relationship of the fictional work to reality from a literary perspective within the text, but merely point to the already ascertained epigonal and meaningless nature of a cliched text. Lelièvre, in speaking of the closeness of the cento to parody writes:

> Certainly centones involve the manipulation of an original work and the application of an author's verses to a situation not intended by him with the contrast which is part of the essence of parody. On the other hand the element of literary criticism which is sometimes found in parody is rare in the cento.[14]

1. Jan van Eyck, *Wedding Portrait of Giovanni Arnolfini*, 1434.

Lelièvre points here to the lack of ambivalence in such a form of parody. The aesthetic and positive criticism by parody of the fictional work is missing, and only the estrangement of the literary word from meaning and contemporary reality is indicated. As with the exaggerated imitation found in the burlesque, the ambivalence of artistic parody is lacking, and the cento form, as for example Peter Handke's play *Quodlibet* shows, is often closer to satire. Yet some parody has given satire the ambivalence characteristic of parody, and made of the process of reduction new works of art. Pierre van Soest's parodistic series of art works, his 'With Van Eyck on a Visit to the Arnolfini Family',[15] illustrates, for example, how the parody of an art work (and, in particular, of meta-art depicting the principle of artistic reflection of the world in the image of the mirror)[16] may expand the corpus of art in the moment of satirically reducing it. For in undressing the Arnolfini family depicted by van Eyck, whilst also alluding to the story of the Fall (a half-eaten apple lies in the foreground while a naked Signora Arnolfini looks askance at her naked body in a mirror in one of his pictures) van Soest was able to fill several rooms with his satirical reduction of the original portrait. The mirrors which van Soest uses both reduce the Arnolfinis to a more 'naked Truth' than the post-Renaissance artist could have drawn − foregrounding diachronic differences between van Soest and his model − while expanding that model into new directions.

The transmission of literary satire through the medium of parody has, of course, been common practice. Pope's *Dunciad* and other satirical critiques of contemporary writers, such as Buckingham's play *The Rehearsal* or Sheridan's *The Critic*, have all put parody to use in their invectives against bad writing, and bad criticism, either as the pretence at being a 'mirror' to the bad style of the poetaster or to show themselves the cleverer.

In the 'Receipt to make an Epick Poem', later to be used in Chapter XV of *The Art of Sinking in Poetry* of 1728 (which parodistically echoed Longinus *On the Sublime*), Pope mocked further those poetasters who had borrowed their poetic machinery from the Ancients, but who had used it without genius. To Pope their use of others' inventions could be seen as a type of home cooking, for which the best cure might be a parodistic recipe. As with Swift's *A Modest Proposal* for curing hunger in overpopulated Ireland, Pope's recipe demanded wit enough in his reader to divine the crucial pinch of irony:

For the Fable.

Take out of any old Poem, Romance, or Legend, (for instance *Geffrey of Monmouth* or *Don Belianis of Greece*) those Parts of the story which afford most Scope for long Descriptions: Put these pieces together, and throw all the Adventures you fancy into one Tale. Then take a Hero, whom you may chuse for the Sound of his Name, and put him into the midst of these Adventures: There let him *work* for twelve books; at the end it being necessary that the conclusion of an Epick Poem be fortunate.

Pope — and other parodists before him — had of course done just this in order to parody the poetasters who wrote thus in seriousness.

But Pope is less ambivalently mocking in his 'Recipe' than in his own mock-epic as he goes on to direct the measuring out of quantities of conceits, gods and heroes. Of the moral and the allegory he writes: 'These you may Extract out of the Fable afterwards at your leisure; Be sure you strain them sufficiently.' Suggesting that the finished work should then be set 'on fire' (either, perhaps, by inspiration or incineration), Pope concludes:

I must not conclude, without cautioning all writers without genius in one material point; which is, never to be afraid of having *too much Fire* in their works. I should advise rather to take their warmest Thoughts, and spread them abroad upon Paper; for they are observed to cool before they are read.

Ironically, however, this parodistic 'recipe' form was itself to become a recipe for apprentice parodists.

When young Friedrich Engels wrote a defence (in 1840) of the poets of the Young Germany movement of the 1830s in the form of a parodistic rewriting of one of his favourite legends, of Siegfried, he also chose to mock his literary opponents as both 'hacks' and unimaginative 'cooks'. Parodying the story of Siegfried's lesson in sword-making, Engels has the reactionary masters of the young Siegfried tell him their recipe for book-making:

Throw everything then onto one big forge,
The public's stomach is very large.
And if you don't have enough iron,
The master will have a good line:
Three heroes from Scott, three ladies from Goethe,
A knight from Fouqué, stern and steel-like,

　　　You don't need anything further
　　　For the stories of twelve narrative writers![17]

Earlier, in 1839, Engels had also successfully hoaxed a journal into
believing that the verses he was sending them imitated its style, while
they were, in fact, parodying the very lack of wit which the journal
demonstrated in publishing the parodies of its articles written by
Engels. Many other examples of satire using parody in the style of
Pope's *Dunciad* might be given. One less often referred to perhaps is
W.E. Aytoun's *Firmilian*, which set out to parody the Scottish
'Spasmodics', a Storm and Stress group of writers of the second half
of the nineteenth century, and which combines a parody of their
writings with parody of literary criticism. W.L. Renwick writes of
Firmilian in his Introduction to Aytoun's satires,[18] that it had begun
as a bogus review in *Blackwood's Magazine* of a dramatic poem by one
Percy Jones. The faked extracts from Mr Jones's 'Firmilian' were so
convincing that some unsophisticated readers took them to be genuine,
and protested at this latest outrage by a brutal 'Scotch Reviewer'. In
both the hoax and the literary satire then (whether these occur together
or in independent works) parody may be used to create, initially at least,
an identity between the parody and its target. In the following section
the differences between parody and one of its techniques in establishing
this 'dissimulating identity' with its target, its use of quotation, will be
briefly considered.

2.5 Parody, Quotation and 'Cross-Reading'

While non-parodistic quotation may be described as leading the reader
to make associations between two related but contingent texts, the
function of the quotation in the parody might be said to be to connect
and contrast disparate texts so that either their concealed identity or
their concealed discrepancy will be foregrounded. This technique of
parodic quotation is similar to the old game of 'cross-reading', described
below, which forces the reader to make associations between texts not
normally placed together, or expected.

　　　The *Nachahmung der englischen Cross-Readings*,[19] of the Enlightenment scholar and satirist Lichtenberg, describes this game as one in
which connections are made between unconnected subjects by the
'player' reading one line of a (vertically set) newspaper article
horizontally into another so that incongruous, unexpected associations
eventuate and the seriousness of each article is relativised. Such incongruous associations have, when simulated in literary works, served

a parodistic or satiric function. Such parodistic quotations do not, like the authoritative quotation, relate contingent texts, to reinforce or support the authority of an author, but to connect humorously unlike subjects to make ironic or startling comments on them of a critical nature. This has the effect of both making the quoted text appear 'strange', the effect described by the Russian Formalists as estrangement, as 'priyom ostraneniya',[20] and of associating it with the work of the parodist. Hence parodic cross-reading creates a semantic shift, a change in meaning and 'inner reform', which accompanies the structural changes resulting from the comparison and contrast of the two texts.

The basic technique used by literary parody in the quotation of parts or of the whole of another text establishes the ambivalence of the parodist's attitude to the object of his criticism in the structure of its own text. Unlike satire, as stated earlier, parody includes the 'victim' or object of its attack within its own structure and its reception is thus also influenced by the literary value of the object of its criticism, the text which is made part of the parodist's text.

The function of the specific techniques used by parody in refunctioning the text to be quoted can only be properly analysed in the context of the parodic works in which they are used. Common types of techniques have, however, been given labels now in general use: Rotermund, for example – following Quintilian – has listed total or partial caricature, substitution, addition, and subtraction;[21] and to these may be added exaggeration, condensation, contrast, and discrepancy. The overall function of these devices used by the parodist is to assimilate text B into text A as its second code, and then (after fulfilling secondary functions, such as the evocation of the expectations of the reader) to ironise and criticise text B, and to use it sometimes as the mask for the parodist or for his audience, as well as an important structural part of the parodist's own text. The use of quotation to establish discrepancy, as well as contingency between texts, distinguishes parodistic quotation from other forms and suggests also the critical attitude of the parodist to the naive imitation of other texts which may accompany his critique of naive concepts of art as the imitation of other worlds. The 'distorting' imitation and quotation of other texts in parody reflects again on the parodist's ambivalent relationship of dependence on and independence from his models, but also on the debt of all literary works to other preformed linguistic worlds.

2.6 Parody — Irony

In a general sense parody is related to irony, in the terms of an older
rhetoric, as the 'dissimulation' of an utterance. And both irony and
parody confuse the normal processes of communication by offering
more than one message to be decoded by the reader, which may also
serve to conceal the author's intended meaning from immediate interpretation. Thus the ambivalent relationship of the parody text to its
target, which it satirises but on which it is also dependent for a part
of its own material and structure, may also conceal an ironic relationship to the multiplicity of messages which the embedding of another
text in its structure may create.

The term irony generally describes a statement of an ambiguous
character, which includes a code containing two (or more) messages,
one of which is the message of the ironist to his 'initiated' audience,
and the other the 'ironically meant' decoy message. In the parody
the complex function of the dual meaning is sometimes matched by
that of the dual text — and while the ironist may use parody to confuse
his meaning, the parodist may also use various forms of irony.[22]

Ironic parody can also be described as attempting the 'Aufhebung'
(supersession) and (in Schlegel's terms) 'Potenzierung' of a text
through the refunctioning of it as a part of another work. Verbal irony
may, however, be more cryptic, and dissimulative, than parody, which
— through the quotation of another text — may create two distinct
codes, in comparison to the usual combination of messages in the
single code of the ironist. With the juxtaposition of two codes, the
parodist steps in to comment on the preformed language of the
quoted text (code B), and in doing so creates what might be called
(in Roman Jakobson's terminology)[23] a 'metalanguage' — a commentary to another linguistic entity. If this commentary were not given,
code B could be interpreted in the expected way (as non-ironic) by
the naive reader. The ironic function of text B in text A can, of course,
be derived from the parodist's code, or from the recognition of its
displacement from one context into another. In contrast to irony,
parody presents its literary 'victims' to the public through the montage
of a text, diachronically involving a literary text and its public and
tradition in its critical perspective, creating a means to the internal
historicisation of literary tradition. The more specifically individual
the preformed language used in the parodic work is, and the closer it
can be identified with a certain person or group, the greater is the
possibility of satirical criticism of its public. Both the 'encoder' of text
B and the traditional decoder who is assumed to have been instrumental

in the acceptance and canonisation of the text may then be placed under attack.

Whereas the ironist creates a contrast between the 'apparent' message of the code and his 'real' message, the parodist also contrasts a quoted text with a new context, contrasting code A of his text with code B of the parodied text. The authorial subject may posit his reader — who is also assumed to have been the decoder of the parodied work — as the object of his satire. Although parody may in this way be more specific in its criticism than irony, the parodied text is, as mentioned, in the ambivalent position of belonging to both the work of the parodist and to the author and reading public attacked by the parodist. Irony and parody are often classed together in classical rhetorics, as being dissimulative, while satire is given a place of secondary importance, and Friedrich Schlegel also wrote of irony and satire, that Romantic irony was of a 'higher' (that is, more reflexive) form than satire:

> Der romantische Witz ist der höchste — Der satirische kommt ihm am nächsten, und ist ihm an ähnlichsten. Auch die sokratische Ironie gehört dazu.[24]

Schlegel had also called irony 'Selbst-Parodie', and the importance attributed to Cervantes by the Romantics is a further indication of the respect shown by them to the reflexivity of literary parody. In summary, it may be said that the object of the author's criticism in the satire is distinguished from the object of irony and parody in being separated from the author's sympathies, and in being the object of his criticism, but not simultaneously part of his code or message, as is the literary text quoted in the parody. The parodied text is both 'victim' and model for the parodist, but the object of the satirist's attack is distinct from him and plays a comparatively minimal role in adding to the structure or aesthetic reception of his work.

While romantic irony may be said to work with one code which conceals two messages, parody, in containing two codes, is potentially both ironic and satiric, in that the object of its attack is both made part of the parody and is more specifically defined than in irony. Satire, like irony, presents one code, but, on the other hand, explicitly describes the object of its attack. The relationships between the author and the object of his criticism in irony, parody, and satire, may be summarised in the following manner:

If A = the code of the author, and B the code of the quoted text, and C the object of criticism within the code of the author:

IRONY = A↔AC
PARODY = A↔BC
SATIRE = A→C

This, like any schema, is only a model.[25] Parody itself, as has been suggested, may also be indirectly satiric when text B, the object of its criticism, is identifiable with a certain reader or with the attitude of a group: for while parody functions as an internalised form of literary criticism (or meta-language), it also involves the reader of the text (especially one who appears to be inseparable from a canonised work, such as the Bible) in its critical analysis. There are, moreover, at least two other ways of using parody as the vehicle of satire. The use of parody as a mask for the author, through which he ironically identifies himself with the object of his attack (as Erasmus has done in his *Praise of Folly*), may be described in the following way as:

$$(A = B) \rightarrow B = C$$

Parody used as a mask to describe the object of the parodist's satire (as in Heinrich Heine's satire of the hero of his allegoric *Atta Troll*, or in the criticism of other poets as unwitting parodists) is often less ironic and ambivalent than the preceding type, and may be described as:

$$A \rightarrow (B = C)$$

Although the purpose of satire may also be 'utopian', in the sense that it clears a path for the propagation of new myths and plans, parody, even of the second more satiric type of the example given above, is both more ambivalent towards its target in using the object of its criticism dialectically as the object of its reform, and as part of the 'reformed work' itself, and may also complicate the satirist's contrast of Reality to an Ideal.

The unique multiplicity of codes which is to be found in the parody offers one explanation of the ability of the parodist to be both satiric and ironic, and to combine both 'engaged' and poetic literature in the one work. In its most sophisticated forms, the parody is also both synthetic and analytic, and diachronic and synchronic in its analysis of the literary work it quotes. For in evoking the expectations of an audience, parody involves the audiences and the tradition of the literary work, its synchronic and diachronic roles, in its criticism. The connection of historical periods is, in the first place, a function of the quotation. Hans Mayer writes: 'Im Zitat findet sich die dialektische Einheit des Vergangenen und des Aktuellen; das Historische wird aktualisiert.'[26] Yet while the 'conventional' quotation of texts evokes the historical period and publics associated with those texts, parody both evokes and critically analyses and refunctions the diachronic level. The role of parody in transforming literary history will be considered in our final chapter of Part Two in Section 4.5. It is but one function of meta-fictional parody, the subject of the following section.

Notes

1.   To broaden the definition to include the parodistic treatment of gestures or 'non-verbal' signs, the argument may be taken from semiotics that gestures and other such signs perform similar functions to verbal or linguistic signs. Non-verbal conventions are also similar to verbal cliche in that they have been formed by tradition into a recognisable pattern.

2.   John Jump, *Burlesque* (London, 1972).

3.   Henryk Markiewicz, 'On the Definitions of Literary Parody', in *To Honor Roman Jakobson*, Essays on the Occasion of his 70th Birthday, 3 vols. (The Hague, 1966), p. 1,266.

4.   See Ian Donaldson, *The World Upside-Down, Comedy from Jonson to Fielding* (Oxford, 1970), pp. 189 f.

5.   David Worcester, *The Art of Satire* (1940), new edition (New York, 1969), pp. 44 f.

6.   Fielding's farce *The Historical Register* was thought to have brought down the Licensing Act of 1737, which enabled the Lord Chamberlain to keep many burlesques out of the theatre, and, hence, no doubt, several more from being written.

7.   See also the discussion of copyright in Section 4.6.

8.   Hans Kuhn, 'Was parodiert die Parodie?', in *Neue Rundschau*, 85/4 (1974), p. 604.

9.   See *Our Exagmination round his Factification for Incamination of Work in Progress* by Samuel Beckett and others (1929) (London, 1972), pp. 193–4.

10.   Wolfgang Karrer, *Parodie, Travestie, Pastiche* (München, 1977). Though the distinctions given in Karrer's title are themselves characteristic of older approaches to parody (which defined it by distinguishing it from travesty, the imitation of the content of a work, as the imitation of form), Karrer launches his main attack against the eighteenth-century distinction between high and low comedy and the form/content distinction. Karrer also criticises a lack of sociological method in modern parody analysis, but fails, in commenting on his silence, to discuss the relationship of sociological studies to the analysis of the question of reception raised in the meta-fictional parody and to comment on the function of such meta-fictional aspects of the parody.

11.   L. Albertson, 'Der Begriff Pastiche', in *Orbis Litterarum*, 26 (1971), pp. 1–8.

12.   Tuvia Shlonsky 'Literary Parody. Remarks on its method and function', *Proceedings of the 4th congress of the International Comparative Literature Association*, vol. 2 (1966).

13. Ibid., p. 800.

14. F.J. Lelièvre, 'The Basis of Ancient Parody', in *Greece and Rome*, 1954 (66–82), p. 56.

15. Van Soest's 'Visit to the Arnolfini Family' was begun 1974 and completed 1977, and exhibited Amsterdam, 1978.

16. See also Section 4.4.

17. I have discussed this and other parodies by Marx and Engels in *Reading the Young Marx and Engels: Poetry, Parody, and the Censor* (Croom Helm, 1978). It is interesting to note further that Engels' Siegfried parody concludes with a mock battle between the opposing camps in the style of the 'Batrachomyomachia' also imitated by Pope in 'The Rape and the Lock'.

18. W.E. Aytoun, *Stories and Verses* (Edinburgh, 1964), xvii. The work of Aytoun was drawn to my attention by Dr George Davie, Edinburgh.

19. Karl Riha, *Cross-Reading and Cross-Talking* (Stuttgart, 1971), p. 6.

20. See Viktor Sklovskij, *Theorie der Prosa* (Frankfurt/Main, 1966), p. 24.

21. Erwin Rotermund, *Die Parodie in der modernen deutschen Lyrik* (München, 1963), p. 9. Wolfgang Karrer comments (*Parodie, Travestie, Pastiche*, 67), that Rotermund's translation of Quintilian's categories of the 'adiectio, detractio, immutatio' has changed their original sense. For Quintilian these were rhetorical methods of changing given phrases, but to go into Quintilian's meaning here is not our purpose, as we are speaking of the way in which the techniques have been given their rhetorical names by later critics refunctioning Quintilian, and the adequacy of these titles to the phenomena which they are now used to describe.

22. For a discussion of various forms of specific and general irony, see D.C. Muecke, *The Compass of Irony* (London, 1969).

23. See Roman Jakobson's paper 'Linguistics and Poetics', in *Style and Language*, Thomas Sebeok (ed.), (Mass., 1968), pp. 352 ff.

24. See I. Strohschneider-Kohrs, *Romantische Ironie in Theorie und Gestaltung* (Tübingen, 1960), p. 36. Kierkegaard wrote (*Über den Begriff der Ironie* (Düsseldorf/Köln, 1961), p. 329), that the more irony there is in a work the more free the writer when he is in control of this irony.

25. I have also described this in terms of Text-World and Reader-World in *Die Parodie*, p. 119, as:
   1) Irony = Text-World 1 & Communication 1 → Target (in Text-World 1) = Communication 2
   2) Parody = Text-World 1 → Target Text-World 2 and Reader-World
   3) Satire → Target.

26. Hans Mayer, *Bertolt Brecht und die Tradition* (Stuttgart, 1961), p. 99.

PART TWO: A THEORY OF PARODY

Don Quixote is the first modern work of literature, because in it we see the cruel reason of identities and differences make endless sport of signs and similitudes; because in it language breaks off its old kinship with things and enters into that lonely sovereignty from which it will reappear in its separated state, only as literature . . . .

From Michel Foucault,
The Order of Things,
English translation (London, 1977), pp. 48–9

INTRODUCTION

The main consequences for a theory of parody which derive from our definition of it as, in its specific form, the critical quotation of pre-formed literary language with comic effect, and, in its general form, the meta-fictional 'mirror' to the process of composing and receiving literary texts, is to see parody both as a problem for textual analysis and a subject of sociological history: for in the internalisation and analysis of other texts in the parody a meta-fictional and diachronic context for the criticism of the fictional work is established which forces our attention on to both the problem of representation in the fictional work, and its interpretation by the reader.

Following on from the discussion of defining parody given in Part One, we shall now consider the problems raised by a theory of parody as a form of meta-fiction, which are implied in works such as *Don Quixote* and *Tristram Shandy*, and which have been made more explicit in the writings of the Russian Formalists, the Prague School linguists, and contemporary Structuralists and post-Structuralists. As mentioned previously, the parodistic criticism of other fictions purporting to represent an object-world has also recently been extended into a theory of the structure and function of fictional texts in the history of discourse in our episteme by Michel Foucault. And the critical attitude taken in the parodies of many 'modernists' to the function of literature as the reflection of other worlds will also be related here to a general theory of the reflexive self-critical form taken by much modern meta-fictional parody, and to a consideration of its dialectical refunctioning of the discourse of the canon of its time. The controls used by this canon to preserve itself in predetermined forms — controls such as censorship and copyright laws — will also be considered.

One of our first questions about modern meta-fictional parody will ask what it means to say — as Cervantes has — that fiction is not a true description of the world of objects and to say this from within the meta-fictional world of parody itself. The meta-linguistic functions of parody and the question of verifying literary statements foregrounded in such meta-fictional works as the *Quixote* will be discussed in both the following chapters.

3 PARODY AS META-FICTION

3.1 The Meta-linguistic Functions of Parody

Parody and irony both complicate the normal process of the communication of a verbal message from addresser to addressee,[1] parody by combining two codes (code B being familiar to the decoder, and code A which 'estranges' the message of text B, strange), and irony by juxtaposing at least two messages in the one code. In complicating the processes of communication they reflect on the communicative function of literary language as a vehicle of the transmission of messages, and offer a form of 'meta-critique' to literary language, a 'meta-language' by which parody, for example, may criticise the communicative function of the conventional quotation. And if fiction may sometimes be used as a meta-linguistic means of refunctioning standard speech, the parodistic meta-fiction may perhaps be characterised as a 'tertiary' form of meta-language.

Jakobson writes on the functions and the nature of meta-language:

> Whenever the addresser and/or the adressee need to check up whether they use the same code, speech is focused on the code: it performs a metalingual (i.e. glossing) function.[2]

The simplest form of questioning of the meaning of the addresser's code may be termed, according to Jakobson, 'meta-lingual'. To question the meaning of the code quoted in the parodist's work would also be to focus on the meta-lingual function of the parodist's code and the results of the parodist's analysis. Jakobson does not discuss the functions of the parodist's quotation of other texts, but writes: 'Poetry and metalanguage, however, are in diametrical opposition to each other: in metalanguage the sequence is used to build an equation, whereas in poetry the equation is used to build a sequence.'[3] Parody may, however, be used in both criticism and poetry, and be both analytical and synthetic, for another function of its 'meta-lingual' criticism of other works is to renew them as part of the parodist's own literary text. In the passage quoted above Jakobson is talking of the rhythmical and sound basis of poetry, but the synthetic function which he attributes to those factors may be said to be characteristic of poetic literature in general. Sophisticated parody may, moreover, be described as using meta-lingual analysis for its pro-creation of poetic language. And like the play within the play, epic parody contains within itself a verbally-like piece of literary material which is made the object of its analysis and renewal and part of its own structure and effect as a literary work.

Manfred Smuda has argued in his study of *Becketts Prosa als Metasprache*[4] that because Beckett takes as his subject the 'Objektsprache' or 'object language' of traditional prose, his own prose is to be characterised as 'meta-language', and to be seen as carrying the function of reflexive self-analysis. Smuda takes his concept of meta-language from Roland Barthes' essay 'Littérature et Méta-Langage',[5] but also connects his analysis of the relationship between meta-language and consciousness in Beckett's work to a phenomenological interpretation of the text as reading-object. In Smuda's conclusion it is the reader who will give meaning to the confusion in Beckett's text, a function of that confusion being (as in many parodies) to challenge the reader to the task of interpretation. Smuda has not explicitly explored the consequence (for his view of Beckett's prose as meta-language) of his phenomenological thesis, that the meaning of the text (and, hence, the meta-language) is only realised in the moment when it becomes an *object* of the reader's perception. And when Smuda implies that it is only as the object of another's interpretation that meta-language itself is subjected to critical analysis, he also implicitly joins philosophers who have restricted the limits of meta-language to the analysis of other (object) languages. The parodistic use of meta-language in Beckett's prose to confuse the definition of the process of interpretation, and the limits of reflexion in meta-fiction, also ironically makes this problem itself into an object of the reader's interpretation, which demands self-reflexion from the reader on both the 'implication' of the reader in the text, and on his own role in giving meaning to its language.

It might also be suggested that it is from a concern for communicating with the reader that parodists have sometimes, as Cervantes in *Don Quixote*, presented themselves as a model of the critical reader, but have also made an image of the naive reader into an object to be represented in the text itself. In doing this the parodist creates a situation whereby the reader must also relate to himself as an object of the author's discourse if he is to understand the status of other objects represented in the fiction. He must, that is, see his own world through the image of himself, the reader, in the text before him, as a part of a fiction which, as he himself, has taken on a different form than in the world of objects.

Sartre wrote of the surrealists in 1947 that one of their techniques of shocking their public has been to present a phantastic object — such as

Duchamp's sugar blocks in marble (1921) – in such a way that its objectivity is at the same time dialectically superseded, and surrealists like Magritte have even 'objectified' the dialectic as a subject in their work.[6] So, too, one might also describe the picture of the naive reader in *Don Quixote* as an artifice which directs the attention of the reader to himself as an object of criticism in the text, while at the same time putting his reality in the fiction into doubt, so that his understanding of the reality of his self in the fiction must also lead him to question the reality of other objects in the book in a manner which is not naive. In this way parody may fulfil a heuristic function in changing, or developing, the reader's horizon of expectations, while also serving the author in the task of freeing himself from earlier models, giving this liberation concrete form in the parody text and in the liberating effect of laughter implied in it. In German where 'Zitieren' (to quote) also describes the evocation of ghosts, the 'exorcising' function of parody can be described as a form of 'Zitieren' in which the ghosts of the past are quoted in order to be overcome. This exorcism may be realised by the author for his or her self and/or for the reader.

When the characters in *Don Quixote* are shown reading about themselves, the external reader is again 'mirrored' in the text. And while these readers were represented within the first volumes in the caricature of Don Quixote as a naive reader of the Romance – suggesting the situation that they are also to be reading about themselves – so Cervantes later takes Don Quixote (and the caricature of the naive reader) this one step further, to make of Don Quixote a portrait of the naive reader, who, when reading about himself in the caricature of the reader in the figure of Don Quixote, may or may not have recognised a caricature of himself. Here the naive reader's tendency to identify with the text before him is utilised to educate him to both a more critical reading, and to greater 'self-knowledge'.

The book itself takes on a concrete and 'self-conscious' form in the parody of the Romance in *Don Quixote*, and perhaps even a 'meta' three-dimensional character in the blank pages or missing chapters of *Tristram Shandy*. And here the parody text may be seen as a represented object within the book which will fall into the hands of the reader. So the book may reflect upon itself in parody as an object in the world of objects outside the fiction, while also reflecting on the limits of fiction in representing this world. When the meta-language of parody has the book itself as its object it may use the image of the book to duplicate the appearance of objectivity which the book in which the fiction is bound will have for the reader, and it may continue its heuristic task of making the reader aware of the different status of objects within and without the fiction by then transforming the objectivity of the book (as when Don Quixote reads of himself in Part II of the novel) into fiction, or a creation of the fiction. A function of this in *Tristram Shandy* — to strip the self of the preconceptions of author and reader — will be returned to in Section 4.2.

A further example of the objectification of the reader in the book may be found in Joyce's *Ulysses*, where, after describing Bloom's and Stephen's walk home together, Joyce parodies the school exam on literary analysis — asking questions about the actions of his characters (before they have been written), such as 'What parallel courses did Bloom and Stephen follow returning?', to write them in the moment of giving the 'answer' and — ironically — to create the material on which similar exam questions are now set. Here the 'reification' of literary works in the school syllabus is mocked, and here also the character Bloom is ironically reified when he finds himself and an embalmed owl reflected in the mirror of 'giltbordered pierglass' before him, and his outer frame, the book, reflected in the reflection 'of several inverted volumes improperly arranged and not in the order of their common letters with scintillating titles on the two bookshelves opposite'. A catalogue of the books follows, amongst which is listed the title, '*Laurence Bloomfield in Ireland* by William Allingham (second edition, green cloth, gilt trefoil design, previous owner's name on recto of flyleaf erased)'.

Bloom — superimposed on these books in the mirror (or they on him) — represents the 'second edition' of this book (or it to him), and like these books (and the embalmed owl), stands reified as a character in fiction in the static reflection of the world of the book in the mirror before him. As a vehicle of Joyce's parody, which serves not only to erase the names of the 'previous owners' of other books which it uses, but to refunction them so that their imitation is ironised, Bloom is however more than a static reflection of the world or of other books, just as Joyce's book is an ever-changing and dialectical game both with other texts and their worlds, and with the idea of fiction as reflection.

Meta-fictions such as *Don Quixote* might be said to differ from the meta-linguistic analysis of language by reflecting the whole process of text-reception within the text itself. When Beckett writes about Joyce's *Finnegans Wake*, 'Here form is content, content is form . . . His writing is not about something, it is something itself',[7] he emphasises the autonomy of a text seen as a meta-language and of a text which has also foregrounded its relationship both to standard speech and to the literary

traditions from which its language might be said to come. Seeing a
work as meta-fiction, as the discussion not just of language but of the
whole process of the composition and reception of literary texts, leads
us, however, to join in the game of interpretation mirrored in the text,
and to see this game mapped out in the meta-fiction itself. In fact Smuda
has implied that Beckett is also engaging in meta-fiction in discussing his
own and others' literary language and works, though he uses only the
word meta-language to describe this:[8]

> Becketts Schreibweise kann als Metasprache bezeichnet werden, weil
> sie sich reflektierend von einer Prosa der Tradition abhebt und die
> Auseinandersetzung mit ihr zum Gegenstand der literarischen
> Produktion wird ... [9]

Beckett's prose is here described as 'meta-linguistic' because it supersedes a tradition of prose, while making this reflective supersession a
subject of another fiction. In doing this Beckett's novels are also
parodistic, self-parodistic and meta-fictional. Parody has served
modernists such as Beckett and writers of the 'nouveau roman', with a
form both of revolt against the past and a way of centering attention on
the way in which the reflexive consciousness of the text is expressed,
and then interpreted by the reader. But within the frame of the fiction
this analysis has less the scientific character of meta-language than the
playfulness of meta-fiction. In self-referring meta-fictions such as
Borges' 'Ficciones' the difficulty of 'using language to escape from
language' is made into the virtue of creating a new form of self-reference
in writing – but even here the limits of self-reflexion have, as will be
argued presently, become problematic.

3.2 General Parody and Parodistic 'Meta-Fiction'

It will be suggested by the use of the word 'meta-fiction' that some
parody provides a 'mirror' to fiction, in the ironic form of the imitation
of art in art, as well as by more direct references to these authors, books,
and readers. It is not suggested, however, that all meta-fiction is parodistic.
In Book 8 of Homer's *Odyssey*, for instance, the first narrator of the
story describes how Odysseus hears of his own exploits from a blind
minstrel (who is possibly a 'mirror' to Homer); Odysseus himself then
brings the story of his journey up to date, before the first narrator takes
over from him. It is, perhaps significant, however, that Homer was for
many authors – as Cervantes was – a paradigm of the 'realistic' author.
 Parody and meta-fiction are also alike in criticising naive views of the

representation of nature in art, and in that parody is, as meta-fiction, able to demonstrate critically the processes involved in the production and reception of fiction from within a literary text, it is also able to show how a literary work exists both within a particular social context and a literary tradition. Much parody is therefore both satirical and self-reflexive, or ironic, while also offering criticisms of traditional concepts of imitation. The 'mirror' used by some parodists will also be seen to be self-reflexive, and to have hence, as well, the function of superseding imitation. For in that self-parody can be seen to foreground the problem of ever completing the task of 'imitating' or 'catching up' (as Tristram Shandy says) with the 'self', it also puts into doubt the thesis that the mirror, held up to its subject in the literary work, will give the reader a 'true' picture of the subject. The concept of 'truth' and its verification will also be discussed with such issues in mind, and it is these problems which will be seen to be reflected *on* in the parody. In serving to criticise the concept of imitation some meta-fictional parody has, therefore, gone further than suggested in Renaissance and pre-Renaissance poetics; and here the restriction of parody to 'Gegengesang' or counter-song in some definitions may also be seen in the context of the time in which these definitions were composed, as reflecting the view that forms of literature critical of imitation were oppositional in a negative sense. That the criticism of imitation might also be 'creative' was doubted even after the Romantic period by some critics, and parody relegated to a form of 'negative' imitation – to plagiarism.

M.H. Abrams comments in *The Mirror and the Lamp* on the popularity of the idea of the mirror in Renaissance literature:

> There are mirrors of fools and mirrors for magistrates. The analogue was especially popular for comedy, the early representation of literary realism, and a great many critics, Italian and English, cited the words that Donatus, writing in the fourth century had attributed to Cicero, that comedy is 'a copy of life, a mirror of custom, a reflection of truth'.

But it will be argued here that the satirist's distorting mirror could also do more than 'reflect truth' – by laying bare the myth of validity in mimetic art. In this sense the parodist's mirror is not merely an 'analogue' to truth, but a tool in the supersession of the limitation of art to imitation and representation.

The criticism of the 'truth' of fiction in novels following *Don Quixote* and *Tristram Shandy*, is part of a critique of unreflexive realism which

has taken various forms in literary history. Even disparate works such as
Diderot's *Jacques le Fataliste*, Proust's parodies of the Goncourt
Journals, and the nouveau Roman, demonstrate a common critique of
the myth of realistic representation in mimetic art; and of the assumption that art may truthfully mirror other worlds.

The complicated structure produced by the use of specific and
general parody in *Don Quixote* created not only a subtle ambivalent
form of literary satire, but a mirror to the author, his book and his
reader which attacked naive concepts of reflection and imitation.
Sometimes this mirror distorts, and sometimes it reflects an already distorted version of the ideal in reality. In the so-called 'Cervantic
tradition', and following it, this meta-fictional device has been used by
parodists to criticise unreflective literary traditions, but also to analyse
the problem of mimesis, the relationship of fiction and reality in their
own work. Through Don Quixote's imitation of the heroes of the
knightly Romance the latter are brought to life in distorted form and
brought into conflict with the reality of Don Quixote's milieu, and
with that of the reader whom the hero also represents. Through this
dialectical confrontation of the fiction with its 'contradiction' – within
another fiction – Cervantes is said to have created the way to the
supersession of the Romance. By this means Cervantes is also said to
have contrasted fiction and reality to establish a more 'realistic' form
of fiction. Yet it is also true that his use of parody in the novel is
directed towards reflecting the fictional nature of the context in which
this conflict of the Romance and reality takes place, and that the
realism of his work was reflexive and self-critical. Not only does
Cervantes ironically mock his own *Galatea* (in Chapter 6 of Book I),
but he represents himself in *Don Quixote* as both a more self-conscious
reader of the Romance than his hero, and as an author capable of
rewriting it and other works to greater effect. The multiplicity of
fictional authors (as well as readers) in the work – of, for example,
Cide Hamete and his 'interpreter' – provides a number of mirrors for
the ironical author. It might also be said that the irony used in *Don
Quixote* creates a sub-textual connection of another kind between Don
Quixote as the heroic Messiah manqué, satirised by Cervantes as a fool,
and Cervantes as the satirist whose book against the knightly Romance
will mean the true 'salvation' of literature. Thus the friend speaks in
the *Prologue* of the book as 'the light *and* mirror of knight errantry'[10]
for it is Cervantes' parody as a whole which reflects the 'true' fiction,
through its self-critical satirically distortive reflection of the world as
book. And, as it is in the nature of the satirist's mirror itself to shed

this light, so the *Prologue* concludes with a description of the friend's advice as 'enlightening' — a covert reference to the fictional friend's identity with his maker, Cervantes, but also to the function of the book both as the product and self-reflexive mirror of Cervantes' thought. Through this method of self-conscious reflection Cervantes created his 'open' structure for the novel. In 'Tlön, Uqbar, Orbis Tertius', Borges describes a fictional world based, moreover, on the rules of fiction:

> The Metaphysicians do not seek for the truth or even for verisimilitude, but rather for the astounding . . .

The paradox of this world — that in it science and reason argue themselves to be fictitious — is one which meta-fictions such as *Don Quixote* (as Borges is obviously aware) have raised. This confusion can itself, however — ironically — be taken to mirror the world. Borges has himself described Cervantes (for whom he says, 'the real and the poetic were antinomies'[11]) as one seeking deliberately to confuse the reader:

> Cervantes takes pleasure in confusing the objective and the subjective, the world of the reader and the world of the book.[12]

The burning of Don Quixote's books is, for example, a typically ambiguous self-referential moment in Cervantes' book. For though it is part of Cervantes' satire of Don Quixote's naivete, and reflects the reductive character of some of Cervantes' parody, it also implicitly condemns the Inquisitorial burning of books to which an untutored reading of literature might also lead, and refers then too to the censorship suffered by Cervantes in his own time.

As, however, a function of Cervantes' parody had been to mock the target of his criticism by bringing it back to life in order to take the logic of its statements to a new conclusion, so Borges' Pierre Menard, 'Author of the *Quixote*', burns, in a suitably self-referential gesture, his *own* books. Borges writes in a footnote to Menard's habit of destroying the products of his attempts to write *Don Quixote*:

> I remember his quadricular notebooks, his black crossed-out passages, his peculiar typographical symbols and his insect-like handwriting. In the afternoons he liked to go out for a walk around the outskirts of Nîmes; he would take a notebook with him and make a merry bonfire.[13]

Don Quixote has been taken both as the model for other parodies — by Fielding[14] and Sterne in England, and Wieland in Germany, to name only a few — and as the paradigm of the novel. As we have seen, it introduces a critique of the truth of mimetic fiction into fiction itself. And more than this, as a meta-fictional work, *Don Quixote* foregrounds many other concealed problems in the literary text, the dependency of supposedly autonomous literary texts on other texts, on expectations of their readers, and the social milieu. When Sterne speaks, in Chapter 12 of Volume I of *Tristram Shandy*, of a 'Cervantic tone', he is both paradoxically — despite the parodist's distrust of authority (auctoritas) — 'canonising' parody as a literary style, and laying bare the self-consciousness inherent in the author's use of parody and irony. In doing this he is both using parody as a model and making it the subject for his text.

This use of parody, which may be termed general parody, can be compared with the Romantics' use of irony as both a form of 'heightening' self-reflection, and an image for a world projected by the ironist as being ruled by the laws of irony. Specific parody, the comic quotation of certain texts within another, need not necessarily be part of a general parody: its primary function may be satiric, and, within novels such as *Don Quixote*, can serve to add further levels to the parodistic mode of the work.

As the comic effect of specific parody is often derived from its evocation of the readers' expectations for a certain text, and the disappointment of those expectations with the distortion of the text, the parodist must assume that the object of his satire will be known to a proportion of the reading public. But with general parody, the reception of its irony assumes an identification of the reader with the parodist's purpose, as well as recognition of the work which is being satirised. In the 'meta-literary' analysis of another text, the parodist is to be seen in the dual role of reader and writer, as both the 'decoder' of the parodied text and its new 'encoder', and here the reception by the reader of the parody can be said to be foreshadowed and foregrounded in the parody itself. The reader of *Don Quixote* may thus see himself satirised as a reader of the Romance, but he may also identify with the parodist as the critical reader, if not with the parodist as author.

3.3 The Parodist as Author and Reader

The dual role of the parodist as reader and author of an other's work is particularly evident in examples of parody in the novel. Jane Austen's *Northanger Abbey* may be taken as a well-known example of the use of parody in a novel which takes its surface plot features from the novels which are the object of its satire. In doing this Austen marks herself as a reader of the text, the value of which she is questioning, and — in refunctioning its plot — also assumes the role of independent author. Foregrounding both her use of the contemporary popular novel for parody, and the peculiar interrelationship of the parodist and reader in the parody (which is one of criticism and identification), Austen ironically mirrors *her* use of parody in the use of parody by one of her characters, Tilney. Just as a function of Austen's use of parody is the education of her readers to more critical, urbane literary taste, the use of parody by her character Tilney to educate the heroine Catherine in more urbane conversation also mirrors the moral purpose of the author. Here the mirror — like the book in the parody — is an object which can be said to supersede itself in the moment of being presented, for not only do the parodist's mirrors reflect in at least two directions at once — back to the target and forward to the author — but their distortion of either or both show them to be mirrors which do not perform in the manner of normal reflectors. Many conventions of the popular novel are parodied in the opening chapter of *Northanger Abbey* in which Catherine is introduced — not least the figure of the girl born to be heroine. But the appearance of Mr Tilney in Chapter 3 puts the characters into roles similar to those of the author and the reader of Austen's parody itself. Catherine Morland is made the amused audience to Mr Tilney's intentional parody of the conventional politenesses of speech which he has overlooked in engaging her in conversation:

> Then forming his features into a set smile, and affectedly soften-
> ing his voice, he added, with a simpering air,
> 'Have you been long in Bath, Madam?'
> 'About a week, sir' replied Catherine, trying not to laugh.
> 'Really!' with affected astonishment.
> 'Why should you be surprised sir?'
> 'Why indeed?' said he in his natural tone; 'But some emotion
> must appear to be raised by your reply, and surprise is easily
> assumed, and not less reasonable, than any other. Now let us go
> on. Were you never here before, madam?'

To emphasise the contrast between the standard use of conventions and their parody, Tilney is shown falling out of one role into that of a parodist. The reader, like Catherine, is given a signal for the parodist's intention by the changes in tone from natural to 'conventional', and from ironic to natural voice. This piece of reported speech also shows, that while the use of parody and irony in speech can ensure the communication of intention through modulations of tone, the novel writer must devise other, literary signals.

In the passage quoted above Austen may both be satirising social conventions and parodying their representation in novels of other writers. Austen's solution to the problem of communicating her intention in the novel as a whole is, as in this case, to mirror herself as parodist in a character, and then to act as commentator to his use of parody. Some subtlety in her use of parody is maintained, in that Tilney's final change of tone and fall out of his role as parodist may be seen as a clue to Austen's revelation of her parodistic intention in mirroring herself in the parodist Tilney.

The reaction of the yet little educated Catherine to Tilney's irony, of mild but amused confusion, appears, moreover, ironically to mirror the possible reaction of the readers of Austen's parody of the popular novel, who are unable to decide in Chapter 1 if what they are reading is intentionally satiric. Here they may see their confusion portrayed in that of the heroine and receive another hint from the author to see the conventions of the Gothic novel parodied, and they themselves re-educated with the heroine. Moreover, Tilney (a mirror-image to the parodist Austen) creates his own mirror to his use of parody by imagining himself written up in Catherine's journal. In a following passage Tilney ironically pre-empts his audience's naive reaction to himself, in a manner similar to Austen's in portraying herself and her reader in the figures of Tilney and the naive Catherine. Tilney has just concluded his parody of polite conventions:

> 'Now I must give one smirk, and then we may be rational again.'
> Catherine turned away her head, not knowing whether she might venture to laugh. 'I see what you think of me' said he gravely, 'I shall make a poor figure in your journal tomorrow.'
> 'My Journal!'
> 'Yes; I know exactly what you will say:— "Friday, went to the Lower Rooms; wore my sprigged muslin robe with blue trimmings, plain black shoes; appeared to much advantage but was strangely harassed by a queer half-witted man, who would make me dance with him and distressed me by his nonsense." '

The mirror to the novel set up by Austen is one which will move with her through her book, sometimes being used to reflect herself as author, sometimes to reflect the reader, and sometimes to distort and caricature those other authors and readers she will satirise. In this sense — and in the sense that its function is to distort that which it is assumed to reflect — the mirror held up to another literary work (or to the poetics of fiction) by the parodist, is not simply 'mimetic' but 'dialectical' in its effect. So too the parody used by Austen works in several directions at once — in pointing to the roles of author and reader outside the book, and to the fictional nature of the world of the characters within. This allows a multiplicity of sub-texts and meanings to be found in the book by the reader. Characters, author and reader are all simultaneously the targets and the tools of satire. Thus too the world of fiction is shown, as in Cervantes' parody, to be both potentially misleading to the reader and educative.

In parodies such as *Northanger Abbey* and *Don Quixote* the clash between the worlds of fiction and reality is shown on the example of the naive readers, who, because they are unable to clearly distinguish the two worlds, cannot cope with either. Like these parodies the play-within-the-play has the function of distinguishing the fictional nature of the work offered to the public from the public world by providing a mirror to the fiction. The play of Snug the Joiner in *A Midsummer Night's Dream* is but one case in which the play-within-the-play is also a means of satirising other works apart from the play in which it is performed: in this sense it has both an ironic, reflexive function and a satiric purpose. When Bottom advises the actor playing the 'Lion' to show he is a human actor to the ladies in the audience, he assumes, on the basis of his own naivete, that they will not understand it to be fiction without specific reference from the players. This ironic identification of the naive Bottom with the audience may also have the specific satirical purpose of mocking naivete in the theatre audience outside the play-within-the-play.[15] The unintentional parody by the naive players of the conventions they admire and seek to imitate also of course serves to satirise those conventions as practised in the contemporary theatre. Yet apart from these specific satirical functions of the play-within-the-play, it — like other parodies — also fulfils the more general function of foregrounding the processes involved in the communication of meaning between author and reader in the fiction.

Another play-within-a-play, Buckingham's *The Rehearsal* of 1671, parodied Dryden and dramatic tragedies of its day, as Fielding was to parody the theatre of his time in his *Tom Thumb* (1730 and 1731), and Henry Carey the same in his *Chrononhotonthologos* of 1734, and Sheridan his age in *The Critic* in 1779. Then as now, in plays such as

Tom Stoppard's *Travesties*, the scope of the parody text could be
enlarged by the parody of gestures and styles of other theatres and
companies, or of older traditions. Sheridan's *The Critic* is, however,
not only a tragedy within a farce and a parody of tragedic practices of
its time, but a satire on the manipulation of theatre by forces other
than the author, audience, and actors, by, that is, critics, management,
and patrons. In Act I.i Mrs Dangle serves to point Sheridan's critical
finger at the influence of the philistine on art:

> *Mrs Dangle.* And what have you to do with the theatre, Mr. Dangle?
> Why should you affect the character of a critic? I have no
> patience with you! – haven't you made yourself the jest of all
> your acquaintance by your interference in matters where you
> have no business? Are you not called a theatrical Quidnunc,
> and a mock Maecenas to second-hand authors.
> *Dangle.* True; my power with the managers is pretty notorious. But
> is it no credit to have applications from all quarters for my
> interest – from Lords to recommend fiddlers, from ladies to
> get boxes, from authors to get answers, and from actors to get
> engagements?

Thus Sheridan does not exclude the author (or, hence, himself) from his
criticism, giving both authors and actors a share in the blame for the
influence of the critic over the theatre. But it is also clear that as much
as authors may sell of their honour in this way as much do they try to
get back in their satire. And while Sheridan's satire is self-referring on
several different levels at once his target remains caricatured in black
and white – lacking both 'the profit of the "plague and trouble" of
theatrical property', or, as Mrs Dangle continues 'the ambiguous credit
of the abuse that attends it'.

The political satire which Sheridan has added to his literary satire
makes it difficult to evaluate the criticism of Dangle's avoidance of
politics for the theatre with the excuse that the stage is the 'Mirror
of Nature'. Though Sheridan's satiric parody may provide a distorting
mirror to Dangle's world which may perhaps influence his public in
wanting to avoid *it*, Mr Dangle's theatre is of another kind, and a mirror
which is shown in the 'mirror' of Sheridan's stage to reflect neither
truth nor nature.

The role of meta-fictional parodies in criticising naive concepts of
art as a mirror to the world, by providing a mirror to the writer's art
itself, may either serve to argue for a more 'realistic' representation

of the world as the world of the writer, and a more self-conscious use of art as fiction, or for a more absurdist picture of the world 'as stage', where reality had been totally fictionalised.

In satires of the poetaster, as in Sheridan's *The Critic*, the self-reflective function of parody comes into play to reflect satirically on audience and critics, but also to reflect on art within art, and to draw criticism back into the text and the fictional character of the play itself. So it turns out at the end of Act I of *The Critic* that the newspaper reports of events in the political world which Mrs Dangle claims to be of greater importance than the happenings of the theatre are themselves products of writers of fiction and theatre reviews such as poetaster Puff. Puff's reporting of current events are no more 'true' than his historical drama, parodied in *The Critic*. All writing is under 'suspicion' in the meta-fiction, a function of which is to sharpen the public's powers of discriminating fact from fiction, and good fiction from bad. Here fiction is also rescued from a naive relationship to its subject, and to itself as the means of representing objects from reality within the 'second' world of the stage. Thus parody could also serve to introduce a critique of 'realism' into literature where, for example, satire might remain bound by its contrast of ideal and reality.

Tom Stoppard's *Travesties* (London, 1975) also uses parody in a meta-fictional way, and as both its subject and form, in basing its action on that of Oscar Wilde's *The Importance of Being Earnest*, produced by Joyce in Zurich at the time of the action of Stoppard's play. Not only does *Travesties* thus present its action as a play within a play, and a parody within parody, but raises questions of the relationship between art and art, art and audience, and art and society, which also reflect the scepticism of the author of meta-fiction towards naive representations of the theatre on stage. The exchange of the manuscript of Joyce's *Ulysses* with Lenin's plan for Revolution brings to life on stage the juxtapositions characteristic of both parody and revolutionary history. It is also no accident that the part of *Ulysses* concerned is the 'Oxen of the Sun' passage, a paradigm of parodies:

> *Joyce.* Miss Carr, did I or did I not give you to type a chapter in which Mr. Bloom's adventures correspond to the Homeric episode of the Oxen and the Sun?
> *Gwen.* Yes, you did! And it was wonderful!
> *Joyce.* Then why do you return to me an ill-tempered thesis purporting to prove, amongst other things, that Ramsay MacDonald is a bourgeois lickspittle gentleman's gentleman? (etc.)⁶

'Oxen of the Sun' is, in the own words of Stoppard's Joyce, 'a
chapter which by a miracle of compression, uses the gamut of English
Literature from Chaucer to Carlyle to describe events taking place in
a lying-in hospital in Dublin'.[17] So too Stoppard compresses Tristan
Tzara, Lenin, and Joyce together, using the concept of Wilde's
'Importance of being Earnest' — of the unwitting exchange of the
manuscript of a novel for the baby Ernest (himself, of course, a
fiction) — to bring together not only classes previously kept apart, but
historical characters who were themselves involved — in revolution
or in literary parody — in turning their worlds upside down. 'Travesties'
and not 'Travesty' is the title of Stoppard's play, and the function of
meta-fictional parody (as found together with 'travesty' in Stoppard's
play) to reflect on itself as well on its subject, is also reflected in the
plurality of parody worlds presented on the stage. The climax of the
scene in which Joyce's manuscript is identified (as Ernest is identified
in Wilde's play), also reflects on a function of parody as a tool of
epistemological change, announcing the entrance of new knowledge on
stage as well as for the audience outside the play. Though Locke may
not have valued wit so highly, Kant — referring to parodies by Blumauer
and Fielding — had attributed a function in changing opinion to wit (in
the 1790s — notably, following the Revolution of 1789), and it is a
function which serves to explain in part at least the place of parody in
periods of epistemological upheaval, and, in Stoppard's play, the juxtaposition and concrete exchange of Joyce's parody with Lenin's plan
for the Revolution. The rediscovery of Joyce's manuscript precedes
(hence with only apparent absurdity) the recognition by the other
characters of their correct (or given) identities: '(Gwen and Cecily
swap folders with cries of recognition. Carr and Tzara close in. A
rapid but formal climax, with appropriate cries of "Cecily! Gwendoline!
Henry! Tristan!" and appropriate embraces.)'[18] Even the 'complete
dislocation of the play' which Stoppard announces at this point may be
said to have the recognisable parodistic functions of disturbing the
presuppositions brought by the audience to the theatre. Peter Handke's
more aggressive attack on the audience in *Publikumsbeschimpfung*
('Insulting the Audience') also made use of parody, but, as in his
Quodlibet, this parody has the function of breaking down the expectations of the audience through an attack on their use of language as a
source of cliches to match (or reflect) their preformed ideas. Carr's
earlier Wilde-like comment on the dangers of irony might be recalled in
interpreting the roles given parody and irony in disturbing the audience
in *Travesties*:

Carr (aside). Bennett seems to be showing alarming signs of irony. I
have always found that irony among the lower orders is the first
sign of an awakening social consciousness. It remains to be seen
whether it will grow into an armed seizure of the means of
production distribution and exchange or spend itself in liberal
journalism.

The cynicism of Carr's words — strengthened by the fact that Carr himself is being used as a mouthpiece of authorial irony — serves also to
express the basic problem of the play of the relationship between art and
society, which is, not least, a problem of communication. In the chaos of
the final scene (which again reflects on the function of revolution, parody,
and Tzara's Dada to overturn the status quo) the audience is confronted
with a confusion in which they may find humour, but also the challenge
to find meaning in it and in the art used to represent it, and to offer
their own answers to the problem of the play. And it can also be said, that
Stoppards's use of Joyce offers not only a comment on his own use of
parody in *Travesties*, but on the role of Joyce's parody in the modern
episteme.

Joyce's parody is, as we have seen, also meta-fictional. The 'author'
of Sterne's *Tristram Shandy* spoke to his reader of the difficulties of
adhering to a rule of unity of time in telling his autobiography, not only
because of the implication that in the act of telling he is adding more
to his life and can thus 'never catch up with himself', but because he can
never hope to give an hour's reading for an hour's living and hope to
progress. Joyce's *Ulysses*, on the other hand, takes Homer's epic to
describe the day in the life of a character. Here literature is made to fit
into the depiction of a life which is itself fictional, and Joyce has
mirrored both the refunctioning of Homer's *Ulysses* for the story of
Bloom, and the mirroring effect on fiction which this creates within his
book in the parodies of the parody of Homer's 'Oxen of the Sun'
passage. These parodies also, as Stoppard comments in *Travesties*, refer
to the process of giving birth to new lives in the 'lying-in hospital' in
Dublin. But they reflect on this further in that while Bloom is 'reliving'
the Homeric epic being parodistically refunctioned by Joyce, the
parodies of works of English literature, which serve to present this
episode, reflect the birth of Joyce's own style, and, so, the birth of the
parody which they themselves are.

Stuart Gilbert wrote in his 'Prolegomena to *Work in Progress*:

The obscurity of that passage, its prolixity and redundancy — all are deliberate, and artistically logical. For this whole episode of the 'Oxen of the Sun' is constructed so as to follow the growth of the embryo from its dark and formless origin to the hour of its emergence into the light of day, a fully developed and perfected child. The style of this section of *Ulysses* is at first dark and shapeless. Gradually the diction takes form and clarifies itself till it culminates in a futurist cacophany of syncopated slang, the jargon of our latest and loudest *jeunesse nickelée*. But, before this outburst, the language ascends in orderly march the gamut of English styles — of Mallory, Mandeville, Bunyan, Addison, Sterne, Landor, Macaulay, Ruskin, Carlyle and others. (It may be noted, however, that, as in the unborn embryo there is often premature development of a certain part, so there are occasional patches in the first section of the 'Oxen of the Sun' where the terseness and clarity of styles are anticipated.)[19]

Joyce's use of parody, to give birth to new children from old parents, is clearly reflected in this complex of parodies within parodies. In the 'Oxen of the Sun' parodies he has given both a genealogy of his forbears, and an example of how the imitative faculties of the self may be refunctioned to serve it in the process of coming to consciousness of itself in distinguishing itself from others. And here Joyce also indicates the role parody will take in modern literature as an 'archaeology' of the text in which both the epistemological and material limitations on its composition and reception are recreated, through the use of preformed language from other works, and reinterpreted in anticipation of the interpretation of the parody by its readers, but also in the attempt to supersede and eliminate these limitations restricting both the parodist and his readers.

Meta-fiction can, as Max Beerbohm's story of Enoch Soames demonstrates, also be at once the vehicle of satire, literary criticism and self irony. The world of 'Enoch Soames' is, Lord David Cecil writes, a portrait of the 'World of *The Yellow Book*', while 'Savonarola Brown' is 'like Buckingham's *Rehearsal* and Sheridan's *Critic*' a 'skit on the pseudo-poetic tragedy'.[20] As in Joyce's 'Oxen of the Sun' parodies Beerbohm runs the gamut of styles in his parodies, bringing to the surface models of the apprentice writer, or memories of the reader for older works, which ultimately serve, however, to disturb that which is of familiar or sentimental value to the reader of the parody, while 'exorcising' the past for the writer. 'The Happy Hypocrite' of 1897 begins, for example, with a parodistic juxtaposition of cautionary tales for children with the stories of the *demi-monde* of the decadents of the 1890s. This juxtaposition serves to parody both genres as they reflect the one upon the other and create an unequal, comic union together. Here Beerbohm also creates a caricature of the addressed reader as an adult child, to signal the 'Romance' that follows as a tale of seduction, in which the language of the Romance serves a less naive purpose for the seducer than the naive reader might have expected:

> None it is said, of all who revelled with the Regent, was half so wicked as Lord George Hell. I will not trouble my little readers with a long recital of his great naughtiness. But it were well they should know he was greedy, destructive and disobedient. I am afraid there is no doubt that he often sat up at Carlton House long after bed-time, playing at games, and that he generally ate and drank far more than was good for him.[21]

It is in 'Enoch Soames' (1912), where Max himself appears, that these parodies also serve a meta-fictional game with the book itself.

Under the mask of autobiography Beerbohm presents to his reader the story of his meeting with the poet 'Enoch Soames' in the Cafe Royal in the days of *The Yellow Book*. Under the guise of presenting a sympathetic portrait of the sorry figure of Soames — who, we later learn, is to sell his soul to the devil for the chance to see his name in the catalogue of the British Museum — Beerbohm writes a satire of the English imitators of the Paris decadents of the *fin de siècle*, using fictitious works which he attributes to Soames in order to parody the writings of the poetasters Soames represents. 'Fungoids', of course, the title of Soames' poems, is said (with ironic dissimulation on the part of Beerbohm) to represent 'strange growths, natural and wild; yet exquisite . . . many-hued, and full of poisons'. Their parodistic echo of Baudelaire's 'Fleurs du mal' foregrounds the irony of this description and their true 'parasitic' or plagiaristic character as literary fictions. For these fungoids grow on other literary trees, and are hence 'fleurs du mal' of another kind than those of Baudelaire's work.

When Soames returns from his visit to the Reading Room of the BM one hundred years hence (the visit allowed him by the devil), and announces to Beerbohm that he has found himself mentioned only once, in a story written by Max Beerbohm, we have self-referring irony as well as satire. This ironic game with the book again raises questions about its relationship to reality which remain unanswered. Beerbohm's professed loyalty to Soames, in letting us know 'he was real', serves, however, other functions than raising meta-fictional questions about the verifiability of his statements. For it allows him to write the book which is to 'upset' Soames on his return from the next century, to give his character a final satirical stab by then questioning his status in the fiction, and to make a story out of the writing of fiction itself. In 'A vain child' Beerbohm parodies his own meta-fictional use of his self as one of his fictional characters, and his own works as the subject-matter of those other fictions, to take the meta-fictional game one step further, though not in order to supersede it. The function of parodistic meta-fiction, to criticise but also extend fiction, will be returned to in the following section.

Such literary examples as the above should show parody to be a critical form of fiction and a multi-faceted phenomenon not only within satire, but within literary history as such. One way of defining parody to include etymological, historical and sociological perspectives would be to define it as a literary work perceived by the reader as juxtaposing preformed language material with other linguistic or literary material in an incongruous manner in a new context, to produce a comic effect. But it should be remembered that the definition serves only as a signpost to further analysis. The heuristic function of dialectical parody in changing opinion is an issue which goes beyond specific textual analysis and may also be linked with its epistemological function of introducing change into the work of a writer, and into the broader context of the inherited literary tradition from within which he or she writes. The limits of meta-fiction, and the limits of meta-criticism as we find it in such parodies, will also be discussed in the next section.

3.4 'Higher-Order Actions' and the Problems of Meta-Criticism

Works of general parody often offer analyses of the processes of composing and receiving texts — and may, in phenomenological terms, also comment on the difference between the processes of understanding and receiving, and between reflexion and recognition. As both a form of reflexion and as meta-fiction, meta-fictional parody also, however, raises the philosophical problems of the independence of meta-language from its own criticism, of the possibility of meta-actions being of a 'higher' order to the statements or actions they describe, and, hence, of the possibilities of revolutionising the functions of literary language or general discourse.

Gilbert Ryle, writing on the 'Systematic Elusiveness of "I" ' in the *Concept of Mind*, has stated that a higher-order action is an action, 'the description of which involves the oblique mention of other actions'.

This higher-order action cannot however have itself as its subject, just as an act of ridicule cannot have itself as its target, for 'A higher-order action cannot be the action upon which it is performed'. Ryle concludes: ' "I" is like my own shadow; I can never get away from it, as I can get away from your shadow.' Having taken the act of ridicule as an illustration of the limitation of meta-statements (or 'higher-order actions') to subjects other than themselves, Ryle then passes to the subject of self-parody, taking the example of the singing master who is able to parody his pupil but not himself, to argue that self-parody is as 'impossible' as any other higher-order action working upon itself. The logical status of meta-critical statements raised here is of interest not only to the discussion of general parody as meta-fiction and of the limits of its critical powers, but to an understanding of the scepticism with which irony, and parody, are themselves treated as ways 'to the truth' in modernist literature. For whereas, as we have seen, Friedrich Schlegel regarded irony both as being of an 'higher order' than satire because of its reflexive character, and a way to the 'liberation' of the self in its reflexion on itself, and Kierkegaard also wrote[22] that control over irony would bring the writer both freedom and closer to the truth and reality, modernist authors have put these theses in doubt. Canetti's parody of the idealist dialectic in his novel *Die Blendung* (*Auto-da-fé*) has, for instance, described the result of the idealist dialectic (such as that on which Schlegel's concept of irony was based) to be the absolute isolation of the self within the book, which lends to the destruction of both. In this novel the book, as also a medium of meta-fictional analysis, meets (like Pierre Menard's *Don Quixote*) its auto-da-fé, which is only 'transcendental' in a grotesque ironic sense. Here meta-fiction and irony — never able to reach the truth about themselves in the sense promised by Kierkegaard — are not shown to have won a new freedom for the author's self, but to have trapped him in a never-ending circle of self-criticism, or, as in the extreme case of Canetti's Peter Kien, in the world of the book. What for Tristram Shandy was yet another irony about irony, authors following the nineteenth century have taken as a final irony of tragic as well as comic character — of, in fact, grotesqueness. The modern parodist has shown the book within the book to be part of a chase in which the authorial self appears to be unsure as to whether he is the tortoise or the hare or (as in the grotesque!) an amalgam of the two. Tristram Shandy wrote: 'Write as I will — I shall never overtake myself' (Book 4, 13) — and yet in making this scepticism the subject of their fiction, modernists have again, it will be argued, 'potentialised' parody in the act of superseding it.

The limitation of self-analysis, and meta-criticism, to other subjects is, as Ryle puts it, also the problem of self-parody. Self-parody, or irony (as Schlegel defined the two), cannot, in this view, be seen as a way to discovering the truth, as Kierkegaard believed it to be. Yet it must of course be remembered that (anachronistically put) Tristram's apparent agreement with Ryle, that one can never 'catch up with one-self', in his game with his autobiography, is concerned with showing the limits of the self's analysis of itself while also, thereby — and through self-parody — expanding the self's knowledge of itself. Just as Tristram's problem is derived from the fact that self reflexion adds to the subject-matter which must be analysed, so it adds knowledge to itself, and expands the autobiography. Parody — being both beside and opposite its subject — shows (though it may not be able to show itself in the process of analysis), that its subject may be both reduced and expanded through the parody. (Even the status of parody before the law is, it will be seen, complicated by this ambiguous treatment of its subject.) For the modern parodist there is, hence, no irony without a victim when the author himself must become the victim of his own irony — forever trapped in the cage of meta-language constructed by his text.

Here again the very opposite of Kierkegaard's promised freedom is argued, even if this argument itself is yet another antithesis — as irony was for Kierkegaard — to a thesis. Here the modern author as ironist is also not necessarily concerned with proving his self-reflective text to be 'more true' than another. Though it may come closer to representing the reality of the author, the parodistic and modernist meta-fiction has also shown itself to be forever short of its mark of analysing the reality of its own fiction, and in knowing its relationship to the category Truth, which Kierkegaard had given as the goal of irony.[23] And here too modern parody begins to question the dialectical form attributed it by nineteenth-century Hegelians.

Yet while, like Tristram Shandy, the critical meta-fictionalist may be able to make more literary 'copy' from his criticism of his own representation of reality, the philosopher's criticism of the 'possibility' of self-parody may prove reductive to fiction if misunderstood. Though Gilbert Ryle and others have pointed to a philosophical problem for meta-fiction, which puts in doubt earlier philosophies of fiction such as those offered by Schlegel and Kierkegaard, his use of the term 'self-parody' must be regarded critically in speaking in more general terms of the 'possibility' of self-parody in literature. Ryle had given the example of the singing master who may parody his pupil but not himself[24] in writing that 'self-commentary, self-ridicule and self-admonition are logically condemned to eternal penultimacy'. While Ryle specifies that the problem of self-parody is that 'a word cannot be a parody of itself' so that the parodist can never complete his parody of his self; it must also be made explicit that self-parody as it appears in literature is not to be described so much in terms of a self acting in imitation or parody of its 'self' as in terms of the self-consciously ironic or satiric imitation of previous works, actions, or texts made by that 'self'. Literary parody, moreover, may not only take the form of the imitation of an author's previous works, but thereby also show the author in both a different role to that in which he or she normally appears, and as more than the literary works by which he or she was previously known – giving a different picture of the author's self than given previously, and again serving to 'expand' that self. Ryle's denial of the singing master's ability to parody himself in the very same moments in which he is singing also turns on a physical and temporal problem of doing two things at the same time. But in the fictional discourse – where the normal elocutionary rules of communication between encoder and decoder do not always hold – the *impression* (rather than the 'pretence') of two things happening at the same time – the author presenting his known self, while parodying it – may successfully be created. This can be said to be possible, (1) as the 'self' does not have the same physical definition as the body of the singing master and may be imagined (in as far as it can be imagined apart from something as concrete as the text of the author) as being of more than one kind – and of being present in different forms as well as in the totality in which these forms are 'aufgehoben' or 'superseded'; (2) because recognition of the self-parodying author's self may only come with the perception of a totality made up of thesis and antithesis (or in broad terms, early text and parody) – in which neither separate form appears to dominate or define the other, or to proceed or to follow the other. For example, is Tilney as a vehicle of Jane Austen's self-parody representative of the 'real Austen', or the Austen 'before' Tilney, or the Austen who has created both forms – her text and its parody – and used them together? The psychological problem – of distinguishing texts in parody – will be discussed further in section 3.5.

If cases of self-parody must imply further parody of themselves this need not of course impair their ability to offer meta-critical comments on their subjects from within a self-conscious 'fictitious' context. As many works, such as *Tristram Shandy*, have shown, the 'open-ended' character of the arguments created in the parody by its contradiction and supersession of others has often been exploited by the parodist to create ambiguity, or to show the process of literary creation to be unfinished and open for further development. As suggested earlier, parody, as a meta-fictional comment on the process of literary production and reception, may hold a mirror up to the literary work to reflect on both the work and the mirror, and so too on the concept of imitation as it applies to the literary work. But in casting doubt on the veracity of the fictional world, or on the veracity of the concept of imitation, parody also extends the process of literary production, to make a new literary work from its criticism of the old, and from its questioning of the truth value of the fiction itself. What was for Ryle a disadvantage may thus appear in the literary world of the parody to have the advantage of offering criticism and self-criticism of that world, while also extending it in a new direction.

Though meta-fictional parody may, as a higher-order action, be unable to describe itself 'completely', it can, as an archaeology of the text, foreground its own origins in commenting critically on the pre-formed language of other works or discourses. In evoking the expectations of its audience for a certain text, or discourse, it also foregrounds both the epistemological and material conditions for the reception of literary texts, which will also affect its own reception and 'realisation' by the reader. But the parodist's reflexion on his text is both 'hindered' and expanded by the appearance of these other conditions, for here his text is shown to be both the object (and victim) and subject (and initiator) of other interpretations.

Jürgen Habermas has written in *Erkenntnis und Interesse* (4th edition, Frankfurt am Main, 1977, p. 213), that standard speech (Umgangssprache) is even meta-linguistic by virtue of having internalised the conditions through which it will be interpreted. But here a linguistic sleight of hand conceals the fact that as this interpretation is post-hoc, no 'awareness' of it can be given in standard language itself. Only in its interpretation in another language (which is thereby meta-language) can the immanent interpretation implied in it be 'realised'. Habermas' claims that standard language can 'interpret itself' might also be submitted to Ryle's comment that meta-language cannot have itself as its own subject. Habermas' critique of Nietzsche's nihilistic 'denial of Reflexion' (*Erkenntnis und Interesse*, p. 353) does, however, point (if only implicitly) to a crisis of reflexion in the modernist episteme, in which the limits of the meta-critical methods which had served to criticise less reflexive ideational modes, such as imitation, are also mapped out. But, in some cases at least, this 'crisis' of reflexion may, perhaps, be less nihilistic than Habermas would have it, in taking the logic of analytical and dialectical statements seriously enough to apply also to itself. Here, however, we must restrict ourselves again to a discussion of reflexion in meta-fiction.

In other mediums too parody has sometimes served to transform its criticism of the truth value of the mimetic role of art into criticism of the superior truth of meta-criticism, or the higher reality of meta-fiction itself. In this sense too parody appears in the role of a tertiary criticism of fiction. In art the parodistic criticism of the mimetic principle has played a similar role, and while, for example, the representation of the artist's atelier or studio – representing the artist and his model, or his work – was a commonplace in nineteenth-century art, as a representation of the 'landscape' of the artist's world, the juxtaposition of this studio scene with a traditional landscape – as in Manet's 'Dejeuner sur l'herbe', which 'secularises' Giorgione's pastoral scene of 1510, produced the effect of shocking its public. There the figures of the artist and his naked model, which were in place either in the idyllic phantasy landscape of Giorgione or within the four walls of the artist's studio (as in the frame of the painting), was looked upon as being out of place in the identifiable landscape of the outer world. The painting had erred, in the eyes of its critics, both morally and in terms of the realistic representation of the credible. Yet now the imitation of the photograph by 'hyper-realists' shows meta-commentary to have led the artist back to his earlier subject of criticism – the 'realistic' object in the art work – and to have 'duplicated' it in the process of 'transcending' it. Earlier, surrealists (such as Duchamp) had parodied the Renaissance artist's self-confident reflection of his own work by putting objects from the outside world – from paint brushes to newspapers – into the painting itself, to blur and confuse accepted distinctions between the sign and the signified, the painting and its subject. René Magritte's 'pictures within pictures' have also parodistically 'laid bare' the devices of artistic representation from within the context of the art work itself. 'The beautiful prisoner' of 1931, in which a board on an easel is superimposed on a landscape, shows how the realist – like the photograph – may 'catch' nature in his painting. But it also implies that this picture in a picture has itself been 'caught', and captured, by the artist, and that the meta-artwork, too, may be caught up within the limits of its representation of itself.

And while Charles Ives' stylistic variations on a musical theme, or the musical parodies of Gerard Hoffnung, have been followed by John Cage's more radical 'Silences', in film Renoir's pictures within pictures and plays within plays have been followed by experiments in the meta-film such as Fellini's *8½*. Fellini's attempt to analyse the relationship of the film to the reality it represents through the medium of self-analysis in the meta-film also leads to a more disturbing juxtaposition of the medium and its message, and to more explicit comments on the limits of the former. The acting out of self-analysis in the film by actors — professional or otherwise — also complicates the process of authorial self-analysis as found in meta-fiction. The limitation of meta-languages, that they can never describe themselves in the act of description, also produces here a metaphorical use of meta-criticism as allusion to the problems involved in such analysis — and this function of meta-criticism in parody — of 'showing how' the fiction is made — will be returned to presently.

The logical status of meta-language has also been questioned by Sir Karl Popper in his dialogue entitled 'Self-Reference and Meaning in Ordinary Language', in *Mind*, NS 63, 1954, where he argues both the case for the exclusion of self-referring statements from 'formalised' language and presents his argument — with irony — in the form of a self-referring play. Here we have again an ironic theoretical undermining of such self-referring actions as parody and irony, but also, at the same time, an apparent affirmation of them as tools in critical method. When in the style of other academic parodists, Popper's Socrates reacts to Theatetus' suggestion that their dialogue of 400 BC will not take place 'before another 2,350 years' (that is, the twentieth century), with the complaint that this latest self-reference reminds him of a play, but that as a victim of the joke he is not amused and must 'draw a line some-where' — he is ironically used to introduce Popper's own conclusion to the criticism of self-referring statements as 'truth-giving'. And where does this leave Popper's argument? While it shows us that he is, of course, aware of the important difference between fantasy and arithmetical and 'formalised' language, it also suggests that Popper/ Socrates has used a form of Socratic self-reference — Socratic irony — which may well undermine yet again the criticism of self-referring speech. But if we believe that Popper's use of self-referring irony in his conclusion shows faith in the use of self-referring statements as carriers of meaning, then we must also believe that this is not to be believed! Socratic irony — saying B and meaning A — ambiguously represents here both the application and the undermining of self-referring statements. Hence while it might be said that an irony always implies a meta-comment and explanation from the encoder to his decoder on another code, it also — like the Cretan liar — warns the decoder of accepting verification from its author.

The Cretan liar — whose statement that all Cretans are liars leaves his interlocutor with the paradox of not believing him if he chooses to believe him — is of course also a paradigm of irony. Similarly, an irony may also appear to be a case of paradox — and within the literary work may offer a satiric challenge to the reader to use (as Laurence Sterne wished he would) his imagination in decoding the text offered him. The aim of parodists such as Sterne, to make their readers think about the written word, may also be seen to be expressed in their meta-literary demonstration of *how* the literary text is composed and received. By adjusting Ryle's distinction between higher order and other statements as between statements of 'knowing how' and 'knowing that', we might say that parody may be distinguished as a higher order action from other literary statements as a case of 'showing how' as well as 'showing that'. When Cervantes suggests to his reader that a certain work of fiction is not to be believed, he may be compared to the Cretan liar. For when an author suggests that another fiction (which may or may not mean all fiction) is false, and makes this suggestion from within a fictional text, he is setting us the problem of deciding whether his judgement is therefore also suspect. Yet in that he offers us another literary text in putting this problem to us, he also shows us how fiction may be generated by meta-fiction — and how it is both more than the verification of fact and a product of the world of social institutions controlling both author and reader.

Whereas Popper argues that a meta-language cannot verify itself (as it might be able to verify an object language), parodies such as *Don Quixote* have established their Cretan-liar-like paradoxes to show that it is not a function of fiction to offer verifiable statements of the world — for the naive reader to take as true — but to lead the reader to interpret the fiction as, in its turn, an interpretation of the world of the reader.

The fact that Epimenides makes himself the subject of his sentence by speaking of 'all' (that is, other) Cretans as liars, should also not be overlooked in analysing how the paradox 'conceals' itself. Similarly, when Cervantes claims in *Don Quixote*, that the reality of the Romance fiction is false, he at first conceals the fact that he has also put the truth value of his own fiction, as of all fictional encoding between the author and his 'absent' reader, in doubt. In that Don Quixote represents the reader of both the Romance and of Cervantes' parody of the Romance, Cervantes' warning against the naivete of the

Quixote is also a warning to the reader of Cervantes' book. Hence
Cervantes does not exclude his own text from those which may lead
the Quixote, and the external reader caricatured in him, into confusing
fiction and reality, or into attributing a verifiable truth value to the
fiction. The parody of the Romance by Cervantes also, as argued previously, makes his target a part (structurally) of his own work, so that
both are encoded by the readers as part of the same textual world.
Hence too Cervantes must also 'imply' a warning about his own text
in warning his reader about the fictional character of the truth of
other fictions.

In so doing Cervantes, like Epimenides, creates the apparent
paradox (or irony) that the truth of his own statement, warning
against the truth of the fiction, must itself be put into doubt. For
Cervantes — as for other ironists — this had, however, the heuristic
function of alerting the reader to a critical reading.

Michel Foucault has also discussed the problem of the paradoxical
sentence 'I lie', but in order to suggest a more problematic paradox for
the modern writer — the sentence, 'I speak' (In 'La pensée du dehors',
in *Critique*, 195/6, 1963). Foucault's explanation of Epimenides' Cretan
liar paradox is also that there the speaking subject is the same as that
about which he speaks, whereas every sentence should be of a higher
type than the sentence which is its object. But for Foucault the
Cretan liar paradox threatened the speaker only as long as language
was (falsely) attributed the function of verifying itself as truth. The
Cretan liar paradox hence, so Foucault argues, put into doubt the
Greeks' concept of truth. Similarly it might be suggested that Cervantes'
attack on the use of texts as authorities (explicitly made in the Preface
to *Don Quixote*) also undermined the role of literature in Rhetorics. A
negative result of this, the trivialisation of fiction as embellishment
(and the reduction of the topos as the place of an argument to a cliche),
might be seen as being counter to the aim of Cervantes' attack on the
Romance. The official trivialisation of parody, in order to censor its
subversive criticism, was, however, another negative result which may
be seen to be counter to Cervantes' aims in his novel, and to have
exacerbated other negative effects of his use of parody.

The Cretan liar paradox shows that we can communicate paradoxes
because the truth/falsity law exists, but also because we know that
language, and particularly, perhaps, poetic language, is more than this,
and that a critical attitude to language, as suggested in parody, may also
serve to protect against the misuse of such laws for deceptive purposes.
Poetic language has often given us new metaphors by its deviation from

the laws of normal speech, and irony is but one other way of subverting
these laws to make us look at them, and at our use of them, with fresh
eyes. But the psychoanalytical foregrounding of repressed meaning in
our speech also complicates our definition of how the Cretan liar lies.
For example, can we establish a distinction between true and false
statements when all statements can be assumed to conceal some other,
unspoken, and often apparently contradictory meanings? Or is it then
such an exception to the 'rules' of normal speech for the Cretan to say
'all Cretans are liars', if it can be said that all speech is a form of
deception? For when we say 'I speak the truth and all Cretans (of which
I am *not* one) lie', we raise not only the need for external verification
of our statement, but the question of whether we 'mean to say' what
we have said, and whether the 'verification' of our statement from
external evidence (of whether Cretans lie or do not lie) can tell us anything about our intentions for speaking the truth – remembering again
Augustine's definition of a lie by the 'intention', or will of the speaker,
to say something false.

The rules of truth and falsity which allow us to see the Cretan liar
paradox as contradicting the normal use of these rules are in themselves problematic and open to misuse, as history has often shown.
Irony (and parody) in creating paradoxical statements, and parody in
also finding paradoxes in preformed literary material, show us this, but
also show us that it is the recognition of such problems which enable
us to continue our communications both critically and creatively.

In presenting his readers with a problem to be thought out, Cervantes,
for example, is also directing their attention to the maker of the statement, to the author, and to the problem of how the literary text can
be perpetuated or transformed by a dialectic of illusion, criticism and
paradox. Unlike some meta-linguistic statements (or those made in
mathematics), parody, in making its meta-comment in a language
and, often, generic form similar to that of its target, is able to both
criticise and extend the medium of the literary text, which is its object.
This important difference between parody and mathematical meta-
statements allows us to see the former as a 'higher-order action' which
makes an advantage out of its limitation to the language of its target
in refunctioning the target into a new literary text, in which target and
criticism appear in a synthesis in which the dialectic of text and anti-
text is still evident and observable.

3.5 'Showing How' in Parody

In his discussion of 'Intentions in Parody',[25] Wayne C. Booth refers to

Gombrich's comment on the duck/rabbit picture (designed by its creator Jastrow to be seen – from different 'perspectives' – as duck and/or rabbit), 'that you can see the figure either as a rabbit or a duck, but you can't *see* it as both at the same time', to describe an effect of irony. Wittgenstein's distinction (in his *Philosophical Investigations*) between 'continuous seeing' and the 'dawning' of an aspect in viewing such ambiguous representations as the duck/rabbit may also be made here. And even if it is in the 'dawning' of ambiguity that we first see both figures, it may be granted that our 'continuous seeing' of the object must also change after its ambiguity has been perceived.

It is also an important point to note, with Booth, that, after the observer has recognised both figures in the one drawing and the drawing as a whole 'as an optical illusion', 'our chief pleasure now becomes our awareness of the duplicity'. The parallel here with the ironic – or parodistic text – is clear: our pleasure in recognising ambiguity lies in the recognition of both the cleverness of the author in showing it and in our own cleverness in perceiving it. Yet though it may be difficult for a reader to decide which text is the target of a parody, it does not necessarily follow from this, as Booth appears to imply[26] (following Gombrich), that we are then no longer able to enjoy or perceive the individual figures in the textual landscape – or one strand of meaning in the text independently of another. Booth writes:

> For both receiver and maker, then, the focusing of attention on duplicity inevitably makes each single effect peripheral and thus makes the full focusing on a single effect impossible.[27]

Unlike perhaps in irony, the perception of a relation of ambiguity in parody does not necessarily exclude our continued perception of the parts of this relation as separate, even though our concept of them may have become more complex than before. Even if we perceive them as separate only by putting ourselves into the position of the naive reader seeing each separately before recognising the relation of ambiguity (and knowing 'how' as well as 'that'), our perception of the single effect may (if only in memory) continue to exist 'independently' of our understanding of the whole. The question of *how* our perception of the individual parts may change is different to this question.

Seeing that the figure can be seen in two ways, and that we may have at least two or three ideas about what it represents (a rabbit, or a duck, or the idea of a duck/rabbit/ is, as in the case of perceiving a parody as consisting of two texts (and as being both 'itself' and something else), a matter of understanding the *how* of knowing. Thus parody, as a form of meta-fiction, and a higher-order activity, also raises our awareness of *how* we receive literary texts, and *how* the world is represented in them.

It is hence also important to point out that ambiguous figures such as the duck/rabbit and the parody focus our attention both on what they represent or interpret and *how* this representation is achieved. The duck/rabbit cannot be identical with either a duck or a rabbit from the world of objects, but then neither can other, single representations of ducks or rabbits in art. Our use of the same word to describe both an object such as a rabbit and its representation in art (as for example Dürer's rabbit) is both explanatory and misleading. Magritte's picture of a pipe, bearing the motto 'This is not a pipe' ('The Use of Language', 1928/9), is symptomatic of the modernist's awareness of the problem of representation — in a time, moreover, when inflation was also reducing the value of money notes and other notes of exchange to undermine their representational value. In *Les Mots et les Choses* Foucault has drawn a parallel between literary and monetary forms of representation, and it is interesting to extend his parallel further to note that the critique of the representational power of the sign, and of the identity between the sign and its object which we find in the works of Magritte, is not only contemporary with the inflationary devaluation of the representational power of paper money in the 1920s in Europe, but can also be placed into the context of scientific thought, in which Einstein's theory of relativity had offered a critique of the simultaneity of events in time. This critique, reflected in many literary works of the early twentieth century, finds, however, its literary prototype (which is perhaps also a more suitable comparison for the attack made on identity between sign and object in the works of Beckett *et al.*) in Sterne's *Tristram Shandy*, in statements such as Tristram's complaint — that write as he may, he can never catch up with himself. Here, however, it is particularly the impossibility of describing an act while also doing that act, and the limitation of meta-

2. Gunther Witting, *'Dürer's Rabbit'*, 1977.

Source: reproduced courtesy of Dr Gunther Witting, Konstanz.

3. René Magritte, *'Ceci n'est pas une pipe'*, 1928/9.

Ceci n'est pas une pipe.

fiction to other fictions than itself, which is Sterne's concern, and which will present a problem for the self-reflexive criticism of the system of signs used by the writer in his meta-critique of simultaneity.

Critically ambiguous forms of representation, such as parody, foreground the concealed ambivalence of representational forms of language, and leave us (like Jastrow's duck/rabbit) with a new 'representation' or conceptual problem. Unlike the self-parody, which Ryle claimed to be an impossibility in the sense that we cannot represent ourselves in two different ways at the same time, or ever complete the task of criticising the self, the literary parody which has been built from passages of another work may — like the rabbit which can also be seen as a duck, or vice versa — be viewed by another to be two things at once. It is obvious that the parallel between Jastrow's duck/rabbit and parody cannot be stretched too far, as we do not — in most cases of parody — have two complete works (or 'representations') before us, but only the indication, or the suggestion, of two. Yet the parallel between the parody text and our perception of the duck/rabbit can suggest that it is not in verifying which of the two images is 'true', or if our perception of them is 'valid', but in perceiving the contingency of these two things, and the effect of this on our normal processes of perception and validation of knowledge, that we pass through the stages of recognition which lead to laughter, to shock, to the destruction of expectations, and to a possible change in our knowledge of the thing observed and in our manner of observing it — to the knowledge of 'how' characteristic of parody and the critically imaginative writing of texts. In demonstrating how a text may be read in different ways, and in its own use of ambiguity and allusion, such parody may also show us how the 'Other', the repressed meanings in our speech acts, may be concealed in normal speech, and exploited by the poet. Thus, while parody allows us to read and compare two texts 'at the same time' (or 'self-parody', two works of the same author), it also serves to change our perception of the previously 'independent' text, and, too, of the fictional world and our reception of it.

The consciousness of the ambiguity of language has, as Paul Ricoeur has also argued,[28] led philosophers and thinkers such as Freud, Marx and Nietzsche to analyse the relationship between language, writing and false consciousness. Parody (which all of the above have used in their writings for different purposes and in different ways) has also been used as a means to both the criticism of deceptive ambiguity and the criticism of false consciousness.

Freud himself has shown in *Der Witz und seine Beziehung zum Unbewussten* (1905) that the mechanisms of the joke — of juxtaposition, displacement and condensing — are those of the dream, but that its function — to foreground these processes, and to comment on the process of repression through consciously recreating its processes — makes conscious what is still concealed to the dreamer in the moment of dreaming. But just as parody may be used to either demythologise or to create new utopias and new myths, so too the joke may either serve to release repressed wishes or fears (in self-reflective cases) or to rein-force them, as in many satires with aggressive or destructive intention.

Freud's connection between the processes involved in the release of repressed desires or anxieties in the dream and the process of juxtaposition used in the joke, also appears to have been used in the surrealist dream films by Du Lac and others. But whereas the speeding up of sequences of dream images in those films was to evoke that of the dream, the logic of the joke — as in Du Lac's apparent parody of the figures of Venus and Mars in *La coquille et le clergyman* of 1927 (Artaud's story of a clergyman's repressed desires and erotic fantasies) — demanded a more reflexive response from the film audience than the associative response required for the dream sequences. (The symbol of the shell in Du Lac's film, evoking both the sexual images associated with it in

Freud's analyses, and parodistically realising the figure of Venus, had also to work on both dream and parody levels at once.)

Parody may, however, also serve, as suggested earlier, to bring to the surface the history of an author's style, or of his reading of other literary works, or his relationship to the language of his public, and in fulfilling this function might also be compared to the 'archaeology of the subject' of which Ricoeur has spoken. In both it is also in the act of self-reflection that this archaeology may find its subject, though for the parodist the act of foregrounding the discovery of a conscious self may also have the function of awakening the reader's consciousness of the ambiguity of discourse and its powers of concealment and confusion.

In the analysis of the 'other' in speech and literary texts we also meet the meta-problem of how we can know we have properly reconstructed the processes of repression determining cases of forgetfulness or error in speech, when we have, at the same time, assumed those processes to be always at work. Freud himself stated in his summing up of Chapter 3 of the *Psychopathology of Everyday Life* that the self-reference complex was the most effective of the interfering complexes. Thus – if we are to believe this (being aware of the basis of self-referential evidence on which the statement is itself based!) – we have the problem that self-analysis seeking to explain the self's repressive mechanisms must at the same time also be illustrative of their workings, bringing (according to Freud's argument) the process of repression even more surely into play (but not always to light) than is the case with other forms of self-reference. Here it is the 'self' itself which is shown to inhibit its own analysis of itself. Again, however, the dual function of parody – to both unmask fantasy and to refunction and perpetuate it – makes an advantage of what is for the scientific analyst a considerable methodological problem. For in the process of revealing the fictional nature of a discourse the parodist (such as Cervantes or Sterne) may be provided with the material for his own fiction, in which his self as author and decoder of other texts becomes both the means to literary criticism and the subject of another fictional world. However, in avoiding the criticism of its avoidance of mathematical answers, parody – like perhaps all fiction – creates the need for an external critical appreciation of its role in other discourses.

Yet another problem comparable to one in psychoanalysis for the parodist is, that, in imitating another work to include it or incorporate it into his text as an object of satire, a parodist may not only make himself aware of older bonds between himself and that work, but may bind his own work even more closely to that of his targets. Not only does the incorporation of the target text in his own work make the latter, to some extent at least, dependent on an audience familiar with the target (so that if his parody is successful in making his target less popular with his readers his own work may, ironically, lose part of its audience, or a future audience), but it relates the language of his self even closer to both his target and to his attack on the target.

In the sense that many quotations may have clearly personal associations for the speaker using them which make them self-referring, much of that which has been said about self-parody may also be applied to parody. It may also be demonstrated in parody that a writer has an affinity with his target text, and this ambivalence may be expressed both in his identification of it with his own work and in the critical drive to distinguish himself from it at the same time as he makes it a part of his own work. In fact, the internalisation of another text in any literary work may express an ambivalent form of identification with another, or the drive to distinguish the author's self through comparison with another literary ego.

For some writers parody may also act as a first step towards establishing a style for themselves on the basis of the imitation of others. But some parodists have also used the idea of Buffon's dictum, 'Le style c'est l'homme même', to make a writer the object of satire through caricaturing his style, to make him into a comic embodiment of his style. So, for example, the ornate writer has been caricatured as an ornate person, or the clumsy stylist as an oaf. Aristophanes made use of this device, but the implication that a writer has *only* the characteristics of his style suggests, contra Buffon, that he may be then less than a whole person. So a parodist may, by imitating the style of another, borrow an identity — but he may also bestow identities, and caricature the person or author in question by imitating and distorting his style, or by reducing the author to stylistic devices.

The self-referring irony of much great parody may also be seen as a comment on the difficulty of identifying an independent authorial 'I' in the literary work, but the 'Lustgewinn' or comic effect of such irony adds another level to the parody to distinguish it from other forms of meta-fiction.

As Booth also appears to suggest,[29] what gives aesthetic pleasure in our perception of the ambiguity of the duck/rabbit figure is the recognition of Jastrow's cleverness in devising it. So, too, the parody often pleases because of the unexpectedness of its juxtapositions and the success of its combination of previously separate texts or ideas. It is, hence, possible to enjoy an attack on our normal way of perceiving literature, or the world, but often, of course, such an attack becomes, as in the case of the grotesque, threatening. For all our praise of parody, it must also be admitted that, like many other literary forms, it has been used for destructive as well as creative purposes. The use of parody in verbal warfare has often been little more than mockery or invective, and it is not this type which is meant when we discuss the great parodies of world literature such as Cervantes' *Don Quixote*. But, as with most meta-languages, parody may be critical in a generalising way, and also direct its criticism towards specific target texts, authors or readers.

In the complex parody, dogmatism, as characteristic of invective, does not appear to be at home. It is, as we have seen, often of less importance to 'know that' than to 'see how', and hence to recognise that the complexity of the production and reception of the text is one of the basic themes of meta-fiction. Great parody may show us that it is in the process of comparing interpretations — rather than perhaps in verifying one against the other — that we come to know 'how' and to understand the processes involved in the writer's representation of 'that' as an object of knowledge. As a 'higher-order' action parody presents the external reader with both a mirror to his reception of literary works and a complication of the normal processes of reception. In this sense then parody, like Ryle's other higher order self-reflecting actions, does not give us a completed mirror image of the literary text (or itself) but an ever-varied one. Only in this way, of course, is parody also capable of introducing change into literary history, and of pre-serving the ambiguously sceptical attitude to representation with which it begins its critique of other works. Thus we were able to speak of a parodistic mirror to author and reader moving with Jane Austen through her novel. In complicating the normal processes of reception in making reception itself the subject of its analysis, parody is not only able to transform the subject-matter of literary works, but also the methods and processes of presentation by which that subject-matter is treated. As with irony, and with other cases of discussing 'how we know what we do', parody often demands both imagination and patience from its reader — not only because it tries the memory of the reader with parts of works he may have forgotten, but because the processes by which knowledge is imparted to the reader in those 'straighter' works are themselves made more complex.

3.6 Self-Parody

It is in self-parody — under the 'suspension of belief' thought character-istic of fiction — that many of the problems which might be raised in a discussion of parody as meta-fiction (such as the author's problem of communicating with an 'absent' receiver, or representing or 'imitating' an absent reality, or of adhering to, or quoting, the rules of genre while writing a 'new' work) are made a part of the discussion within the text itself, and related to the author 'present' in it. For in self-parody the function of meta-fictional parody to reflect upon its own medium is pre-eminent. In other words, it might be pointed out again, that the problems of self-reference in meta-fiction, discussed in the preceding chapters, have shown meta-fictional parody to imply criticism of itself, and a form of 'self-parody', in parodying other fictions.

In self-parody the problems of the reader in interpreting the parody are often also brought to the fore. In addition, the self-parody demonstrates how the change in consciousness effected in the reader by a parody (its heuristic function) may also be related to an epistemological function of effecting self-criticism and change within the work of the parodist: self-parody may — like the parody of a model — be used by a writer to refunction earlier texts, his style, or his arguments. The ambivalence of the parodist towards his target of satire as both his model and the subject of attack is transformed in the self-parody into irony. In self-parody the critical element in the distorted quotation of texts must appear in an ironical light — as an attack by the author on himself, and as being not totally condemnatory. The ambivalence of the parodist to his target — of emulation and condemnation — is made clear in the self-parody, where the source of the comic effect is less the condemnation of a model than the ironic pretence at self-'emulation'.

In many parodies the author himself appears in some guise, to add self-parody to satire. In Chaucer's *Canterbury Tales*, for example, we have in the Prologue to the Tale of Sir Thopas one of the most complete literary portraits of the author as parodist, self-parodist and reader satirist. When Chaucer himself is asked by the 'Hoost' to 'Telle [us] a tale of myrthe, and that anon', he gives us one and a half cantos of the Tale of Sir Thopas, before being interrupted by the Host's plea for him to stop his rhymed 'dogerel'. Ironically the author is then told that his tale shows less literary talent than those of his characters. In an apparent reversal of roles when author as character is accused of not being able to tell a tale by the naive host, and characters are praised as authors, Chaucer's reader appears to be at first forced into the situation of sympathising and identifying with the host, and decoder of the tale within the text, but must then recognise the irony inherent in the author's depiction of himself in the role of artless storyteller, and also the ironic suitability of parody to the tale of the author. For if it can be said that each pilgrim's tale reflects his standing or profession, as does, for instance, the Knight's Romance, so it might be agreed that one of the most appropriate literary forms for the author would be the self-parody, in which is reflected not only his literary models, but his own style, and in the interruption by the host, the role of the reader as decoder of his text. Here, too, as in many self-parodies, the author is able to ironically 'pre-empt' the criticism of his work which *he* may expect from others. Hence, as parody elicits the expectations of the naive reader for a certain text, such self-parody may be said to foreground the author's expectations about the 'critical' reader.

The picture of the characters in the novel reading the work of their author (and later, in the case of Don Quixote, reading about themselves in an earlier part of the text) confuses the naive verification of the 'truth' of the text by forcing a comparison between text and text as well as between text and the world represented in it and outside it. But – in its fictional way – it also presents an inverted image of the reality of the parodist as reader of other texts. In the 'topsy-turvy world' of fiction characters read their authors, but in this inversion there is also an ironic self-portrait by the author of himself as one who has read and extracted his characters from the works he is parodying. It is logically consistent with Cervantes' criticism of Don Quixote as a naive reader who has confused the world of fiction with the real world, so that he cannot distinguish the two or recognise them to be different, to see him challenging his own readers. This challenge is, moreover, a challenge to the reader to understand that the ironic picture of characters reading their author is both a reflection on the reader reading Cervantes and a fanciful inversion of the reality of the parody, in which the author has taken his characters from the pages of other books, where their fictional reality gave them an existence (or 'pre-existence') prior to their distorted reflection in Cervantes' work. The 'reality' of their pre-existence is thereby also shown to have been fictitious, and is superseded by their caricature in the parody.

In *Partial Magic in the Quixote*,[30] Borges takes the logic of this situation to an extreme to suggest that what the reader finds disturbing in reading the *Quixote* is the implication that he, too, may be, or become, a fiction:

... Why does it disturb us that Don Quixote be a reader of the *Quixote* and Hamlet a spectator of *Hamlet*? I believe I have found the reason: these inversions suggest that if the characters of a fictional work can be readers or spectators, we, its readers or spectators, can be fictitious.

Borges then concludes with a reference to the idea of the world as a history book in which men are at the same time authors, readers, and participants:

In 1833 Carlyle observed that the history of the universe is an infinite sacred book that all men write and read and try to understand, and in which they are also written.

When history repeated itself as a farce, post-Hegelians like Marx, aware of Hegel's description of history as a drama rather than a book, took to speaking of it as parody, using the word in its popular derogatory sense, while at the same time parodying Hegel (and other texts) to refunction his work in a dialectical, non-imitative way.[31]

In another work, *The Parable of Cervantes and the Quixote*, Borges suggests an identity between Cervantes and Don Quixote, the 'credulous reader':

In gentle mockery of himself, he [Cervantes] imagined a credulous man who, perturbed by his reading of marvels, decided to seek prowess and enchantment in prosaic places called El Toboso or Montiel.[32]

Cervantes' sympathy with his Quixote, the adventurer, can be found in the concealed autobiographical notes on Cervantes' adventures in the novel, but this does not perhaps go so far as to make an identification between Cervantes, the critical reader, with his naive reader.

Borges has also argued that Cervantes was a realist who believed the poetic world of the Romances 'unrealistic', and who believed in a distinction between the real and the poetic. We will return to this question presently. In other cases it has, however, been the ideal, and the world of the mind, which has been attributed a greater reality than the world outside. In his novel parodying the Kantian dialectic, *Die Blendung*, referred to earlier (and which was originally to be titled 'Kant fängt Feuer', or 'Kant catches Fire', a parodistic reference to Kant's thesis 'Über Feuer'), Elias Canetti has analysed the relationship between the outer and inner worlds in the bibliomanic world of the sinologist Peter Kien (originally noted as 'K', or 'Kant'). David Roberts has analysed this as a study of the complex relationship between the individual and the crowd in his study, *Kopf und Welt*,[33] and it is a novel which, as also suggested earlier, takes the concepts of reflection and representation in the book to grotesque conclusions. Its dialectic — Kopf ohne Welt, Welt im Kopf, Kopflose Welt — reflects the transformation of the outside world into the world of the mind, and the bibliomanic Kien's replacement of his lost library of objective books with an imaginary library which turns his head into both the illusion of another world, and the source of other illusions about the outside world.

In parody used together with literary satire the book has been treated as both an object of the external world and the means to its criticism. A meta-critical attitude to the use of the book as a critical tool against other books is often also found in parody, as we have seen, but it may present itself as a subtle justification for its criticism, or as anarchy which must also, eventually, turn against itself. In Canetti's *Blendung* it is anarchy which finally takes hold of Peter Kien. The consuming fire in Kien's mind which concludes the novel, marks the destruction of the book as inner world (and its supersession and self-negation in terms of the distorted dialectic), and, as Roberts writes, its encompassing of the outer world after which the individual has longed. But when the subject and object are identical — as they have now become in Kien's mind — then this destruction is ambiguously (as fire is both ambiguously creative and destructive) infinite. Borges also points to a case of 'infinite suffering' in literature in Scheherezade's victory over the King to whom she has told the tales of the 1001 Nights:

> The necessity of completing a thousand and one sections obliged the copyists of the work to make all manner of interpolations. None is more perturbing than that of the six hundred and second night, magical among all the nights. On that night the king hears from the queen his own story. He hears the beginning of the story, which comprises all the others and also — monstrously — itself. Does the reader clearly grasp the vast possibility of this interpolation, the curious danger? That the queen may persist and the motionless king hear forever the truncated story of the *1001 Nights*, now infinite and circular ...[34]

Yet such an infinite occurrence could only be speculated on in texts
such as the Märchen. Borges' conclusion itself reflects on the
'paradoxically' fictional character of the problem discussed in meta-
fiction. And in the world outside the book, the world of the reader,
as Borges himself has shown in his masterly story of 'Pierre Menard,
Author of the *Quixote*', each reader makes his own text of the work
he receives, not only in the phenomenological sense of realising the
work in his interpretation of it, but in the sense of giving it a new and
different reading from another which may itself make a new text with
more 'reality' than the original.

It is in self-parody that the meta-fictional character of general
parody is most clearly to be seen and the locus of a hermeneutics
of fiction established. The general function of parody, of analysing
the nature of fiction from within fiction, is spotlighted in the refunctioning of an author's own work in the self-parody. In the
mimicry of his own style the author provides a commentary to the
essential features of his writing as well as to the nature of fiction as a
creation — or 'product' — of the writer: self-parody (like the play-
within-the-play) both mirrors and questions the act of creating
fictional worlds. It is moreover significant that a self-parody such as
that found in Chaucer's Prologue to the Tale of Sir Thopas describes
not only the reader of other texts (as in *Don Quixote* or *Northanger
Abbey*), but the parodist's own, hypothetical audience. In both
satiric and ironic (reflexive) parody, the parodist shows himself to be
concerned with the limits of the fictional world and the related problem
of the reception of texts by the reader. Again, a theory of parody cannot ignore the reception of the parody by the contemporary reading
public, which is often explicitly or implicitly mirrored by the parodist
in a figure of the decoder within the text, and empirical studies of
reception must join with the theoretical analysis of parody texts.

Apart from its contribution to the analysis of the structure and
reception of texts, modern linguistics has much to offer to both the
empirical study and theoretical analysis of parody. And many linguists
have, as mentioned in our Introduction, developed their theories of
textual analysis on the basis of examples which are recognisably
parodistic works. The Russian Formalists — among them Viktor
Sklovskij, Jurij Tynjanov and Michail Bachtin — were amongst the
first linguists of the twentieth century to base the analysis of the complicated structures of continuity and discontinuity in narrative on
examples of parody in the novel, on *Don Quixote* and *Tristram Shandy*.
And though it can be argued that a general theory of the text cannot be

extrapolated only from examples of parody, the foregrounding of structural problems raised by such meta-fictional works as the parodies mentioned, together with the work of later schools, including Roman Jakobson's analysis of codes, and recent work on the concept of 'intertextuality', has done much to raise the student's awareness of the structural complexity of literature. It has also spotlighted the complexity of the relationship of the fiction to that which it 'represents', which parodists had earlier sought to demonstrate from within the literary work itself.

The importance of a study of parody to an understanding of the modern literary text and its history has recently been raised again by the theories of the text offered by post-Structuralists, as well as by 'deconstructionists' such as Derrida. Terry Eagleton has also pointed to this trend in commenting on the view implied in Macherey's work that literature is parodic in deforming rather than imitating its target, and has, thereby, also pointed to the role of modern parody in undermining the belief in art as imitation:

> For Macherey, the effect of literature is essentially to *deform* rather than to imitate. If the image corresponds wholly to the reality (as in a mirror), it becomes identical to it and ceases to be an image at all. The baroque style of art, which assumes that the more one distances oneself from the object the more one truly imitates it, is for Macherey a model of all artistic activity; literature is essentially *parodic*.[35]

It will be shown that Magritte and other 'modernists' have in fact implied that imitation itself unwittingly 'deforms' its object in pretending to reflect it. And here, too, parody and the concept of art as mimesis are shown to be in conflict, and art no longer conceived of as reflecting the world. As in fiction itself, the function of introducing parody into a critical debate on mimesis has often been to reopen our eyes to the presuppositions buried in our Platonic or Aristotelian concepts of literature as the reflection and imitation of reality. But though we may now more frequently reconsider the nature of this reality, we cannot forget that much literature has been written on the assumption that it was to have the function of imitation, and that parody has been written both as a way of commenting on the limitations of the individual author in achieving this aim, on, for example, the plurality of the worlds being imitated, as well as — through its meta-fictional reflection on the limits of representation in fiction — on the impossibility of the concept itself.

Historically, as we have argued earlier, parody has meant many things
to different critics when writing of literature; but here parody not only
represents the rejection of an older concept of imitation, but comes to
stand for a new idea of what 'really happens' — for, that is, the
'deformation' of reality which is necessary to its reconstruction in the
literary work. It is hence also important to note that such 'deforming'
imitation has now also come to describe parody, and to equate it with
'mimesis'! Also suggesting a concept of 'deformation', Adorno wrote
in his notes to an Aesthetic Theory (*Ästhetische Theorie*, Werke,
volume 7, Frankfurt am Main, 1970, quoted here from the Suhrkamp
edition, 1973), that an artwork had to free itself from the drive to
identify with the world it would represent in order to represent it, but
that it was only through its estrangement from itself ('Selbstent-
fremdung') through the initial attempt at imitation ('Nachahmung')
that it would free itself from a naive concept of mimesis:

> Erst in seiner Selbstentfremdung durch Nachahmung kräftigt das
> Subjekt sich so, dass es den Bann der Nachahmung abschüttelt.

So Adorno's concept of imitation has been used to describe the
relationship to reality in works such as the novels of Proust or Joyce
which we would rather term parody. And Adorno himself might appear
to be describing a method of dialectical parody — of the supersession
of imitation through the ironic imitation of a target — in the above
passage. For Adorno, however, a Hegelian concept of dialectics which
posits a synthetic solution to the supersession of a thesis must remain
attached to that thesis. The 'negative aesthetics' excludes a concept of
dialectical parody which is 'both beside and opposite' its target.

Though a metaphoric use of parody, such as that suggested in
Macherey's work, may allow us to find a new 'parodistic' function in
the anti-mimetic literature of other ages as well as our own, the specific
historical functions of 'parodia' cannot be overlooked. Some specificity
in definition (based on historical usage of the form as well as its
theoreticisation) is moreover necessary in order to enable us to distinguish parody from other forms of literature, so that we understand
the point being made when the concept of imitation is replaced by
that of parody, and the word for imitation then (as in 'negative
dialectics') used to describe what has previously gone under the name
of parody. (Perhaps it might even be suggested that here too a continuing distrust of parody as an unacceptable form of negativity has
influenced the replacement of it with the word imitation.)

Going back to the etymology of the word parody, outlined at the beginning of this study, it seems clear that the complex meta-fictional functions of parody, which critics are again bringing into the discussion of ideas such as imitation and representation, are implied in both the ancient definition of the word — as 'beside and in opposition to another work' — and in its use (even with Platonic traditions of seeing poetry as the reflection of the world) as a way of both criticising and supplementing other literary texts.

Harold Bloom's argument for the 'Necessity of Misreading'[36] also offers us a description of the processes at work in the parody as a distortion of another text. Though Bloom may be said to have confused an effect of strength with a criterion for strength, in arguing in the above mentioned article that 'A poet is strong because poets after him must work to evade him', what Professor Bloom says about the necessity for 'strong readings', which change, or seek to evade their models, also holds true (and has always been true) for the parody which attempts to reconstruct critically a literary work from within another literary text. When seeing themselves as critical, if not 'higher-order' actions, many parodies have offered strong readings of texts by carrying the logic of arguments to new conclusions (sometimes of course with comic, or absurd effects), or by relating the target text's argument to the world of the reader, to show discrepancy between the two. Yet the parody is often at the same time more than the misreadings offered by the literary critics, who can only assume — from their place outside of the fiction — that they are also 'one with the text'. For the 'misreadings' offered by a parodist are made from within the fiction, so that his criticism has the function of simultaneously renewing and rewriting literary tradition.

In parody the internalisation of the fiction text within a form of criticism which is itself a fiction-text, thus achieves a 'strong reading' of another work at the same time as it expands the creative literary tradition. In this sense the parody could also be said to have more permanence in literary history than the external non-fictional critiques and readings of texts, though it has also been suggested earlier that a danger of redundancy is built into the parody when it limits itself to a weak text (easily eliminated from the literary scene) or to an audience of initiates. Yet for longer than literary criticism, parody has also, as we have tried to emphasise, represented the combination of analysis with the agonistic principle — the sense of play now also being championed by de-constructionists. And here, too, the parody has made creative use of the principles it has put into practice, by not only using them to 'deconstruct' what was false in earlier prose works, but to show what was latent and in need of 'reconstruction'. But in that its meta-fictional criticism has, as has been argued in this section, also shown the limits of parody in criticising its own world, it must be added that the concept of 'strong reading' advanced in some modern criticism has still to solve the problems of self-reflexion and self-criticism raised in modern meta-fictions and in other schools of criticism.

Notes

1. Jakobson, 'Linguistics and Poetics', in *Style and Language*, Thomas Sebeok (ed.), (Mass., 1968), p. 353.
2. Ibid., p. 356.
3. Ibid.
4. Smuda, *Becketts Prosa als Metasprache* (München, 1970).
5. In Barthes, *Essais Critiques* (Paris, 1964).
6. For example, Magritte's 'In Praise of Dialectics', 1937, mentioned again in Section 4.4.
7. Quoted in Smuda, *Becketts Prosa*, p. 62.
8. Another term which might be used here is Gide's concept of the 'mise en abyme', discussed by Lucien Dällenbach in *Le Récit speculaire* (Paris, 1977). Valerie Minogue quotes Dällenbach (p. 52) in her review of his work: ' . . . est mise an abyme tout miroir interne réfléchissant l'ensemble du récit par réduplication simple, répétée, ou spécieuse'.
9. Smuda, *Becketts Prosa*, p. 10.
10.. Cervantes' *Don Quixote*, transl. J.M. Cohen (Middlesex, 1964), p. 27. As Quentin Skinner has argued (referring to A.J. Close's 'Don Quixote and the Intentionalist Fallacy', *British Journal of Aesthetics*, 12 (1972), pp. 321–30) in his article 'Hermeneutics and the Role of History', *New Literary History* (Autumn 1975), pp. 201–232, *Don Quixote* may be taken as the paradigm of a 'heteronomous' literary text, the context of which must also be understood. In arguing that parody is not typical of all literature, Skinner appears, however, to underplay the role of parody in the *Quixote* in foregrounding the processes at work in all literature which otherwise may remain silent.
11. 'Partial Magic in the *Quixote*', in *Labyrinths*, Donald A. Yates and James E. Irby (eds.) (Harmondsworth, 1976), p. 228.
12. Ibid., p. 229.
13. Ibid., p. 70.
14. Fielding's *Joseph Andrews* was subtitled 'written in imitation of the manner of Cervantes, Author of *Don Quixote*', and begins as is well known, as a parody of Richardson's *Pamela*, before developing (as Cervantes had done) its own narrative.
15. Later Heine was to use this as a metaphor to describe events on the political stage, to satirise the timidity of the 'lions' in the Revolution of 1848, intimidated by the opinion of their audience so that they felt it necessary to reassure them that their Revolution was not 'real' (e.g. *Heine – Sämtliche Werke*, Elster (ed.), vol. 6, p. 540).
16. Tom Stoppard, *Travesties* (London, 1975), pp. 96–7.
17. Ibid., p. 97. Dwight MacDonald has suggested such a key to the styles

parodied by Joyce in *Parodies* (London, 1960), pp. 522ff.

18. Stoppard, *Travesties*, p. 97.

19. *Our Exagmination*, p. 55.

20. *The Bodley Head Beerbohm*, David Cecil (ed.) (London, 1970), p. 15.

21. Ibid., p. 21.

22. Søren Kierkegaard, *Über den Begriff der Ironie*, transl. Emanuel Hirsch (Düsseldorf and Köln, 1961), p. 329: 'Je mehr da Ironie ist, um so freier und dichterischer schwebt der Dichter über seinem Dichtwerk'.

23. Ibid., p. 333.

24. Gilbert Ryle, *The Concept of Mind* (Middlesex, 1966), p. 186.

25. Wayne C. Booth, *A Rhetoric of Irony* (Chicago, 1974), pp. 123ff. Many of the issues raised by Booth in his discussion of irony are also relevant to a study of parody. Some points, however, such as that a parody contains an implied author and implied reader, can bear with elaboration, as when, for example, the idea of an implied author is explicitly caricatured in a text. Arnt Lykke Jakobsen has criticised Booth's emphasis on reading irony through the intentions of the author, and implied author, in his review of 'A Rhetoric of Irony' in *Orbis Litterarum*, vol. 32, no. 3, (1977), pp. 173ff. In his work on the 'implied reader' (*Der implizierte Leser*, München, 1972) Wolfgang Iser deals with texts – many of them eighteenth-century parodies – in which the author speaks of, and to, his reader, often with didactic purpose, or to ironically chide him for not taking an active enough part in the conversation between himself and the author suggested by the text. Yet, despite his recognition of the importance of the role of the implied reader as 'constructor of the author' and as silent receiver of the literary text, Iser approaches the parody in his English texts from an eighteenth-century 'Gottschedian' viewpoint as a negative 'destructive' style, when he writes the following: 'Die beim Wort genommene Ich-Form des *Tristram Shandy* ist nicht durch eine bloss parodistische oder gar destruktive Absicht allein zu erklären.' It has, on the other hand, been argued in this study that parody need not be excluded from meta-fiction, and that it may, in fact, be seen as a hyper-critical form of the same, rather than as a 'destructive' form of literature.

26. Ibid., p. 127.

27. Ibid., p. 128.

28. Paul Ricoeur, *De l'Interpretation. Essai sur Freud* (Paris, 1965).

29. Booth, *Rhetoric of Irony*, pp. 123ff.

30. Borges, *Labyrinths*, p. 231.

31. See Rose, *Reading the Young Marx and Engels* (Croom Helm, 1978), part 2, ch. 5.

32. Borges, *Labyrinths*, p. 278.

33. David Roberts, *Kopf und Welt* (München, 1976).

34. Borges, *Labyrinths*, p. 230.

35. Terry Eagleton, *Marxism and Literary Criticism* (London, 1976), p. 51. And see also Eagleton, *Criticism and Ideology* (London, 1976), p. 95.

36. Bloom, 'The Necessity of Misreading', in *Georgia Review*, 29 (1975), pp. 267–88.

4 THE PARODISTIC EPISTEME: QUESTIONING REFLECTION AND REFLEXION

The analysis of the reader's reception of other fictions which may be made in the meta-fictional parody also contributes to the external reader's understanding of the peculiar relationship between the parodist and the preformed literary material used in the parody, and his relationship to it as both decoder and encoder. Explicit reference to the role of the reader made in some parodies has been seen to have this 'hermeneutical' function, as well as the meta-literary function of analysing the distinctive nature of the fictional world. The relationships between the author of the parodied text and the parodist as passive encoder to active decoder should also be made the subject of closer attention. For the dual nature of the role of the parodist as both decoder and encoder is one factor which must be considered in explaining the ambivalent attitude of the parodist to his model which was recognised by those understanding 'parodia' as 'Beigesang'. But yet another factor of ambivalence is that of the structural role played by the parodied text as a second text-world (and not just as a sub-text) in the parody. For as a structural element in the parody the imitated text contributes to both the aesthetic and comic effect of the whole work. The parody must thus be seen as consisting of two fictional worlds — the one 'preformed' and the other, the parody itself, a new world which offers a critical context for the re-coding and re-reception of the former. The parody has, moreover, been described here as a form of 'meta-literary' criticism which is distinguished from other types of literary criticism by its presentation of an argument within the confines of fictional reference. In focusing on problems specifically associated with the interpretation of texts, and on the role of the reader outside the text, as well as on the role of the parodist as reader of the text parodied, the parodist raises questions about the role of the reception of literary texts played in both the formation of the author's expectations of the reader and of theirs for his work. Although a pragmatic approach cannot explain all the phenomena contributing to the effect and the particular structure of the parody, it can be applied to questions, such as those raised above, on the nature of the relationship between texts and readers in fiction. On a more specific level, the inter-relationship of the history of the development of a society and its literature is also necessary to an understanding of the types of material contradictions facing the parodist, and to an understanding of the use of parody at certain historical moments, whether it be as a way around censorship, as the cynical expression of a present overburdened by the past, or as the development of modern forms. This problem, together with the question of the role of the reader, will be the subject of analysis in the following chapter.

4.1 Parody and the Verification of Statements made in Fiction

We have said that a theory of parody could aim to explain the complex relationship between the parody text, its target, and its reader which is peculiar to parody. We have also suggested that the parodist's analysis of the reception of literary texts from within fiction itself may be accompanied by meta-fictional 'reflections' on the role of fiction as reflection and imitation, and on the reader's problem of 'verifying' these fictional statements and others which may bear the appearance of similarity with standard language statements, but which are uttered in a different context, and in the absence of the decoder reading the text.

The naive reader who, like Don Quixote, takes the fictional world to be 'true', in the sense of being an accurate reflection of the external world, or, that is, his own world, and of being subject to the same rules as the language of this external world, has been seen to be the target of parody in meta-fictional works such as *Don Quixote* and *Tristram Shandy*. And such reader-satire may also reflect the author's fears of being misunderstood. But the parodist's foregrounding of the 'mysterious' ability of literary statements to both evoke and suspend belief in their truth, in the parodistic juxtaposition of different perspectives, may also be seen as both an attempt to educate his reader to a more critical understanding of the workings of the literary text and an ironic game with the mysteries of fiction as such, which has as its aim not the total demystification of its secrets, but their refunctioning and renewal. In the parodist's foregrounding of the composition of his text as a dialectic of decoding and encoding the preformed language of another, the processes of reception – also foregrounded in the satirical caricature of the implied reader – are made the subject of analysis, and of reception itself.

Siegfried J. Schmidt has maintained that in speech acts the recipient may be said to match his world to that of the speaker in understanding his meaning.[1] But if statements in the fictional work can be said (as they were by Frege and others) to be 'neither true nor false', and are not subject to verification by reference to the world of the decoder, then

it might also be said that the reader of imaginative literature is not
expected to match his world to the text-worlds in order to verify those
fictional statements. Indeed, the reader who does so (such as Don
Quixote) will, if sight of the distinctions becomes lost, be accused of
lacking critical judgement. Thus Laurence Sterne spoke of encouraging
his reader to use his imagination — thereby also counteracting the fear
expressed in the story of King Thamus and Theuth (the 'creator of the
written word') in Plato's *Phaedrus*, that writing would lead men to
laziness or to the manipulation of others. The exaggeration of discrepancy is but one technique used by parody to achieve its 'awakening'
shock effect, to demonstrate to the reader the fictional character of a
given text-world, or to arouse the reader to a critical reading similar to
that demonstrated in the parody. Through utilising discrepancy as a
source of humour the parodist also distinguishes himself from the
literary critic who assumes to give a verifiable literary criticism of
literary texts. More significantly, perhaps, is the fact, referred to before,
that the parodist also distinguishes his form of criticism from the
critic's by making it a part or function of another fictional work.

Parody of a more satirical kind, as is often found in political literature and rhetoric, may, however, aim at changing the opinion of its
audience about a text or its supporters, and may dispense with the
more ambivalent reflexive method of analysing the truth of the fiction
within the non-verifiable fictional world. It may offer verifiable statements which break the illusion of the fiction, or which ignore its
peculiar rules. It may, of course, also use the cover of the fiction to
make apparently verifiable statements which are (even in their
apparent objectivity) not verifiable.

In some literary parody aesthetic and literary norms are, on the
other hand, made the measure for judging the amount of discrepancy
between texts and the truth of the author's new message. There
'Poiesis' may be described as providing the context of another world,
separate from that of the public world. In this other world of
fictional form an apparently different set of criteria for the verification of statements is set out by the author. Parody may set up a
contrast between its criteria and that of its target, but it may also
foreground the difference between these literary norms and those of
the public sphere. As its own statements cannot be directly
challenged by the reader and brought into a two-way discussion of
their validity, they remain within the world of the fiction, apparently
differing from literary criticism in their avoidance of objective criteria.
Yet while some parodies clearly differ from literary criticism in their

individualistic approach to other texts, as well as in their use of the
fictional form to refunction those texts as literature, the theoretical
discussion of the nature of statements made within the fiction, and of
the element which distinguishes them from others, has not yet produced
any entirely confident conclusions.

Distinctions between 'normal' and fictional language have been
frequently discussed, and linguistic systems applied to literary texts
despite the inconclusive nature of these discussions. Like definitions,
then, such distinctions must be approached critically and with care.
Because, however, parody as meta-fiction often itself raises the question
of the nature of the fictional world *vis-à-vis* that of the reader − these
distinctions between fictional and 'normal' language, as they have
been made by critics and authors, must also be considered here.

For the philosopher John Searle, fiction has a 'set of extra-linguistic
nonsemantic conventions' in which the normal rules of illocutionary
acts (such as the 'preparatory' or 'essential' rules which govern the
provision of evidence for the truth of statements and the commital to
that truth) are suspended, while language used in fiction has the function
of 'the pretence at making an assertion'.[2] If we may interpret this to
mean that fiction appears to follow the rules of speech while the author
intends in fact no application of those rules to be made, we may ask
what the purpose of such a pretence could be in the political work
which ironically uses a fictional world, as in Orwell's *Animal Farm*,
which is sub-titled 'A Fairy-Tale'. While it has often been the case that
to escape censorship the political writer has offered a pretence at non-
verifiability, it is rarely true that the ultimate aim of the committed
author is that the reader take this pretence at verifiability at face value
to be his only message: the prime aim of the political work must surely
be to convince its readers that its message is valid for their world. The
question to be put here concerns the form taken by verification in
fiction.

The critic distinguishing fiction from speech-acts and from other
forms of literature (scientific, etc.), and parody in fiction from literary
criticism, must be able to explain the use of fictional forms by political
writers and satirists, who appear to make statements which behave
according to the rules of standard speech and which express certain
attitudes and intentions. Neither Searle, nor other linguists who have
interested themselves in such questions, have felt themselves able as
yet to offer solutions to this basic problem.[3]

Parodies which offer a political message often provide a fictional
form for statements which are to be verified by reference to the world

of the reader. Such statements do not appear to be beyond verification, and appear to have the perlocutionary function of effecting a change in the world of the reader. In this they differ, theoretically, from statements of 'pure' fiction. The purposes of using fictional forms for the presentation of normally direct political utterances may, for example, be the avoidance of censorship or the gaining of the reader's sympathy, though it may also, of course, be the means of attacking fellow political writers. Such was the case with Heinrich Heine's satirical allegory, *Atta Troll* of the 1840s, which, like Orwell's *Animal Farm*, clothed the political writers and activists of the day in the animal skins most expressive of their characters. In both the aforementioned satires the reader is asked to interpret the allegory as having a meaning for the author which is not apparently immediately related to the world of the reader. The reader must then verify this meaning for his world, or even adjust and change his presuppositions, for communication to take place as in the manner described by Siegfried J. Schmidt when speaking of the reception of speech acts. Such communication may go beyond the normal processes involved in reading a fiction which does not seek to make verifiable statements about the world of the reader. For in the political allegory the use of the fictional form obliges the reader to make more than the single step taken in decoding the standard speech act. In the political allegory at least three steps must often be made — from, for example, the fiction of the speaking animal, to the general meaning of its statements (or to the recognition of cliches from the world of humans), to the world of the author (and to his evaluation of these cliches), and to the world of the reader, who may associate with or dissociate himself from the allegory and its key. This multiplicity of verifiable and non-verifiable worlds is also to be found in the parody, where at least two text-worlds and the world of the reader are deliberately set into conflict. Yet the multiplication of texts or of codes in the political allegory and the parody shows that they also have in common with other works of fiction the communication of covert messages — of sub-texts — all of which need not be agreed with by the reader; but it will be his recognition of their existence, which facilitates his understanding. The recognition of the structure of the literary work is, for these reasons and others, of significant importance to an understanding of the received text.

While communication in standard speech could be described as resulting from the two-way adjustment and matching of the worlds of encoder and decoder, the apparent one-way communication of messages in literary fiction (though these messages may be multiple,

and though in parody a fictional reader may appear in the text as a
target of satire), often makes the reader dependent on the recognition
of patterns of meaning beyond the sentence. For this reason the
verification of statements in the political allegory, or of any political
or direct messages given in fictional form, is problematic. Yet, as
suggested earlier, the question of verifying the truth of statements made
in fiction is perhaps only as suspect as claiming a statement in standard
speech to be either true or false without reference to external evidence.
Frege's definition of fiction as neither true nor false (pre-dated by Sir
Philip Sidney's) appears, however, to imply belief in the possibility
of comparing statements in fiction with others which are true or
false — and the possibility of knowing the latter's relationship to the
fiction. Above all we come back here to seeing parody as a form of
meta-fiction which, unlike some meta-linguistic methods, is not
necessarily concerned only to show other statements to be true or
false, but to show *how* these statements were composed and received.
Frege's definition may also be seen, however, as another variation on
what Wimsatt later termed the 'Intentionalist Fallacy' — for it also tells
us that verification of an author's meaning is not given by the text alone.
Nor by hypotheses about the author's intentions.

The limits of defining fiction as neither true nor false are made clear
not only by reference to the case of political literature in which the
intention of the author appears hidden for tactical as well as aesthetic
purposes, but by the case of irony, which is also often found in parody.
For how is irony to achieve its particular effect through simulation
and dissimulation without a contrast being made in the fictional text
between its deliberate use of 'insincerity' and 'sincerity' statements in
which the speaker 'commits himself to belief in the truth of the
expressed proposition'?[4] Here Searle's definition of fiction as the
'pretence' at offering verifiable statements (such as 'sincerity statements')
may seem to be of use. Yet what may more accurately be said to occur
in irony is the pretence at belief in a certain argument, countered by
the implication of there being a more — or another — valid position. It
is not the case, as Searle's argument implies, that it offers a pretence
at the verifiability of its arguments by social standards outside the
fiction. The ironist may suggest that his message is verifiable, but will
also have to describe the conditions for verification, such as, for
instance, a change in the expectations of the reader. It is in irony and
parody that the mock duplication of meaning by the author foregrounds the power of the author over the transmission of his meaning
or message to the reader, which the cautious interpreter may acknowledge

to exist, but because of the problems of deducing the author's intention from the text may choose not to positively define.

The meta-fictional parody, such as *Don Quixote* or *Tristram Shandy*, may demonstrate that, rather than say that fiction is neither true nor false, it may be more accurate to define the fictional world created by the author as being the subject of 'verification' within the text by the author. This verification may be made within the confines of the fiction and its set of norms (two texts may be compared with each other – as in the parody), or the author may choose to introduce criteria from the world of the contemporary reader, or to indicate their applicability, as through allegory. This wider definition of fiction still distinguishes it from other forms of literature (such as the critical study or the scientific work), but the definition may also be applied to political literature, where the step out into the world of the reader is implicitly or explicitly made from within a fictional form. Finally, it can be argued that the rule of 'sincerity', of the speaker's belief in the truth of his statement, may hold in the non-ironic fictional work, even if the preparatory rule, or evidence for truth, or even the essential rule (the speaker's commitment to the truth of his proposition) cannot. In the case of political literature the question of intention may not concern the reader as much as the verification of the author's statements for the reader's world. In the work of irony or parody the figure of the author and the role of his intentions in shaping the work are often, however, foregrounded, and the reader's verification confused – though this may have the function of emphasising the complexity of interpreting the literary work. We have seen that parody may mock the naive reader's undirected or confused use of standard rules of verification in the fiction or, as in the political work, may imply that these rules of verification should be operative. Broadly speaking, these modes may be seen as typical of ironic and satiric parody respectively, of, that is, parody which 'mocks', or foregrounds its own literary conventions or another fictional work in an ironic (reflexive), meta-literary way, and satire that uses parody to attack a living person or current idea within a fictional world in which illusion is consistently broken. It must not be overlooked, however, that, while the parody complicates both the normal structure of the work of fiction by weaving together two texts, and the problem of interpreting intention and meaning by depicting a reader in the process of interpretation, it creates humour from this exercise as well as raising theoretical questions about the nature of fiction. But, while pointing to the distinction between the rules of standard speech and those of the fiction in which the author determines the character and applicability of such rules, parody has also served to point to the subjective character of some of the 'objectively-given' rules of standard speech and has for this reason too played a role in political satire and in the de-masking of propaganda, in which rules of verifiability or sincerity are used or misused as authority for the arguments given.

4.2 'The Implied Reader': Phenomenological Approaches to Parody

In his study of the reception of the literary text in *Das literarische Kunstwerk* (1931), Roman Ingarden suggested a phenomenological distinction between 'Konkretisation' and the recognition of the literary work and 'Rekonstruktion', the critical objectification of the text in the reading given it by the reader. This distinction has also been described as a distinction between understanding and explication, and has been developed further in studies of the reader's role in the reception and composition of texts, as by, for example, Wolfgang Iser. It is interesting in the context of this study of parody that when phenomenologists have gone to a literary text to explain their view of the interconnection between the text and its reception they have, as Wolfgang Iser in *The Implied Reader*, reached for meta-fictional texts such as Sterne's *Tristram Shandy*, where the explication of this relationship is itself the subject of the book.

Earlier Hans Robert Jauss had also spoken in his *Konstanzer Rede* of 1967 of the role of parody in evoking the 'Erwartungshorizont' (the 'horizon of expectations' spoken of by some phenomenologists) of the reader. By its imitation or partial quotation of another text, for example, the parody functions as a means to evoking the reader's expectations for a certain text, genre, style, or literary world, before then destroying or disappointing these expectations 'step by step'.[5]

We have already seen that Quintilian had described a technique of wit as the disappointment of the expectations of the audience of a speaker,[6] while philosophers such as Kant also saw the disappointment of expectations for a certain conclusion to be a function of wit. Parody has served to fulfil a meta-fictional task, in view of these arguments, in foregrounding the role played by audience expectations in the reception of texts, and so also the role played by the author's awareness of the effect of these expectations on the reception of his text in the composition of his work.

A phenomenology of the parody text will then not only take into account the role of the expectations of the reader in the actual reception of the work, but the function of the author's foregrounding of this process of reception in the explicit or covert depiction of author and/or reader and/or book in the text itself. While the expectations of a reader may for the parodist be treated as a stumbling block to the understanding of his work, and as prejudices which must be shaken, these expectations can, on the other hand, serve the parodist in defining his audience by the expectations he expects them to bring to his text, or by the literary work from which these expectations may be declared to have originated. In this sense the expectations of the reader attacked by the parodist (such as the expectations for the knightly Romance attacked by Cervantes) have also served him in the composition of the work, and in defining its 'horizon' of communication with the reader. Again, of course, the knowledge brought by the reader from a reading of other texts to a new text may both inhibit his understanding of the new work in the view of its author, and assist him in placing it within the limits of his experiences. It is, however, the limits of the familiar, or the reader's persistence with the familiar, which parodies such as *Don Quixote, Tristram Shandy, Ulysses*, and Borges' meta-fictions have attacked or shaken, to introduce new and revolutionary developments into literary history.

Particularly in periods of political crisis or religious dispute preformed beliefs and prejudices have been seen by satirists and parodists as the locus of the expectations of their public, and their attacks on the 'Erwartungshorizont' of the reader determining his interpretation of their texts, have hence also been presented as attacks of broader social significance. The satirist and ironist Karl Kraus wrote in 1933, in explaining how it was that the people of the Third Reich could not *know* what crimes were being committed in the name of justice, that 'belief is always stronger than knowledge (Erkenntnis)'. Thus, because they saw but did not *believe* the crimes around them to be possible – neither did they *know* them. Though perhaps Kraus would not have wanted to have seen this in Freud's terms of repression, the parallel is there, and especially in Kraus's portrait in that same work (*Dritte Walpurgisnacht*) of the authority which would not *let them know* – or, that is, come to know – the knowledge of what was, in fact, happening. Kraus's ironic beginning, 'Mir fällt zu Hitler nichts ein', implying at once that Hitler was not worth thinking about, had overstepped the bounds of the imagination and was, most importantly perhaps, imposing a censorship on thought which excluded or obliterated his subject's power even to think of him, pointed to the effects of censorship on knowledge, not least in its own use of the Aesopian language of irony. (Even Kraus did not feel safe enough under the partial cover of irony to publish the

4. John Heartfield, *Der Sinn des Hitlergrusses*, 1932.

book in 1933.) In Kraus's argument the control which censored knowledge of the external world had also been internalised as a control
which forbade belief in any knowledge which was obtained: his use of
irony then was not only an Aesopian language designed to escape that
censorship but to foreground the duplicity of thought produced by
such a censorship and to point to the necessity of making conscious,
through self-reflexion, both the knowledge censored, and the control
censoring that knowledge, which, internalised again as censor, prevented
belief when that knowledge was given.

In times of political crisis and religious dispute polemical as well as
ironic self-reflexive parody has been used to denigrate the beliefs held,
or propaganda given, by the opposing party. When the expectations of
the hypothesised reader can also be traced or attributed to specific
texts, then parody has also been used to attack specific expectations or
beliefs through the satire of these specific texts. (The various Bible
parodies and theological 'pasquilles' of the Reformation provide many
examples.) John Heartfield's photo montages of the 1930s also comment
on how the camera was made to lie in the propaganda of the Third
Reich. By creating fictional, shocking, and unexpected juxtapositions
of photographic material and texts Heartfield both refunctions and
comments on the methods of distortion available to the photographer
for purposes of revelation or deception. Thus his famous montage of an
x-ray photograph on to a photograph of Hitler, to show him gulping down
pieces of gold coinage, carrying the motto 'Hitler schluckt Gold und
redet Blech', foregrounded a hypocrisy by (like the x-ray photograph
itself) a distortive 'hyper-realistic' presentation of two realities at
once.

Heartfield's interpretation of Hitler's claim that 'millions were
behind him' (Millionen stehen hinter mir!') as meaning that the millions
of marks of financial and industrial moguls were supporting him, led
to a picture montage in which the Hitler salute becomes an open hand
awaiting the financial millions behind him. And here the function of
the fictional montage was – as in much parody – to arouse a critical
attitude in the public to the determination of other statements as true
or false in the propaganda offered them.

In each case the montage both attacks the interpretation of a phrase
or image assumed or expected to be given by the believing recipient,
while foregrounding the process of distortion itself, demanding a critical
rather than a naive reaction from the decoder. By contrast, Heartfield's
montage of Delacroix's 'Liberty on the barricades' behind a group
depicting freedom fighters in the Spanish Civil War does not create a

5. Klaus Staeck, *For the Union of German Authors*, 1977.

shock effect, or effect of discrepancy. Rather it creates a new 'myth' for the encouragement of the cause which it supports, supporting belief in that cause rather than attempting to undermine it with new contradictory knowledge.

A recent poster by Klaus Staeck for the Union of German Authors, entitled 'Autoren fordern Tarifverträge' has mounted the motto 'Nur die Armut gebiert Grosses' ('Great works are only produced in poverty') − describing it, ironically, as 'an old publisher's saying' − on to the well-known picture of the 'poor poet' by the nineteenth-century painter of philistine life, Karl Spitzweg. The parodistic juxtaposition ironises the 'truth' of the motto, for the poor poet in his sleeping cap can be taken as an image of the unsuccessful poet, and also the poetaster. When the viewer of this parody is also aware that Spitzweg's own picture has been based on earlier caricatures of the night-capped German as an example of the complacent dreamer (even Gillray, in the eighteenth century, has such a caricature), this aspect of the poor poet, as poetaster, must be clearly evident. Whereas, however, Spitzweg's painting made use of such caricatures without foregrounding a discrepancy between his use and theirs, Klaus Staeck's parodistic juxtaposition has used Spitzweg for a different purpose than proposed by Spitzweg, to create an ironically sympathetic image of the impoverished poet in the mind of the viewer, and to then undermine the truth of the motto which is to represent the policy of the publishers under attack, that literary greatness is helped by impoverishment.

Sterne's expressed aim of encouraging the reader to use his imagination freely in the moment of interpreting the literary text is symptomatic of the concern of many parodists to free the reader from preformed beliefs and expectations which might inhibit his interpretative faculties. The history of 'successful' parodies − of their break with the past of which their own work may earlier have been a part − demonstrates in broader terms the process by which new discourses enter into written history as the supersession of others. Yet the processes by which these discourses are themselves then canonised as part of a tradition raise other important questions which must also not be forgotten.

Though phenomenological readings sensitive to the interaction between the reader and the text, and to the possibility of the construction and reconstruction of fiction by author and reader, have focused on subjects also dealt with by many meta-fictional or self-reflexive parodies, the specific techniques of parody − as, for example, its caricature of the reader or his expectations, or its encoding of two text-worlds within one text — have also to be considered by the phenomenologist taking a parody as his text for a general theory of literature.

As already mentioned, however, it has been to parody texts that some phenomenologists (like the Formalists of the 1920s) have gone, in order to explain their general theories of the literary text. So that not only are distinctions between parodies and other texts blurred, but the parody made the measure, or norm, for the latter.

In *Der Akt des Lesens*,[7] Wolfgang Iser, referring to *Tristram Shandy*, as he had earlier in *Der implizierte Leser* (*The Implied Reader*), and to Sterne's demand that his reader use his imagination, argued that meaning is realised in the interaction between text and reader in the moment of interpretation by the reader of the text. This concept of reading as a creative activity, requiring the reader to exert himself in the use of his imagination assumes, however, an understanding of reading activity as a specialised competence. And though it is often in parody that such a special 'strong-reading' of another text is realised in its refunctioning of the other work, Cervantes' contrast of naive and critical readers in *Don Quixote* also foregrounds the problem of assuming an ideal state to be always realised in the reading of texts. And while directing his reader's attention to this problem Cervantes has thus also expressed the author's fears for being misunderstood by his reader. Such parody has, thereby, also shown that one man's reading cannot always give us a rule for another's, and it may also be argued that it is, for this reason alone, difficult for the phenomenologist to extrapolate from his reading of one work, as of, for instance, a parody text, to a general theory of the text.

The parodist's 'strong reading' of other texts has been taken as reflecting either his creativity or his plagiaristic mentality, according to the attitude of the reader to the text parodied or to the activity of parody in general. However, in that the parody has made its reading a part of a new text, it has a claim to having realised its reading in a concrete form which has contributed to the corpus of fiction as well as to text-reception, which the critic cannot have claim to in the same way. The problem of some phenomenologists, of distinguishing the meaning of the text from that given it by the reader, to speak of the interaction between the two in the 'realisation' of the text, may, however, be avoided or repressed in the parody which presents its target either through the parodistic reading of it given it by the parodist or by a poetaster satirised by the parodist, or by the figure of another reader being caricatured in the work. The 'objectification' of the process of interpretation thus offered in the parody cannot, of course, tell us all about the process of interpreting this objectification by the reader outside the text, and although it may suggest guidelines and distinctions which foreground, and to some extent direct, the interpretative moment outside the text, it may also represent a manipulation of interpretation.

But here the parody may also assume that the reader will compare readings of the target text. It also shows, thereby, that a text may exist in both a public and a private reading for the individual reader (as it has for the parodist who, as Cervantes, sets out to compare his reading with that of an hypothesised reader). And while both of these images of a text offered by the parodist may then be privately interpreted by each reader, they also relate to the concept of a public readership for the book, which will always be distinct from the individual self of both parodist and reader. Yet the parodist's attempt to make his strong reading of his target a 'public reading' may also tendentiously attempt to exclude other readings or, more ambivalently, challenge his reader to a more critical reading of both the parody and its target. In parody then both author and external reader may be represented as readers in the text in several forms.

Wolfgang Iser has concentrated on the figure of the implied reader in *Tristram Shandy*, but according to James E. Swearingen's recent phenomenological analysis of *Reflexivitiy in 'Tristram Shandy'*,[8] that novel is a meta-fictional analysis not only a study of the reader, but of the author, of the Lockean concept of words as the presentation of ideas, and of the author's reflexive search for the idea of the self in those words.[9]

But if we may see the author-parodist as also playing the role of reader in decoding the text of another, then the 'reflexive' analysis of the self as author which a phenomenological analysis of *Tristram Shandy* may find in the irony and parody used in that work, must also be seen as the ambiguous analysis of the self as both subject and object as, at once, the encoder of a text, the object of the text, and the means of interpreting itself in all three of these activities. The more general problem of deciding how each of these roles may be limited and defined in parody may be raised in different ways in each text. Yet even in individual works of parody this confusion may be functional in forcing the reader into interacting actively with the text by, for example, using his imagination (as Sterne desired). Thus the external reader, who may have already been caricatured in the parody, or reflected in the figure of the author in his analysis of his 'authorial' self, or role, may be required to exert himself in an interpretation of the text, but may also serve to aid the author in the analysis of the authorial self — as it is created in the composition and projected reception of the literary work — and this is also suggested in *Tristram Shandy*.

In his interesting and complex study of reflexivity in Sterne's novel, Swearingen suggests Tristram's narration to be at the same time reflexive, and interpretive of his self, and audience orientated.[10] As Swearingen has also implied, Tristram creates this self in the moments of interpretation and composition. It may perhaps be less clear as to how, or in what form, the audience with which he seeks to establish a friendship is established apart from the image of his own self as interpreter of his text. But it can be said, that in the sense that Sterne's reflective narrator.may also be seen as a product of Sterne's reading, he reflects back on Sterne's dual roles as (as parodist) author and reader, encoder and decoder, as well as on ideas of the reader formed through Sterne's reading of other authors as encoders and decoders. Moreover, Tristram also appears to represent an interlocutor who is himself involved in processes of interpreting and concretising his self as object in the text, as narrator, and reader. And in the language used by Tristram we have an indication of the horizon of expectations his reader may be assumed to have, and, in the continuous parody and disappointment of these expectations, a playful but perhaps 'friendly' communication with the reader about his 'horizon'. As this communication can, however, only take place through the medium of the text, it is Tristram's discourse, through which he both communicates with himself and the figure of a reader, which must be the locus of our interest. Here the idea of the author, revealed in the parodistic foregrounding of that role in Tristram's reflexions, may also serve the reader with the idea of an author to which he may relate his self as interpreter of the text. For in that the parodist's view of the author as both encoder and decoder reflects the processes of understanding and reconstructing the literary work in the process of interpretation, then the reader is also given a model for his 'act of reading'. Here an epistemological function of parody — the interpretation of the self — also serves the author's heuristic purpose in educating the reader to a more 'reflective' reading of the text, in which the idea of the author and the act of interpretation has already been 'concretised' and offered as a subject for interpretation. Sterne's idea of the autobiography as an act of self-interpretation, and realisation for the author, itself connects the two subjects treated separately by Wolfgang Iser and Swearingen, the subjects, that is, of implied reader and author.

Swearingen has particularly emphasised the 'ontological' significance
of these processes of analysis for Tristram's reflection on the self and
for the process of 'writing a life which makes its own composition a
part of its subject'.[11] But this account of these processes also implicitly
describes Sterne's meta-fictional concern with the book, which reflects
on the processes of reception and interpretation by both author and
reader. Swearingen writes:

> Tristram reflects upon himself and, in the act of reflection, writes a
> book about the process. The book includes an account of its own
> composition and thereby takes on a relation to itself that parallels
> Tristram's own self-relatedness . . .

As we have argued earlier, the 'objectification' of the book within
the narrative of the fiction may also function as a challenge to the reader
to regard the book in his hand critically as an object presenting a
different kind of world to his own (which, in the case of parody, is also
more than one text-world), and a challenge in interpretation, which
will also involve the reader in self-analysis and a critical understanding
of his role, as implied or hypothesised decoder, in the composition of
the text before him.

Sterne's ironic comments on the difficulties of writing an hour's living
while preserving the unities of living, writing and reading must also imply
differences between these contingent activities, and 'wheels within wheels'.
Much of the dislocation of the expected structure of the novel also
derives from this game with time, as when Tristram's statement in
Book 3, 13, that he is living faster than he is able to describe his life,
leads to the introduction in 3, 20, of the 'spare moment' in which he can
write his 'Preface'.

The later reversal of the order of the chapters has been seen by Viktor
Sklovskij as foregrounding Sterne's technique of retarding the action of
the main plot. It also might be said to have another function in the
autobiography, of showing these 'retarding' moments to be themselves a
part of the 'plot' of the autobiography, in that they both add more
material for the autobiography, while retarding Tristram further in the
task of completing it. In this sense the main plot of the novel becomes
subsidiary to the story of writing the autobiography. The reader has,
therefore, not only to read across different stories at once (in the
manner of 'cross-reading' suggested by the satires of Sterne's friend
Hogarth), but to see them all as part of a complex process of reflexion
in which the wheels within wheels, the stories within the autobiography,

also serve as mirrors to the author, the book, and his reader which, at the same time, 'deconstruct' the accepted process of imitation and reflection in the world of fiction. The role of parody in deconstructing the concepts of imitation and representation in art will be explored in reference to Foucault's analysis of the developments of our 'episteme' in more detail in Section 4.4. One of Foucault's theses, that the liberation of art from the mimetic representation of reality has been accompanied by the disappearance of the author as the structurer of representation, may also be compared with Jacques Derrida's rejection of the concept of the implied author for that of the 'absent' author. Here too, with the elimination of the authorial self, the limitation of meta-fiction to the analysis of subjects other than itself is also circum-scribed, and the self-reflective author's dilemma of having to catch up with his self 'solved' by the elimination of the concept of the self as author.

4.3 The 'Absent' Reader and the Iterability of the Text

While Wolfgang Iser has spoken of an 'implied' reader, Jacques Derrida has suggested we should rather speak of an 'absent' author and reader. In his talk 'Signature evenement contexte' of 1971,[12] Derrida argues this in criticising Condillac's history of the text as a continouus develop-ment from oral communication (between a present encoder and a present decoder) to written communication between absent author and reader. For Derrida, the break between presence and absence in the history of the text is much more radical. And the consequences of Derrida's reading of Condillac are, for our understanding of the relation-ship between text and context, also radical.

For Derrida, though the absence of the reader might also be described by some as being — like the state of the implied reader — a 'distant presence', it is much more than this in representing, in fact, the 'death of the reader'. The next question asked by Derrida is how a written text may continue to function, and be received, under these circum-stances in which reader and author are both 'absent'. Moving from his premise that author and reader are absent to the presence of the text, Derrida concludes (in a precariously circular argument) that it is the 'iterability' of the text — its ability to be repeated anew — which is 'implied' in the continued existence of the text in the absence of the reader, and that it is then not the 'implied reader', but the 'implied iterability' of a text which structures its 'presence' (and iterability!) in the absence of either (or both) author and reader. Implicitly rejecting statements such as Sartre's of 1947 that the text cannot exist without the existence or presence of a reader, Derrida writes:

In order for my 'written communication' to retain its function as writing, i.e. its readability, it must remain readable despite the absolute disappearance of any receiver, determined in general. My communication must be repeatable – iterable – in the absolute absence of the receiver or of any empirically determinable collectivity of receivers.[13]

The radical conclusion Derrida draws from this 'death of the reader' (implied in some other Structuralist analyses of discourse) is that the context of the work – the subject of sociological and historical analysis, and also of hermeneutics – is no longer to play a part in the interpretation of the text. It is the iterability of the text which, for Derrida, 'structures the signs of the text itself' – no matter what type of variability – or difference – we find between these texts. How iterability structures its own presence (iterability) is given, but how iterability structures difference has still to be adequately explained.

Parody, on the other hand, as we have described it previously, not only structures change within texts, but in saying something new about repeated texts, and by its role as a catalyst of change in literary history, shows that repeatability has not only ensured the life of texts within the passing of time in the absence of author and specific readers, but has often condemned these texts to either becoming the subject of parody – or to being ignored, even by the parodist, and condemned to an untimely death. And iterability – even if this word is intended to imply the rebirth of something in the moment of repetition (as Derrida suggests in giving its etymology from 'iter' meaning 'anew' and the Sanskrit 'itera', 'differently') – does not appear to offer an explanation of why a text may become an anachronism in a different time. Alone iterability neither ensures life to a text, nor explains why one text may survive at the time it does, and why another does not. To ignore the sociological factors which affect principles such as the usage or control of iterability is not to transcend them, and Derrida's devaluation of the importance of context in interpreting texts might also be read as an avoidance of the question of anachronism. For if the relationship of a text to its own time, and to that of its reader, cannot be taken into account, then too the conditions affecting its 'iterability', but also offering the criteria for evaluating this iterability, cannot be properly judged.

It might also be argued that it is in fact the assumed presence of the receiver, as a condition of the communication of the author's message, rather than his 'absence', which creates the *need* for the 'iterability' of texts, but it is the unknown variations within the assumed group of readers which also makes iterability alone inadequate as an explanation for the reception of the text. A text repeated in circumstances which have seen changes within the original audience of the text may not only come under attack as anachronistic, or dated, but as incomprehensible, despite its 'iterability'. It is here that a discussion of parody helps us to see that authors have often resorted to devices such as distortion, juxtaposition, and refunctioning of other texts to ensure the 'iterability' of a text through time. Parody shows that although the idea of a present reader is constant in literary history, the awareness of the changing characteristics of this reader has also led to, or been accompanied by, attempts to rewrite, or to change, parallel characteristics in the texts being received. Parody can, hence, show repeatability to be the essence as well as the Achilles heel of literature: and in its ambivalent attitude to and 'dialectical' treatment of a repeated text, Cervantes' *Don Quixote*, has, for example, represented a way in which parody can produce change in literary history while preserving continuity.

In works in which a reader may at least appear in an implied or caricatured form, the physical absence of the interlocutor could be seen to have allowed the author the freedom, limited in an actual speech situation, of defining the characteristics – and even role – of the reader before the latter is able to fill it himself.

The parodistic definition of the horizon of expectations of the reader (as different from those of the parodist) is yet another example of the advantage made by the parodist of the physical absence of the reader which, at the same time, however, would appear to assume the existence of a reader as receiver of this 'self-image'. In establishing a contrast – even discrepancy – between the expectations of another reader and his own reading of the text, the parodist presents himself as reader and implies the existence of another reader as both target and interlocutor, while also attacking the work or the image of another author. In parody then both the 'absent' author and reader are made present in the text itself.

The writer of fiction's ability to suspend the normal rules of speech acts within the fiction – to offer, or demand, at will, for example, verification of a statement – is also made possible by the absence of the interlocutor, though oral literature also surely demanded the reader's suspension of belief which his absence (or 'distant presence') in written literature exploits, while also giving rise to warnings and meta-comments from the distant or absent authors to recognise this as a function of the fiction.

If fiction itself could be said to have the status of a meta-language
to an object language, and to the context of those objects, and to be
not subject to the particular rules of verification which hold for the
object language, the success of its iterability might also be seen to exist
in – or be contingent to – the success of its communication of meta-
statements on the discourse of others and on itself. But though this
might appear to imply iterability to be determined by the meta-function
of fiction, though still independent of the presence of the reader, the
parody texts we have looked at have also shown meta-statements to
have implied, by their critical foregrounding of the processes of communication, the presence of a reader and his expectations as the subject
of the meta-language, and the reception of the parody to be dependent
too on the 'iterability' of their internalised target texts.

Above all the parody text shows iterability alone to be inadequate
to an explanation of the presence of change and transformation in
literary history. For in itself initiating change through the refunctioning
of another, or of several other texts, parody also establishes a contrast,
based on discrepancy, which implies the existence of conflicting readings,
and the presence of a decoder independent of the parodist.

A crisis of modern fiction and its analysis, of defining the role of the
author of the literary work, is also symptomatic of the act of communication in self-parody, where the author has taken on the roles of
both encoder and decoder, author and reader, to investigate the arche of
his style, or his authorial self, and then to be faced with a dilemma of
meta-analysis, that it cannot have itself as its own subject. The question
– as now also put in many linguistic debates about the nature of discourse – then appears to be a question of what the idea of the subject
in fiction can represent if not itself. Theories of the absent author, and
attacks on the humanist 'anthropological' analysis of discourse which
posits an author as subject reflect this dilemma of meta-analysis, though
without always making their roots in this problem clear. But such
theories also may represent an extension of Beckett's claim for Joyce
that he had made form the subject of fiction, and a drive to find new
subject-matter in the questioning of form itself. While Structuralists and
Deconstructionists have questioned the sovereignty of the figure of the
author in giving meaning to the text, hermeneutic interpretations of a
mutually reflexive relationship between text and context may be said to
have circumscribed, on the other hand, the problem of meta-analysis,
that subject and object must remain distinct from each other for meta-
comment to take place.

In the meta-fictional parody the parodist may indicate the limits of his analysis to another subject, but also use that subject (or target) to reflect back on his own activity as parodist. Yet this presents less the idea of an absent (or indefinable) author than the idea of the text as having (like the author's style of which it presents an archaeology) a set of multiple authors. The dual role of encoder and decoder of other texts assumed by the parodist may, moreover, provide a model for the communication between the author and his absent reader, which may complete the process of analysing the fictional world, suggested in the parody's critique of another author or text, but which was unable to be applied by the parodist to his own parodistic activity.

It is, however, not our purpose here to offer a critique in general of Derrida's writings — for we have taken only a small part of one of his texts to compare the concepts of implied and absent readers, and to relate them to our discussion of parody. Michel Foucault, however, has explicitly discussed *Don Quixote* in the context of an analysis of the critique of representation, and, thereby, also implied a role for parody in the development of the modernist episteme. A consideration of his theories is, thus, of central importance in our discussion of parody as a critique of imitation in fiction which leads to the reflexivity and self-criticism characteristic of modern works.

4.4 Les Mots et les Mots: The Function of Parody in our Episteme

Michel Foucault's development of a concept of an absent author in *Les Mots et les Choses*, where the idea of the author represents the moment of individualisation of the principle giving order to discourse, can be seen as both a way of explaining modernism in the literary work, and as a product of the same. But Foucault's analysis of the development of the modernist episteme from the critiques of identity and representation made in parody in *Don Quixote* also suggest that his theories, like those of the Formalists in literature, have been developed on the basis of parody texts and structures. Foucault's development of the Formalist (and Structuralist) concept of discontinuity as structure-determining in discourse — in *The Archaeology of Knowledge* which follows *Les Mots et les Choses* — also reflects upon his use of parody texts and their role in his canonisation of self-reflexive parody in the modernist episteme as a method of discourse. Foucault writes in the opening pages of *The Archaeology of Knowledge*:

Discontinuity was the stigma of temporal dislocation, which the historian had to remove from history. It has now become a basic factor in historical analysis.

In a conversation with M. Fontana, Foucault has emphasised that *Les Mots et les Choses* offered questions, rather than preformed answers, about discontinuity, and in that work the implication of a role for parody in developing a self-critical method of analysing representation in discourse also implies a role for it in the development of a concept of discontinuity in discourse.

The discussion of the status of parodistic meta-fictional statements as 'higher-order statements' in Section 3.4 of this study has implied that the aim of meta-fictional parody is not the 'destruction' of the text, or of the reader. For in presenting its criticism of fiction from within another fictional discourse, such parody both reflects ironically on its own dependency on the fiction and on the reader of the fiction, and adds further to the literary corpus while acting as its critic. Here, too, the possibility of parody initiating a revolutionary break in the discourse of its age through the meta-fictional criticism of other texts is also raised.

For Derrida, however, the text is not given its meaning by the reader but 'reads itself' — excluding hermeneutical interpretation of its code and its relationship to its context. But though the author also 'disappears' in Michel Foucault's *Archaeology of Knowledge*, Foucault's concept of the author as the moment of individualisation in the structuring of discourse also describes discourse as controlled by such epistemological strictures as censorship, verification, and rationality, and (as Foucault also implies in conversation with Paolo Caruso, 1969) does not necessarily exclude the context of discourse from its interpretation. The concept of a discourse which is, moreover, concerned more with its own system of signification than with the representation of things, also reflects the present modern episteme's meta-critical questioning of language, practised in fiction by authors such as Beckett and Borges. Foucault's concept of a discourse, which has, furthermore, come to this stage of self-criticism through a rejection of naive concepts of reflection and imitation and a questioning of representation, also gives a place to parody (from *Don Quixote* on) in the exchange of one episteme for another. While this foregrounds one aspect of parody, the role of transforming the discourse of an age cannot, of course, be attributed to parody, or to the epistemological function of parody alone. Yet in that parody internalises both its past and its present in its 'text-world', in the form of the preformed language of its target, and in its 'objectification' of the expectations of its readers, it is also able to illuminate both the material and epistemological conditions for change present in its world. Foucault's use of parody texts to both illumine the relationship of discourse to these epistemological conditions, and to characterise the self-reflexivity which has helped authors transform such conditions, will be the subject of the following section.

Inspired by Borges, and taking *Don Quixote* as his text for *Les Mots et les Choses*, Foucault carries the Formalists' use of parody as a model for the discontinuous structure of fictional texts several steps further, to develop a model for the breakdown of the concepts of identity and representation in the epistemes of the sixteenth and eighteenth centuries, and an explanation for the creation of a modern, self-reflexive episteme. For though Foucault does not explicitly connect the Quixote with the latter, the 'crisis of reflexion' discussed by Borges in his comments to the Quixote and evident in the work of Beckett, Magritte, and other modernists, owes much to the discussion of the possibilities and limits of self-analysis in post-Cervantic literature. The problem implicit in *Don Quixote*, of how fiction can be questioned from within fiction itself (which we have compared to the Cretan liar paradox), and how, despite the logical limitations on meta-fiction, it can be used to create new literary works, has been foregrounded in modern parody, and itself made into the subject of other literary works. Michel Guérin's praise for Don Quixote in his novel *Lettres à Wolf ou La Répétition* (Paris, 1977) represents moreover a variation on Foucault's argument that Quixote's foolishness exists in his search for 'identities' between the world and the fiction. For here Guérin sees Quixote's heroism as consisting in his willingness to put in jeopardy 'the principle of Rationalism, the principle of identity', and also 'to lose his identity'. Here, it is rather the fool who is given the role attributed to Cervantes by Foucault, of undermining the principle of identity. And here the fool, the theatrical mask, and the grotesque are taken as symbols of a modern condition, and Don Quixote seen as a 'Bildungsroman' in the art of learning how to live the fictional life, and the art of masking.

In his Preface to *Les Mots et les Choses* of 1966, Foucault wrote that it was a text by Luis Borges ('The Analytical Language of John Wilkins') which had given rise to his book, adding that Borges' text had produced a laughter which shakes all of our familiar, accepted, ways of thinking, the thinking of our time and place which we had thought above doubt. This, in essence, is what many of Borges' parodies, the parody of Beckett, and other older parodistic meta-fictions have aimed at, and this is why so many parodies – such as Borges' admired *Don Quixote* – can be described as having played a role not only in

changing the course of literary history, but the episteme of their age.
Like Borges, Foucault too goes back to *Don Quixote*, to find in it a
crisis of representation which marks a break with the Renaissance
ideology of the world as mirror of a larger plan, and the text as a further
reflection of that world. Where the fool (as in the 1515 frontispiece to
Till Eulenspiegel) was often shown holding a mirror up to the world, the
parody of *Don Quixote* is seen by Foucault as criticising the foolish
hero's search for mirror identities between his world and the fiction of
the Romance.

Quixote represents for Foucault a pilgrim searching for similarities
without ever discovering the centre of identity, until he himself becomes
a symbol, and, hence, one with the text from which he comes. The book
is for Quixote a guide through life without which he cannot move,
and to which he must give meaning by his enactment of its adventures.
Quixote believes he must prove book and world to be similar, as for
him meaning consists in similarity. Foucault finds in *Don Quixote* not
only Cervantes' attack on the unreality of the Romance, or on the
naivete of its readers in Cervantes' time, but an attack on the whole
episteme of his age – on the obsessive search for a mirror to the world
in the text, and a mirror to the book of God in the world.

The opening sentence of Samuel Beckett's essay on Joyce's work-in-
progress on *Finnegans Wake*: 'Dante . . . Bruno. Vico . . . Joyce',[14] might
also be seen to express the scepticism in mimesis and reflection,
characteristic of the modern episteme. Beckett is also describing the
difficulty, however, of describing Joyce's revolution in writing without
resorting to analogy:

> The danger is in the neatness of identifications. The conception of
> Philosophy and Philology as a pair of nigger minstrels out of the
> Teatro dei Piccoli is soothing, like the contemplation of a carefully
> folded ham sandwich.

Like this analogy (which, furthermore, supersedes the use of analogy
it attacks by its parodistic form), parody, as the criticism of a pre-
vailing manner of thought, does not aim to be soothing, but to disturb
preconceptions and prejudices.

For Foucault *Don Quixote* shows the negative aspect of the
Renaissance world in which writing no longer represents the world, but
leads to the searches for identities which must necessarily end in
absurdity, and so, also to lead to the criticism of its discourse. Parody
– through carrying out this criticism through a new form of discourse –

shows how the latter may be the carrier of both its own transformation, and dialectical continuation. Foucault's choice of *Don Quixote* to discuss the end of the Renaissance episteme, and to point to the critical self-reflexive character of the modern episteme, as we have it in Beckett and Borges, has pointed, if only implicitly, to the broader historical function of meta-critical parody in the exchange of one discourse for another in times of epistemological crisis,[15] yet here it must also be claimed for parody that it has been only one, literary-oriented, means to the refunctioning of discourse.

When the characters of *Don Quixote* speak in Part 2 of that book of having read of themselves, then, Foucault says, some meaning is given the written word. Here the word is seen as possessing meaning in the self-conscious reflection of the book on itself. Yet what makes the meta-fictional 'mirror' productive of more meaning? Is it because as a meta-language it does not appear to demand the verification of its representation of itself in the fictional text, but offers the reader the chance to make his own comparisons or, because, as Foucault suggests, it offers Don Quixote the chance to be true to himself in Cervantes' text rather than true to the roles given in the knightly Romance? Naturally these need not be the only possible answers, but regarding the latter it can be said (as Foucault also shows), that Don Quixote is still naive in the sense that he is not fully aware that 'he himself has become a book' — and indeed, in the books within Cervantes' book — Don Quixote's self-consciousness would need to be poly-reflective. It is, of course, also a fiction of Cervantes' text that Quixote has become — as Foucault claims — the book 'in flesh and blood'. And the poly-reflexive nature of such parody must also be taken into account in asking how new meaning may be produced by the deconstruction of established norms, as well as perpetuated by norms.

Henri Lefebvre's *Introduction à la Modernité. Préludes* has made a case for saving modernism, or for it saving itself, in the reflexivity of irony. For Lefebvre irony represents not the undermining of truth but its salvation. For Foucault, however, paradox and irony had served to shake the dogmatism of philosophy, and to introduce the critique of representation into art. In warning against the 'inwardness' associated with reflexivity (1969) Foucault also distinguishes his position from that of Lefebvre's.

How then can irony (and parody) be viewed both as a means to revealing truth and a means to undermining it? And how have writers used irony and parody to both undermine the past and to create new forms of discourse? This question, and a 'resolution' of the differences between the arguments put forward by Lefebvre and Foucault appears (despite Foucault's warning against some dialectical methods) to be answerable dialectically. For the structure of irony and parody, consisting of the dialectical 'dialogue' between two codes or two texts, also consists of a contrast between positions which 'anti-dogmatically' puts its own contrast into doubt, while showing it, nevertheless, to be of a higher kind (as meta-statement) to its object.

The use of irony in fictions such as *Don Quixote* to reveal the fictional character of the text-world uses a paradox self-critically to reveal its own text-world to be 'false' in its relationship to the reality it is assumed to represent, but to prove the paradox — its meta-comment to its object text — to be of a higher order than that text's naive representation of reality. Even in self-parody — where the object is the author's earlier work — the 'meta-text' B is different from text A, though the 'identity' of the author with the author of his object text may (as in the Cretan liar paradox) appear to create a paradox. Through its 'higher-order' meta-comment to its object the irony or parody offers a critique of falsity, undermines the false concept of the truth of the fictional world, and offers a 'higher' form of truth from the other fiction which is its object. In this way irony and parody may both serve to criticise falsity (as in Lefebvre's argument) and (as Foucault argues) undermine the theory of representation to produce new meaning, and a new method of reading meaning.

For Foucault *Don Quixote* is the 'first of those modern works in which the rationale of identity and difference is made into an unending game of signs and similarities'. There — as later in Borges' work — language for Foucault breaks its established relationship with the world of objects to take on an autonomy which will express itself in the self-reflective fictional worlds of literature. In this argument parody is attributed a role as the carrier of the 'discontinuous' in epistemological history. And it is an argument which re-establishes, within post-Structuralist analysis, the relationship between discontinuity and parody suggested by Sklovskij as a model for literary change as such, and which was taken by Structuralists as a central category in the analysis of discourse in diachronic and synchronic systems. But in extending this to the history of the episteme of an age Foucault has also pointed to the important psychological and historical function of parody often overlooked by Structuralists, as well as by non-Structuralist historians of literature. For in political propaganda, as well as in the criticism of ideological texts and literary fiction, parody has often played a role in the changing of opinion, a task also given it in rhetorics. Controls such as censorship on parody as a literary form have tacitly acknowledged the potential power of parody in fulfilling critical tasks. Though the traditional conflict between empirical methods and those described in this section has tended to keep sociological questions distinct from those of a more epistemological nature, Foucault may be said to have suggested ways in which a sociology of parody may provide evidence for the analysis of epistemological change.

But Foucault's analysis of *Don Quixote* is above all enlightening for an understanding of the anti-imitative character of modern parody. As we have seen, parody has often been described in Rhetorics as a form of 'simulatio' or 'dissimulatio', and defined according to its relationship to its model in terms of imitation. Foucault has shown how parody has served to criticise such categories, and how modern parody has taken on a meta-critical form which raises the specific critical functions of the parody of texts to the role of a critique of its historical episteme. For this reason, too, a sociology of parody may be treated as a sociology of both specific and general, meta-fictional parody.

Foucault has also, of course, suggested ways of criticising his method used in *Les Mots et les Choses*. In *The Archaeology of Knowledge* (*L'archéologie du Savoir*, Paris, 1969), for example, he criticises the impression of totality, and lack of discontinuity in discontinuity, given in the description of epistemes in *Les Mots et les Choses*. ('Archaeology' is now described as designating the general theme of an analysis of pre-formed speech, which questions the signifying function realised in it, the 'discursive formation' to which it belongs, and the general 'Archive' of knowledge under which it stands.) But in describing the episteme at the conclusion of the 'Archaeology', Foucault again implies a coherency of knowledge under which various discontinuous moments of knowledge are gathered. Here the tendency of descriptive terms to give coherency to the incoherent is evident when the episteme is described as the totality of the connections which can be discovered within a given age in the various sciences. In arguing that parody may be seen as critically refunctioning the discourse of a certain episteme I am describing an attitude of the parodist to the extra-textual significance of his paro-distic use of the preformed language of other writers or speakers, and am not attempting to divide history into certain broad epistemological categories, as Foucault might be said to have done in *Les Mots et les Choses*. But I also want to suggest that Foucault's choice of the parodies of Cervantes as his texts has influenced his own categorisation of historical epistemes, and that this has suggested a broader role for parody in the exchange of discourses than suggested previously in literary criticism.

Parody understood as the archeology of the text deals with its own
pre-existence (or 'Arche' in the meaning of pre-knowledge of itself) in
the sense of rediscovering and recreating its own models. In this way too
the parody also multiplies the subjects of its own discourse before
turning them (itself and its models) into the object of analysis. It is
also through this process that the impression can be created of the disappearance (behind a multiplicity of authors) of the subject from its
discourse.

Literary history alone, as an 'Archive' or collection of texts, does
not necessarily represent the self-conscious archaeology of its past practised by the parodist. Foucault's use of parody texts by Beckett and
Borges to illustrate his epistemological history of the critique of representation serves to support, moreover, the archaeological function of his
own enterprise, reflected too in his use of Kant.

In his *Anthropologie* (translated by Foucault) Kant had praised the
Realism of Richardson's novels. But he had then also praised the 'corrective'
to the image of the world represented by Richardson given in the parodies
of Henry Fielding. Wit, and parody understood as a form of wit, is also
described in the 'Anthropology' as a means to the liberation of the mind
from preconceptions. For Foucault, whose attribution of a role to
parody in changing the preconceptions of an episteme bears some
apparent resemblance to Kant's description of the epistemological
functions of parody, it is not the single subject but the structure of the
episteme and its determinations which effects and is affected by the
parodistic criticism of pre-established identities, and of mimetic representation in art. But this also reflects the multiple author of parody.

In section 7 of his essay on 'Nietzsche, Geneaology, and History' (in
Hommage à Jean Hippolyte, Paris, 1971), Foucault both associates
parody with critiques of the concept of identity and uses it in the two
senses used by Marx before Nietzsche to describe parody in history as
(1) the unwitting repetition of identities from the past, and (2) a mode
of discontinuity, and a means to the critical dissociation of the present
from the parodistic-farcical identification with the past of (1).

Hegel had written that man parodies the past when he is ready to
dissociate himself from it, and (2) is somewhat related to this view. The
simultaneous use of the two contradictory concepts of parody found
here may be explained by the fact that parody in both its technical
sense (as literary parody), and used metaphorically, as here by Foucault
to describe an attitude to history, may serve to criticise the belief in an
identity between historical periods, or between present reality and the
signs and terms of written history or literature, by first imitating its

target (to apparently identify with it), and by then distancing itself
critically through distortion, satire, or irony. Parody as farce, or unwitting parody in the sense of (1), fails to make this second step itself,
and becomes the subject of mockery from other critical sources.

Foucault's analysis of Velasquez' 'Las Meninas' of 1656, in *Les
Mots et les Choses*, has described it as a representation of representation.[16] But this type of representation cannot simply be reduced to
the 'conventionalisation' of a 'genuine realistic representation' as
Jurij Lotman has suggested in referring to Foucault in his *Introduction
to the Semiotics of the Film*.[17] The game with the conventions of painting in Velasquez' work is, as Foucault has shown, much more complex.
Lotman's suggestion that the picture of the painter, which Velasquez
gives us, shows us his picture 'from the reverse side', gives support
to his general interpretation. Yet if it is not the painting of the court
ladies and of himself which the painter within the painter is painting,
but, as Lotman appears to imply, elsewhere in his argument, the King
and Queen reflected in the back mirror, then the picture being painted
in the painting cannot be the picture before us. This puts into doubt
not only the equation: outer painting = inner (unseen) painting, and
the equivalence of Velasquez' representation to his subject, but also
any claim that Velasquez' painting is purely a realistic depiction of the
processes of painting.

One of Foucault's theses for his conclusion, that representation is
freed of its subject in 'Las Meninas' to become 'representation pur', is
that the subject of the inner painting – the King and Queen – is
missing, or naively represented. But this also tends to underplay the
double function of representation in the work. For though the
reflection of the artist and his easel within the work reflects on realistic
concepts of reflection, it also functions symbolically within the work
as a whole – contributing to the function of the painting as a
'symbolisation' of the real which attributes to reality an ideal form,
and establishes a hierarchy of realities which reflects the hierarchy of
the court, and which will also be reflected in the way in which court
and monarch are represented.

The reflection of the King and Queen at the back of the picture –
which suggests that they are the subject of the painting being painted
in 'Las Meninas' – shows them not only reflected 'through a glass
darkly' in the art work of the human artist, but places them at the
centre of the perspective of the painting, so that they look at themselves and also serve to reflect the eye of the artist represented painting
them, as well as (as Foucault suggests) the eye of the painter, and his

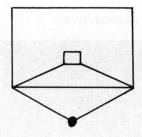

public, observing them from outside the painting. Thus while Foucault has spoken of the 'reciprocity' of communication between the artist inside the painting and the viewer (here also, however, in Velasquez' time, the court) in 'Las Meninas', this reciprocity must also be seen as having been established in the painting, as a reciprocity between the artist outside the picture and his representation of himself and his subject within. This 'double representation' of the artist may also serve as a key to the doubling of the functions of representation within the painting – as symbolism and realism. Here too the complexities of the sixteenth-century neo-Platonists' view of the hierarchy of realities in the cosmos must also be taken into account.

The concentration of our vision on the image of the monarchs at the back of Velasquez' painting – through their place by the centre of its perspective – 'reverses' the image of the situation depicted in the work (where the represented artist appears to be seen through the eyes of his subject, the King and Queen, before him) to give us a representation, in symbolic form, of the eye of the painter outside the painting.

It is in this way that the 'realistic' representation of the artist within the painting is taken a step further, and also symbolised. For the eye of the creating artist could also be taken at that time as an analogy to that of the world-Creator, within whose hierarchy of spheres the King and Queen have both a symbolic and a realistic (or 'natural') existence. But within this hierarchy of spheres we also have the hierarchy of a social order, which in Velasquez' picture might also be seen to be reflected in the use of a realistic depiction for the lower orders of the court – the court ladies, the Church and the artist – and a symbolic representation – through a glass darkly – of the rulers of the court, the royal couple. For the eye of the artist, in which the image of the King and Queen rests, not only gives them the place of the first creatures of creation, but refers us to the fact that it was the discovery of perspective in the Renaissance (of which Velasquez has made symbolic use to put the royal couple into the centre of his picture) which made the three-dimensional 'realistic' representation of

6. Diego Velasquez, *Las Meninas*, 1656.

Source: reproduced courtesy of the Prado Museum, Madrid.

nature (and of the court ladies, the Church, and the artist) possible, while also making the eye of the painter of central importance.

Is this then realism or hyper-realism – or does it function to foreground the symbolic character of realism which it had in Velasquez' time? The juxtaposition of realism and symbolism may have, as just suggested, its own symbolism, in using the realistic depiction of the situation of the artist as a contrast to the darker reflection of the higher sphere of the court in the mirror behind the artist depicted within the painting. The 'higher' meta-level of the painting is then not the 'realistic' representation of the painter within the picture, but the reflection of the King and Queen in the 'eye' of the painter outside the picture, which gives the perspective of the work. What is perhaps 'subversive' in this is the power Velasquez has shown art to have in reproducing the hierarchy of realities determined in the court within the types of representation used in his painting, and in symbolising himself in symbolising his 'higher' subject. For here, as suggested earlier, the artist also appears in the role of creator determining the type of representation, and its symbolism, appropriate for his royal subjects. The Church, however, represented by 'nun and monk', remain in the background of the realistically represented figures.

Reflected on the back wall of the room – at its centre (in the mirror which appears to reflect the eye of the painter) – the symbolised figures of King and Queen have already become fixed within a painting in a painting. Here again the object in the artwork is seen to have at least two functions – of reflecting the artist's subject and of reflecting on the nature of the reality of its representation. And here representation does not, in fact, appear to supersede but to reinforce itself. In this, then, 'Las Meninas' cannot be equated with the *Quixote*. As an ambiguous mirror/painting the picture of the King and Queen also comments on the two representational, reflective and symbolic functions of the artwork, as well as on the representational function of the worldly court as symbol of a heavenly hierarchy. But that the edges of the canvas are evident of the panel partly concealing the painter in 'Las Meninas', this too might be taken as being ambiguously either mirror or picture, thus reflecting the ambiguity of the (finished?) portrait of the King and Queen in which its (the canvas's) contents are reflected on the back wall of the room. Ambiguity characterises this work in many ways, in fact. The ambiguous look on the face of the Princess, for example, may be either that of the curious observer of another subject (the King and Queen), or that of the painter's subject itself. The attention given the front of the picture by all can also be interpreted as either respect for the persons of the monarch, or for the artist. This, too, may be taken as symptomatic of the potentially subversive importance given to the artist through the identification of himself (as creator) and the monarch which is suggested by the system of mirrors and the use of perspective in the work. What Foucault takes as an example of the liberation of representation from its object, or subject, may hence be interpreted in such a way as to leave this liberation itself ambiguous. In the modernist meta-pictures of artists such as Magritte (discussed by Foucault elsewhere), the criticism of representation based on the principle of reflection is however explicit, and, moreover, made through parody — the ironic antithesis in form to the principle which sees reflection as a means to the 'truthful' representation of reality. It may be of some significance, in fact, that 'general parody', of the type used by Cervantes to criticise the 'search for identities', is not evident in 'Las Meninas', though we may find satire and specific parodies, perhaps, of the conventions of other artists.

Parody in the works of modernists like Magritte (whose combination of images and signs can sometimes be compared with the game of 'cross-reading') appears as a symptom of a new episteme — one in which not only standard forms of representation and communication are questioned, but meta-criticism itself ironised. As in the language scepticism of Kraus and other Austrian writers of the 1920s (continued by writers such as Handke, in his early works, and Jandl) meta-criticism of the sign not only seeks to foreground the fiction of the sign's representation of the objects it names, but points to the problem that it, too — as a meta-language or other meta-form of communication — must subject itself to another's criticism. Magritte's 1928/9 picture of a pipe with the words underneath 'This is not a pipe', entitled 'The Use of Language', was part of a series of experiments in analysing the relationship between world, object, name and representation. In these experiments the world is ironically represented as a semiotic system — pieces of scenery bearing the name 'cloud' or 'sky' wait to be put into their appropriate place by the painter or viewer, while the representation of painted and 'unpainted' canvas, on canvas itself, reflects ironically on the fiction of the 'deconstruction' of art in meta-art. For here it is in the process of deconstruction that a new artwork is again constructed.

The caricatures of Saul Steinberg (born 1914) depict the world as a parody of art, or as parody of the 'picturesque', as Robert Hughes suggests in his portrait of the artist in *Time* (17 April 1978). Steinberg's 'Self-Portrait' (1945) of the artist drawing the artist (also reproduced in

7. René Magritte, *Reproduction Interdite*, 1937.

the same edition of *Time*), radicalises the Renaissance concept of the artist's work as a reflection of his self, as well as the Realistic Atelier drawing of the nineteenth century, by objectifying a self-reflexive image of the artist in a cartoon of the artist drawing himself as cartoon. Here the artist is shown seated at his desk — as Steinberg — with pen and ink, sketching — as Steinberg then — himself drawing himself. The abstract, grotesque squiggle (almost a signature) with which the head is drawn, shows the 'representation' of the artist to be of another kind than that of the nineteenth century — but it also shows again the limits preventing self-reflexion from representing itself in the act of self-reflexion. For only an unfinished portrait can suggest the situation of the artist still in the process of recreating his image for another. Here one might also challenge the artist to the perhaps more complex task of drawing himself in the act of parodying himself. The 'open-ended' character of dialectical parody will also, as implicit in our discussion of Ryle, enable the unfinished character of meta-art (and, hence, itself) to be suggested, if not 'represented'.

In his parodistic 'Reproduction Forbidden' of 1937 René Magritte not only parodies the expectations of his public for a reflection of the face of the subject, but suggests an uncanny experience for the subject itself. (Poe's 'The Narrative of Arthur Gordon Pym' lies on the fireplace.) In this sense Magritte both undermines any expectation for a reflection of normal reality in the picture (the mimetic function of art being symbolised, as in seventeenth-century Dutch art, by the reflection of its subject in a mirror), and represents a surreal situation through the medium of the artwork. Ironically he also achieves this refunctioning of reflection in the art work by literary 'doubling' the reflection of the subject. As in 'In Praise of Dialectics' (also of 1937) the subject 'supersedes itself' in a reflection which is the opposite of that which is expected. And Magritte also implies that the attempt to reproduce reality in mimetic art was itself a distortion of the mirroring process known to us. The parodistic distortion of reflection in Magritte's picture thus functions as its supersession and 'correction'. In 'In Praise of Dialectics' the window of a house opens into an interior in which is depicted the outside of the front of another house to, moreover, realise and ironise the 'interiorisation' of the external world in art. The parody of art as the reflection of its subject, made through the parodistic use of the mirror (as also in Pierre van Soest's 'Visit with Van Eyck to the Arnolfini Family' of 1977), offers a clearly more radical break with the concept of art as representation of reality than made by Velasquez or the complex neo-Platonic use of the mirror.

8. René Magritte, 1896-1967, *In Praise of Dialectics*, Oil on Canvas, 64.5 x 54cm, Felton Bequest, 1972.

In this way the modernist episteme might be characterised not by its criticism of static forms of reflection in art, or discourse in general, but by its sceptical subjection of its own meta-critical forms and subjects to a projected third level of meta-criticism, such as we have described as occurring in parody. Magritte's denial in his pipe picture 'The Use of Language', of the equivalence between language, the image, and the external world, is part of the language scepticism of its episteme of which parody was both a central symptom and an important means to the further meta-criticism of discourse.

Further passages from Samuel Beckett, analysing the inadequacy of identifications between words, concepts, and objects could be taken for comparison with Magritte's 'language experiments'. So, for example, in *Watt*, the idea of a pot produces no objective reality when thought or spoken:

> . . . it was in vain that Watt said, Pot, pot . . . For it was not a pot . . .
> It resembled a pot, it was almost a pot, but it was not a pot of
> which one could say, Pot, pot, and be comforted . . .

The self-referring character of criticisms of art made from within the work of art itself also appears to have led Magritte to complicate his critique of the identification of sign and object made in 'This is not a pipe'.

Magritte's 1966 'reproduction' of his famous 'This is not a pipe' of 1928/9 was entitled 'The two mysteries', and depicted the original pipe picture on an easel alongside another representation of a pipe. In this way Magritte both described the mysterious quality of the artistic world and showed how the representation of the problem of representation must itself remain trapped within the limits of that which it is attempting to describe — within, that is, the limits of pictorial representation — because its description is made from within the same medium which it would criticise. Magritte also thereby directs our attention to the 'paradoxical' character of parodistic analysis made from within art or fiction, whereby as meta-fiction or meta-art the parody criticising another artwork or text reproduces and criticises its own fictionality in reproducing and criticising the fictionality of its target. So parody of fiction made from within fiction (parody as meta-fiction) has been shown to imply itself in criticising other fictional worlds, and, as with Magritte's representation of representation in his pipe pictures, to define its own representational (and critical) limits as being within those of the fictional world which is both its medium

and its target. The representation of other fictional worlds (and of
other representations) in parody may, like Magritte's 'Two mysteries',
also present itself self-critically as the representation of representation.

In his *Negative Dialektik* Theodor W. Adorno wrote that the supersession of a thesis through its contradiction in the dialectic was the
'index of the falsity ("Unwahrheit") of Identity'. Adorno's criticism of
the understanding of mimesis as the static reflection of reality, is, as
his critique of Identity theories, 'modernist' in a sense similar to the
critiques made by Magritte of the identification of image, language,
and object. And although Gablik, for instance, suggests that Magritte has
argued in his *The Use of Words* that the pipe cannot be both itself and
its contradiction ('This is not a pipe') at the same time – it is the contradiction which is thereby given as 'true', and used to contradict,
further, the belief in the identity of an object with its sign which the
picture of the pipe alone may have suggested. (Magritte's analyses of
the use of language often also parody the baroque emblem form, where
all three elements – of picture, title and motto – formed a, by contrast,
harmonious whole.) But in Adorno's attack on the ultimate elimination
of the contradiction in the positivising synthesis of the Hegelian
dialectic, he has also offered a critique of the dialectical thinking used
by surrealists such as Magritte.

For Adorno the Hegelian dialectic must produce a false synthesis of
its contradictions, while the dialectic of the surrealists must produce
the 'appearance of subjective freedom in a situation of external un-
freedom'. The surrealists had taken up Hegel's idea that mimetic art
was of a lower order than a transcendental realism. And in Magritte's
pictorial and verbal explanations of how a sign can appear to give
content and reality to an object, or appear to possess that reality itself,
we find Hegel's idea (also quoted by Suzi Gablik in her study of Magritte,
London, 1970, p. 67), that 'man can frame to himself ideas of things that
are not actual as though they were actual'. It cannot be overlooked that
Magritte's surrealism consisted, in part at least, in the parodistic foregrounding of the 'falsity' of the reality represented in the artwork
attempting a mimetic representation of the external world. But the
revelation of this falsity has the function of both defending reality
against misrepresentation and releasing the artwork from the limits of
representing objects of the real world.

Both Magritte's 'Reproduction Forbidden' of 1937/8 and his 'Two
mysteries' (the two pipes of 1966) serve to illustrate Magritte's statement (quoted Gablik, p. 142), 'that the appearance of the figure
rediscovers its mysterious virtue when it is accompanied by its

reflection. In effect: a figure appearing does not evoke its own mystery except at the appearance of its appearance'.

In his mirror pictures then Magritte used resemblance to both question the identity of image and object (signifier and signified), and to foreground the 'mysterious' quality distinguishing the image from its object or content.

So too the parodistic meta-fiction might be said to have the ability to both 'demystify' the 'reality' of other fictions, or the truth of their representation of reality, and to focus on the 'mysterious' irreality of fiction — on, that is, that element which distinguishes its world from others, but which can only be described in a meta-language of a 'higher order' than itself.

This difference need not imply that the artwork is 'autonomous' in the sense of being unrelated to the other worlds it signifies, but that it represents them and relates to them while remaining character-istically but 'indefinably' different. It is both the 'mystery' of the representation of objects in art (as represented by the stories of E.A. Poe drawn in 'Reproduction Forbidden') and the demystification of this representation as real or realistic, which occurs when the reflection of the figure seen by us from behind shows us not the expected front view of his person, but our image of his back, doubling that view and hence — through its 'ironic representation of the mirror image (which is the means to mimetic representation) questions and challenges our view of its reality. Ironically it is also our foreground view of the subject's back which we see projected in the mirror into which he looks, and which is thereby projected back at us to 'parody' (to mimic and supersede) the projection of our expectations for mimesis on to the art work.

In the work of Magritte the mirror image or the representation of reflection so serves not to create identity but to criticise and supersede it. And the principle of identity is also undermined in Magritte's work in his attempts to evoke the 'mystery' of the art work as the nature of its 'difference' from other objects.

Gablik writes (p. 13) that for Magritte this mystery also consisted in the fact that attempts to explain it might be made — but that it 'never explains itself', and this again refers us to the limits of the meta-artwork in explaining its own activity whilst in the midst of that activity. Here, as in meta-fiction and the meta-fictional parody, the identity of the activity with its explanation must limit higher-order comment to other works or activities. For this reason too — for the reason, that is, that identity excludes higher comment — the realistic,

mimetic representation of objects in art could, for Magritte, give no
new knowledge about the world. And here, too, we may find an
answer to why, as Foucault claims, self-critical reflexivity in the artwork may appear to produce new meaning.

A general conclusion for a theory of parody to be drawn from the
above arguments is that it can be said that while meta-fictional parody
has been used to criticise the identity between object and sign in
mimetic art — as an attack on the false concealment of differences
between the representational world of art and the real world in mimetic
art, it has also had to point to its own limits in describing that with
which it is identical — its own activity, that is, as meta-fiction. In
presenting its parody of other texts as a different, more complicated
activity than given in the target text (in that the parodist is implied as
both an encoder and decoder of the other fictional work) the parody
does distinguish itself from the fiction which it criticises — but it can
never, it would seem, describe itself in the process of parodying the
other works. In this the parody does not attempt to mystify the
difference between sign and signified, or to suggest an identity
between itself and its object as in the mimetic art which parody has so
often been used to criticise, and its identification of the limits of its
own activity may in itself be said to have given a new if problematical
direction to fiction.

Meta-art and meta-fiction reflect on other works of their own media,
but, as Henri Lefebvre writes in his *Prolegomena to a Metaphilosophy*,
to his concept of reflexive mimesis: 'The mirror has not all the dimensions
of that which it reflects, and imitation not all of those which it imitates.'
It is clear that both the imitation and the meta-fiction which dissociates
itself from the reproduction or imitation of nature (as has been the case
with some parodies) can give only an interpretation of their subject — the
imitation an approximation to the natural world, and the meta-fiction
an approximation to its interpretation of itself in the process of interpretation.

Also related to the critique of identity made in the works of surrealists such as Magritte (often made through the medium of parody) is
their confession of faith in a dialectic (for them the Hegelian dialectic)
in which the principle of identity is replaced by that of contradiction.

In the apparent 'synthesis' of opposites in Magritte's pictures these
oppositions do (contra-Adorno) still appear as contradictions and not
as identities — as, for example, in 'In Praise of Dialectics' where the
outside of one house is shown within the window of another, or in
'Hegel's Holiday' where a glass of water is shown resting on the top of

an umbrella.

In paintings such as 'Hegel's Holiday' ('Les vacances de Hegel', 1958) Magritte also gave visual form to his admiration for Hegel's dialectical method. That portrait of a glass of water on an umbrella ('synthesising' antitheses) may also remind us of Hegel's own comparison of irony to

dialectics, and of how some forms of wit have shared with dialectics the epistemological function of transforming old ideas into new. In the 1920s other surrealists had, as mentioned, explicitly taken up Hegel's attack on naive forms of Realism, on, that is, the naive imitation of nature in art. Like another 'Hegelian', Heine — who had, as we shall see, described *Don Quixote* as the transformation of the Romance into the novel — Magritte also used irony (and parody) dialectically, to show the transformation of an object in the artwork, as its alienation and transformation into something else — again to criticise mimetic concepts of art. But the criticism of representation which is to be found in the artwork of modernists such as Magritte is, we have argued with other critics, already there in works such as *Don Quixote*. In *Tristram Shandy*, where this critique becomes through the 'dialectical' supersession of the object in the subject, self-reflexive, the modernist author has also found a way of transforming the dialectical transformation of the subject's reflection on its object into its critical reflection on itself as object. Through fixing the role of parody in this development, the canonisation of discontinuity, as well as claims made for the 'absence' of the subject in modern poetics may be seen as part of the development of a self-reflexive, self-critical discourse, which — like the parody texts on which it has been based — is not conceived of as a negative reduction of the text, but as its expansion into new epistemological as well as literary fields. The canonisation of parody as part of a negative aesthetic would run the risk, however, of abstracting it both from the target and context internalised in it, and from the ambivalent sympathy with that target which that structural internalisation implies.

Hans Robert Jauss has now also offered a critique of Adorno's 'Ästhetik der Negativität' in his recent work, *Ästhetische Erfahrung und literarische Hermeneutik* (München, 1977), pointing out (p. 39), that the role of negative works (critical of or in opposition to empirical reality or to other texts) in the development of new (affirmed) canons is difficult to explain from within the negative aesthetic. Jauss sees the artist's criticism of established norms (as in parody) also as a negation of a pre-given reality, and it is the development of new traditions from the breaks with older norms which he sees as offering a problem for Adorno's theory.

A dialectical, Hegelian view of the role of parody in transforming literary tradition and the relationship between text and world (as with Ortega y Gasset's analysis of *Don Quixote*) gives, as seen earlier, the role of antithesis in the dialectical development of new forms from old to the parody, and sees the parodistic synthesis of text and anti-text as a complex anti-textual supersession of the target text which preserves a part of it in the parody, and serves to complicate and foreground the processes of encoding and decoding which occur in both the composition and reception of the literary text.

In the sense that a parody can offer a meta-fictional critique of its target and also subject itself to its questioning of its own fictional medium (the medium, that is, which it shares with its target) its dialectic (and 'dialogue' with its target), is however, both synthetic and open-ended. It hence does not (as in the form of Hegelian dialectic criticised by Adorno in his 'Negative Dialektik') necessarily attempt to posit itself as a 'totality', or closed goal or 'telos'.

The understanding of parody as a form of dialogue is made explicit in the works of the Russian Formalists, and, in particular, those by Michail Bachtin. In terms of our earlier description of the duality of text-worlds, and of the processes of encoding and decoding characteristic of meta-fictional parody, the 'dialogic' character of dialectical parody may be summarised as:

(1) In the sense that dialectics is, in the ancient meaning of the word, a 'dialogue', dialectical parody can also be described in terms of having set up a dialogue with another text — making a new argument of its target's argument and the parodistic counter-argument.

(2) The communication between the parodist and his reader complicates this 'dialogicity' further by offering the two texts which constitute the 'dialogue' between the parodist and his target text

to the external reader to decode.

(3) In the sense that the parodist holds both a dialogue with his target
text and a dialogue with his reader he presents himself in the roles
of both decoder and encoder, reader and author. In this way he also
creates a representative model of the dialogic communication
between text and reader which occurs by means of the monologue
in the author's text. Though it can be suggested that both
'dialogues' (between parodist and target text and parody text and
the external reader) are given in monologue form in the written
parody, the first dialogue spoken of — the dialogue between the
parody and its target, where the parodist is also shown in the role
of decoder, and reader — also reflects on the decoding of the parody
by the external reader, and on a second dialogic characteristic of
the dialectical parody.

When in parody a literary target is attacked as having falsely identified
itself with the reality it would represent, it is the parodist's meta-
perspective which may also (as suggested previously) be shown to be
limited by the limits of representation in describing itself. In this sense
too the parody constitutes its world as one based on a self-reflective
dialectical tension between representation and the supersession of its
limitations, which threatens its own 'completeness' as a world as well as
its status as criticism. The parodist may also thereby offer an attack
(implicitly or explicity) on theoretical oppositions between reality and
irreality in the artwork or as given in the canons of literary criticism.

In the open-endedness of parodies such as the *Quixote* or *Tristram
Shandy* negativity can be given a role in the positive development of
a literary canon — but it is, hence, a dialectical 'negativity' which does
not exclude an Hegelian dialectic. The *affirmation of the negative* in
literary criticism, however, both reflects the new normative power of
parody and distorts the ambivalent character of the parody by again
emphasising the negativity of its activity. The *affirmation* of the
negative in literature is of course in itself problematic. Too often the
dialectic contained within the parody (of text and 'anti-text') is, moreover, confused with the 'negative' effect of the parody on the reception
of its target. But the affirmation of the negative effect of the parody
may also neutralise the parody's ambiguous internal 'negativity'.

Though his negative aesthetic implies a criticism of the idea of an
internal dialectic, such as we have suggested for parody, in which
various texts may be synthetically brought together, many of Adorno's
statements on art do not, in themselves, appear to deny the concept of

positive diachronic dialectical change in literary history. Such a case is
Adorno's development of a concept of mimesis in which the art work
must first 'negate' the reality it imitates in order to transform it into art.
For while Adorno here also redefines mimetic art as a possibility of
breaking with naive forms of realism, he also writes in his *Ästhetische
Theorie* (p. 425), that there would have been no Joyce without Proust,
and no Proust without Flaubert, and that it is 'through' imitation
('Nachahmung'), and not apart from it, that art has constructed its
autonomy and 'won its freedom'. As suggested earlier, however, confusion between Adorno's concept of mimesis and concepts of mimesis
as the static reflection of reality, has, however, to be avoided, in order
to make it possible to describe the historical, diachronic role of modern
parody in criticising the older, static concept of mimesis rejected by
Adorno.

In turning parody against realistic 'mimetic' art Joyce, for example,
can be described as having created a structural discontinuity in the
text expressive of the discontinuity of the text's relationship to its
outer world. Though thus 'mimetic' in Adorno's sense of the word,
Joyce's parody (like Proust's) must be seen in its historical context as
also an attack on older static mimetic art forms.

In 'The Uses of Parody: Parody in Proust and Robbe-Grillet' (a paper
given in Canberra, 1976, and to be published in the volume on Parody
in *Southern Review*, University of Adelaide, in 1980), Valerie Minogue
relates Proust's use of parody to his critique of the 'realism' of the
Goncourt journals, and describes Robbe-Grillet's meta-fictional parody
as a further look back — over the writer's shoulder — into a mirror
which is also self-reflecting. And here continuity in the use of parody
as a self-critical mirror to the writer's activity also suggests its
archaeological function in revealing, and perpetuating, the literary
history of the parodist, which enables him to both evoke and transform
his past. Magritte's 'Reproduction Forbidden' also refers to an aspect
of the use of parody which will be returned to in Section 4.6 in the discussion of copyright. For while the title of 'Reproduction Forbidden'
repeats a thesis of surrealism that the function of art was not to
reproduce reality, it also parodies a copyright phrase which had been
used against parody itself, as the supposed imitation of another work.
Here the supposition that as imitation the parody could not be original,
but must live parasitically off the originality of other artists, is also
ironised and repudiated by the undeniable 'originality' of Magritte's
work. And here imitation is itself both parodied as a principle and
superseded, while parody is used to create the critical confrontation

of one type of art with its antithesis, and to make a new synthesis from this confrontation. The originality of this dialectical form of parody, which confronts the thesis with its antithesis to create discrepancy and incongruity but also a new subject, has also served modernists such as Magritte in superseding the scepticism of their episteme to give their meta-languages the further function of breaking the existing canon to develop new literary or visual art works. The function of parodistic meta-fiction, stressed earlier in this study (in Section 3.4), of transforming the analytical limitations of meta-language into advantages in the fictional work, and in the development of new forms in literary history, can now also be placed in a historical context in the modern episteme, as a means to the transformation of analytical language-scepticism into problematically reflexive and self-critical, but also revolutionary artistic and literary forms.

It is perhaps due to the critical form taken by meta-fiction in parody, that parody has also served as a tertiary meta-language, in the criticism of other meta-linguistic and meta-fictional forms of literature. It is in this sense too that parody may be said to characterise the modernist episteme, and has served it in the meta-criticism of art as the reflection and reproduction of its object. As the distorted reproduction of imitation, its contradiction and supersession, parody has served the criticism of imitation from within fictional works — creating new literary works from its criticism of older works and their aesthetic and, consequently, further evidence for the claim that art need not exist in imitation alone.

The dialectical character of parody was foregrounded, and potentialised (as noted earlier), in post-Hegelian nineteenth-century writings, some examples of these being the works of Heine. Heine's unfinished novel, *Der Rabbi von Bacharach*, was begun in the 1820s after Heine had heard Hegel lecture in Berlin and taken part in the activities of the 'Verein für Kultur und Wissenschaft der Juden', of which several members, such as Eduard Gans, were also Hegelians of the old school. The book was taken up again, however, only after the Damascus pogrom of 1840. The first chapters indicate that the subject of the novel was to be about the exile, internment and liberation of the European Jews, and is set around the time of the 1492 persecution of the Jews in Spain. What is interesting here is that Heine returns to his novel in 1840 to conclude it by parodying his original plan, incongruously synthesising such oppositions as apostate and Messiah, ghetto and liberation, on which the narrative of the early chapters was built, to suggest that the supersession of these oppositions, the goal of a free community, had been parodied by history in the pogrom of 1840, and that now only a false, parodistic synthesis of these oppositions could reflect the actual world outside the fiction. Hence the hero is 'replaced' by the Quixotic figure of the sensualist Don Isaak, an apostate ironically happy to find satisfaction in the kitchen of the ghetto.[18]

Examples such as this demonstrate that the dialectical use of parody against a writer's own work is not peculiar to the current modernist episteme. But it is the application of parody to the problem of reflection in the artwork as such, as well as the direction of its criticism towards itself and its language which characterises its use in the works of Joyce, Beckett, Borges and others. Here parody has been used to take its criticism of other fictions to the logical but radical conclusion that it, too, must be subjected to meta-fictional criticism — but with the consequence that other new fictions have been developed from this meta-critique.

From its role as a mirror to another text (as a form of 'simulatio', or the imitation of other works) parody has progressed to its role in Cervantes' *Don Quixote* as the means to the critique of the naive identification of the text and its subject, and to a critique of fiction as the reflection of another world. In thus raising the question about how this criticism can be made from within fiction, parody has also been used as a tertiary form of meta-criticism, to the parody itself, but it has also shown that the criticism of imitation and reflection has not led to the death of literature but to the development of new, if self-consciously 'negative', or, rather, 'contradictory' literary forms.

In its distortion of reflected texts and world views parody comes to play the role of an antithesis to reflection in literary history, an alternative form of writing, and a means to the transformation of other literary works and trends. The dialectical role of parody in transforming the direction of literary history has been foregrounded in the nineteenth and twentieth centuries, as in Ortega y Gasset's interpretation of Cervantes' *Don Quixote* (which he, like Heine and other dialecticians, describes as having given birth to the novel from the death of the Romance), but also in Beckett's comments to Sterne and Joyce. In the modernist episteme parody has been seen through the dialectic as offering a way to the supersession and refunctioning of older traditions, as an antithesis to imitation rather than a form of imitation and, hence too, an opposition to imitation in art, which leads to its supersession.

In the modernist episteme a work such as *Tristram Shandy* hence comes to represent for the Russian Formalists discontinuity in the text as a creative device, while its implicit undermining of the theory of language as a representation of ideas has also made of this eighteenth-century work a model for the modernist novel. The language scepticism of the 1920s (paralleling, as suggested earlier, the general inflationary devaluation of the notes of exchange which Foucault sees as having been created by an older episteme of representation) may also be seen as leading to meta-linguistic forms (such as meta-fictional parody) being used not only to comment on other object languages, but to reflect back on themselves. It is here, in the meta-analysis of meta-languages, that we might in fact find the duplication of representation which Foucault saw as releasing representation from its subject in Velasquez' work. It has been argued here, however, that in Velasquez' 'Las Meninas' the double reflection of the artist (inside and outside the painting) not only functions to give an ideal as well as a 'natural' reality to the person of the artist, but also to his subject, the monarch, and that here representation serves to represent both objects and symbols realistically and symbolically.

In the dream pictures of Magritte representation is, however, literally shown as having separated from its subject, when named pieces of landscape wait to be painted, or to be put into position in their landscape, or left (untouched). And Foucault's way of viewing Velasquez as releasing representation from its subject reflects in fact rather this, his own modernist episteme.

In his Preface to *Les Mots et les Choses* Foucault wrote that it was between the use of the codes ordering the world of things, and the reflection on this order, that the essence of this order was experienced. Here parody, which Foucault has analysed in Cervantes' work, and praised in Borges, also appears in the role of a method of analysing *how* a discourse is constructed, and received, to give parody a place in the development of self-reflexivity in the modernist episteme.

And Foucault's theory is also symptomatic of this episteme in dialectically seeking itself in the past — in the discontinuous development of the relationship between discourse, the order of things, and the self-reflexivity of discourse — to deconstruct the historical context of the past to find its own roots. So Foucault also seeks to give us the historical context of his subject. As in parody, the process of self-analysis in this discourse proceeds diachronically, to see itself in an antithetical, discontinuous relationship to its past. The dialectical structure of the parody, as well as its epistemological function in 'archaeologically' freeing author and reader from the past, in bringing it (or an idea of it) to the surface for critical analysis, is characteristic

of the modern episteme as Foucault has described it. Whether this is
our only episteme, and whether it must only be described in these
terms, or even whether its discourse might have been described
differently by Foucault if he had not begun with Borges and Cervantes,
are other questions.

The identification here of the specific, parodistic character of some
of the texts taken by Foucault in *Les Mots et les Choses* to trace the
epistemological rejection of identity and representation in the discursive formations of the sixteenth, eighteenth and nineteenth
centuries should be seen as supplementing his own self-criticism, given
in 'The Archaeology of Knowledge', of the method of his previous
works. But our identification of the epistemological function of parody
in transforming the discourses of an age may be seen as an extrapolation
from Foucault's general theory of epistemological discontinuity and
change, which allows us to see parody within the context of
epistemological history, and to explain its ability to transform literary
traditions.

Recent parodies continue to show not only the modern writer's
awareness of this function of parody in transforming literary history,
but (often with reference to Foucault's writings on the imaginative
life of our episteme and its official suppression) to analyse the relationship of the dialectical meta-critical form of parody to dialectics itself.

Recently, for example, Thomas Bernhard has shown in his comedy
Immanuel Kant (1978) the transformation of Rationalism into the
Irrational, the Rationalist Kant into the victim of Rationalism's en-
lightened institution, the madhouse, the supersession of Rationalism in
its negation, the Irrational. In 1947 Max Horkheimer and Theodor
Adorno published their essays on the 'Dialektik der Aufklärung',
arguing that the dialectic of the Enlightenment could now be seen to
have led to the supersession of the ideals of Reason and Freedom it
had helped establish in the eighteenth century. As we have seen,
parodists have also used the dialectic to analyse and 'supersede' other
discourses and traditions, and it might be asked if meta-fictional
parody, too, has faced the danger of also being used for its own supersession. For where the form of parody is also made the subject of
parody, parody itself becomes the subject of criticism. But here the
difficulty of meta-criticism taking itself as its own subject appears
to offer an obstacle to the supersession of parody by parody.

Like the higher-order actions described by Gilbert Ryle as always
being one step behind themselves, so too parody — used to criticise
other works — is always one step behind its supersession of itself. As I

have argued in *Reading the Young Marx and Engels*, the conscious use of parody to parody parody may be seen to lead the parodist only deeper into a maze of self-reference. Though this may be due to the un-dialectical use of parody as a mirror to other parodies, the meta-fictional critique of parody may rather eventuate in the refunctioning of parody for fiction. But though parody may lay bare the self-referring character of other parodies it cannot free itself from this same type of self-reference while still using parody. The criticism of the dialectic of self-reflexion in some modern parodies might, however, be seen as an attempt to supersede its own method of criticism while distinguishing the parodist's use of parody from the dialectic which is now its target. Again, however, this distinction of parody from dialectics saves it from the criticism used to supersede the dialectic because of the principle limiting meta-criticism to other subjects than itself.

Like Foucault several years after him, Adorno also suggested the character of modern art to lie in its use of discrepancy as a criticism of the search for identities, when he wrote with Horkheimer in the *Dialektik der Aufklärung* of 1947 (Frankfurt am Main, 1969, p. 127):

> Das Moment am Kunstwerk, durch das es über die Wirklichkeit hinausgeht, ist in der Tat vom Stil nicht abzulösen; doch es besteht nicht in der geleisteten Harmonie, der fragwürdigen Einheit von Form und Inhalt, Innen und Aussen, Individuum und Gesellschaft, sondern in jenen Zügen, in denen die Diskrepanz erscheint, im notwendigen Scheitern der leidenschaftlichen Anstrengung zur Identität. Anstatt diesem Scheitern sich auszusetzen, in dem der Stil des grossen Kunstwerks seit je sich negierte, hat das Schwache immer an die Ahnlichkeit mit anderen sich gehalten, an das Surrogat der Identität. Kulturindustrie endlich setzt die Imitation absolut.

Here Adorno suggests that a characteristic of great art has been its con-frontation with the concepts of identity and imitation, taken by Foucault as the concepts of past epistemes, broken with in the modernis reflexion on reflexion. We have, moreover, argued that the dialectical form of parody enables the parodist to posit identities, or the belief in identity, only to supersede them. But Adorno, writing before Foucault, also pointed to the role of industry and commerce in rein-forcing the demand for imitation in art, which Foucault has not explicitly discussed. Walter Benjamin's essay on the role of art in the age of technical reproduction had suggested the reinforcement of the older epistemological concept of imitation by the commercial world (where the identity of the imitation with its model is also a criterion for its success), despite its supersession in the anti-imitative movements of anti-art and anti-literature of the modernist period. Here the gap between art as entertainment and art as a critical moment in the episteme of its age is ironically widened — reducing the broader effectivity of the latter's criticism, despite the radicalisation of its anti-forms. In fact, the more radical anti-art has made itself in its attempts to criticise the imitative art of the popular cultural industry, the wider the gap between it and its target has become. The use of parody to reduce the gap between the critic and his target was, ironically, also undermined by this development, for parody too had now become representative of modernist anti-imitative art.

The role of parody in transforming earlier trends in literary history to relate text and context more closely to each other cannot, however, be overlooked as a positive function of its meta-fictional critique of other fictions, and of its criticism of the demands and assumptions of the poetics of older ages.

4.5 The Role of Literary Parody in Transforming Literary History

As Christopher Ricks writes in his Introduction to Graham Petrie's edition of *Tristram Shandy*, Sterne was using a tradition of parodying 'learned wit' in *Tristram Shandy*, which was also to be found in Burton's *Anatomy of Melancholy*. So that when Sterne complains against the 'plagiaristic' use of old texts to make new books (in Book 5, Chapter 1), there is the added irony that he is himself using an older book — Burton's *Anatomy of Melancholy* — to do so. Yet though Ricks suggests this to be in itself a form of plagiarism, it is clear that Sterne has not simply 'poured' Burton's book into his own, but has created a new anatomy of the book from within the fiction of the novel itself, in which the mirroring of the past serves not simply to recreate older texts, but to create a dialectical relationship between the past and his text, of criticism and renewal, to transform the past. In this case then Sterne may have used Burton (and others) to complain about the plagiarism of the past, in an ironic self-reflexive manner, but in creating a new function for this statement has given a new answer to his initial, apparently rhetorical question — 'Shall we forever make new books, as apothecaries make new mixtures, by pouring only out of one vessel into another?'

But when the transformation of trends in literary history is attributed to parodies such as *Don Quixote*, *Tristram Shandy* or *Ulysses*, and these

works themselves canonised as classics of literary history, or taken as
models by other writers, then we are faced with the task of explaining
how parody has functioned as a catalyst in literary history, and how
it may introduce significant changes in the episteme of an age.

In what specific ways then has parody played a role in transforming
literary history? To put this in the form of a question to literary
critics, as to how it has been possible to describe it as playing such a
role, would involve a discussion of categories and presuppositions of
criticism, which cannot be gone into here. The necessity of critically
evaluating presuppositions might, however, be kept in mind in reading
(in a meta-critical way) the following answer to our first question, as to
how parody has played a role in transforming literary history.

(1) The structure of the parody — based on the imitation, quotation,
or distortion of the target text creates a dialectic of imitation and transformation, superseding the act of imitation itself, and uniting the
parody work with another text and literary tradition, while at the
same time changing the direction of this tradition through its refunctioning of its model. Hence parody has been able to transform the limits
of other genres in the act of defining them. While the literary critic may
also criticise a certain literary tradition his critique must remain external
to it (unless, or until, it is also made part of a fictional work), while
the critique offered by the parodist extends (while also criticising
and changing) a literary tradition, because, as another literary work,
the parody itself is a part of the corpus of work against which its
criticism is directed.

(2) The role of parody in reflecting the reception as well as the
composition of literary texts, and in defining the expectation of a public
in the quotation of certain works, means that the parody contains
within itself an internalisation of those historical subjects it criticises,
and to which it relates. Both diachronically, as the analysis of the
transference and refunctioning of historical traditions and discourses,
and synchronically, in internalising its own relationship to this
tradition, a parody may contain within itself elements of the historical
traditions it supersedes.

Heine wrote of the dialectical function of parody in *Don Quixote* as
having given birth to the modern novel from its destruction of the
knightly Romance:

Aber indem er [Cervantes] eine Satire schrieb, die den älteren
Roman zu Grunde richtete, lieferte er selber wieder das Vorbild
zu einer neuen Dichtungsart, die wir den modernen Roman nennen,[19]

and this view (which also revives the Ancients' understanding of parody)
has been frequently repeated. But it is also interesting to note that
parody has established its own dialectical tradition of works following
in the tradition of Cervantes, to transform his *Quixote* in its turn, and
to give parody its place in literary history as a means to transforming
older genres or works so that not only content and form, but their
own function in literary tradition (such as *Don Quixote*'s as catalyst of
a new genre) is renewed. It might be suggested, for example, that it is
from Laurence Sterne's transformation of the 'Cervantic novel' in
Tristram Shandy that the eighteenth-century novel of idealism was born
from the Cervantic novel of realism. For while in *Don Quixote* we
have (in summary) the satire of the naive 'idealistic' reader, we have
in *Tristram Shandy* — if not the figure of Don Quixote as self-conscious author[20] — then the analysis of the book as the creation of the
ideational world of the author.

Hence, it might be suggested that *Don Quixote* not only sets up a
'realistic' genre in criticising the Romance, but, in doing this through
the self-reflexive method of 'dialectical parody', in which the worlds of
the reader and the book, of reality and ideas reflect on each other, has
also set up the conditions for its own dialectical development, through
idealist and 'realistic' forms of meta-fiction, into a critique of both
fiction and meta-fiction.

James E. Swearingen has described a function of parody in *Tristram
Shandy* (though without naming it as such), in writing of Tristram's
search for his Self:

> Tristram's enquiry is stimulated and shaped by a need to under-
> stand himself through discovering his relations to a tradition.[21]

And in parody Sterne has himself looked back to traditions such as
that of the Cervantic novel, from which his own novel develops. In
refunctioning these traditions he has, moreover, found his own individual form. Sterne's altering of literary tradition is, like Tristram's
'altering of the facts', not just part of an epistemological process (as
Swearingen suggests[22]), but part of the process of creating new 'facts',
whose history in those which they supersede foregrounds not only the
dialectical function of criticism of such alterations, but their role in
confronting the past with the present, and the present with its past.
This aspect of the author's method of self-analysis, the role played by
parody in confronting the authorial 'self' with its past, as well as the
past with the facts of progress and time, cannot be ignored in discussing

either Sterne's achievement or the meaning of Tristram's actions in the
novel. But here, perhaps, Swearingen appears to have undervalued the
epistemological function of parody, as well as its other functions in the
novel as a catalyst and metaphor for transformation and self-reflexion:

> The historical question has a history of its own. Sterne does not
> regard his predecessors — Rabelais, Montaigne, Cervantes or
> Burton — as historically different from himself. Their historical
> thinking is not only contemporaneous with his own, as in all
> interpretative encounters, but to his mind it is contemporary as
> well, since historical differences are not observed. He is fully aware
> of altering the original meanings when he borrows from one or
> another as the issue of plagiarism shows; but that is a process of
> imaginative appropriation that raises no historical problems in his
> mind . . . [23]

But 'imaginative appropriation' does raise historical problems both in
and for the mind in *Tristram Shandy*, where the functions of its parody
of the past are both epistemological and critical.

As a 'history of the mind' (Book 2, Chapter 2), and the study of, in
particular, the mind of an author, *Tristram Shandy* is not only a study
of the contingency of apparently unrelated ideas, but of the role of
historically different texts in the work of the author. Not only may a
Lockean history of the workings of the mind as a continuing series of
contingent but sometimes disconnected thoughts be reflected in the
discontinuous juxtapositions of thoughts and 'cross-readings' in the
novel, but the parodist's technique of juxtaposing unlike texts is used
to reflect on this system of thought, and on the way in which texts are
received in the mind of the author, as well as suggesting how they are
thus transformed and renewed throughout history. As a multi-levelled
analysis of the history of the mind, of the author, of the history of
literary traditions, and of discourse, and the role of parody in transforming these, such parody truly takes on the role of an 'archaeology'
of discourse.

The motto of *Tristram Shandy*, that 'it is not things themselves, but
opinions concerning things, which disturb men', points out from the
beginning of the completed book that it is the world of words, and their
epistemological function, which will be a subject of the text. Sterne is,
moreover, an author who makes his own rules in *Tristram Shandy* in
the realisation of his analysis of the history of the mind. His concern
to defend himself against the 'hypercritics' who find his account of

time not accurate enough is ironic. When he defends himself by
arguing the Idealist's case (in Book 2, Chapter 8), that 'the idea of
duration and of its simple modes, is got merely from the train and
succession of our ideas' he not only equates the time being described
with the time taken to describe time, but makes the latter the measure
of the former. Hence too the history of the mind reduces objectively
historically different works and events to contingent moments, as in
the parody where past and present texts are united in the one work.
But as in parody, the historical difference of these texts may also be
suggested and upheld by the use of discrepancy or satirical anachronism,
and made a part of the author's analysis of the history (or
'archaeology') of his work, to link diachronic and synchronic analysis
in the text.

In his use of time for his history of the mind Sterne obviously
differs from Cervantes to whom he refers so frequently in Volume 1.
The self-reflexive author of *Tristram Shandy* is not to be restricted by
the prejudices of his hyper-critic, the critic demanding hyper-criticism
for the novel, for this is a non-reflexive position as naive as Don
Quixote's demand for reality to be identical to that represented in his
books. Sterne attempts rather to disturb this expectation of the hyper-
critic by creating the illusion within the novel that the book itself has
become an object. Hence the author in *Tristram Shandy* is allowed to
begin a new chapter when he wants (as at the end of Book 2, Chapter
8), or to write his Preface in the middle of his book – because 'it is
the first chance he has had to do so' (Book 3, Chapter 20): ' . . . All my
heroes are off my hands; – 'tis the first time I have had a moment to
spare, – and I'll make use of it, and write my preface'. Or the thread
of narration is illustrated by different lines, and blank pages by
seemingly blank pages.

Sterne's representation of the book as a concrete object is, in its
role in foregrounding the author's consciousness of the centrality but
also elusiveness of the authorial mind, very different from Don
Quixote's naive treatment of the book as representing a reality no
different from that of other objects in the world. We must thus
imagine Don Quixote as a self-conscious author to find a figure close
to that of Sterne's author in Cervantes' novel. And this may perhaps be
one way of explaining the nature of Sterne's genial transformation of the
tradition of the Cervantic novel (followed by other writers of the time
in a less creative manner). For while *Tristram Shandy* begins with many
references to the Cervantic tradition, we soon find its author using
Cervantes' idea that a naive reading of fictions such as the Romance

would lead to a distorted perception of both reality and fiction, to imply the figure of a self-conscious 'Idealist' — rather than the caricature of a naive 'idealistic reader' — and to establish an author able to transform the reality represented in the book at will, and to satirise the un-reflective reader, caricatured by Cervantes, from within an analysis of writing itself, from the book's centre in its author. Hence, while Don Quixote rides on the periphery of the fictional world, having misunder-stood its distinctive character, in *Tristram Shandy* the reader is con-fronted with a meta-fictional analysis of the creation of the work in the mind of the author himself which also reflects on the role of the author as reader of other texts. And while this has the epistemological functions of reflexivity as described by Swearingen, it also has the heuristic function of educating the naive reader, and the historical function of refunctioning Cervantes' novel for a history of the mind, as well as for the education of the reader in this history.

From the centre of the authorial mind recreated in the novel (which parody also serves by bringing literary models such as Cervantes to its surface before transforming them into a new text) Sterne confronts his reader with the reality that what he is now experiencing in the act of reading is a fiction involved in the reflective process of recreating itself (on which the technique of parody also reflects) and which can apparently do what it likes to its own structure because it is both real (and an object in the hands of the reader), and reality-giving. A phenomenological reading of *Tristram* is certainly suggested by the author's appellations to his audience, but it, too, must be seen as a part of the author's game with the book as a concrete and meaning-giving object, through which the mind may also be objectified, as well, that is, as in the reading given the object by the reader.

Tristram Shandy is above all an author's book, and for this reason too, perhaps, it, like *Don Quixote*, has been accepted by other authors, and by critics, as a significant turning-point in literary history. But its own dialectical relationship to the *Quixote*, and a clue to how the parody text may transform a tradition before it itself is canonised, is to be seen in its parodistic refunctioning of Cervantes' satire of the naive reader. For, from Sterne's juxtaposition of the oppositional roles of the ironist with this naive reader in the figure of the self-conscious Idealist as author the novel of realism becomes the basis of a 'novel of Idealism', which raises the imagination from a target to satire to its role as the principle structuring meaning in the novel. In this way Sterne also creates the means to reflecting on the specific differences between fiction and the world of objects, also foregrounded by Cervantes, by showing the author in the process of letting the fiction determine its own form of objectification.

The transformation of Don Quixote (and the Cervantic novel) in Sterne's self-conscious author is also symptomatic of the inversion of the world which occurs in satire and the inversion of the book which occurs in parody. This inversion then also has the function as acting as a 'mirror' to the reflective author, but it is a mirror which, when recalling the images of other literary characters such as Don Quixote, also shows itself to be only a negative stage in the dialectic of transformation. Indeed parody which has led to a criticism of the concepts of fiction as a reflection of the world of objects (as in *Don Quixote*) has also used the mirror in this negative way to show discrepancy between object and reflection. In this way imitation itself is made into a negative stage in the development of new forms in the literary work – and, indeed, if reflection were to be taken literally as the reproduction of one image by another, the concept of progress would be subsumed in that of repetition. Here progress is rather the result of a parodistic use of imitation, and when Kant attributes the function of transforming ideas about reality to wit and to parody in his *Anthropologie* he also implicitly reminds us of Sterne's use of parody in *Tristram Shandy*. Later both Nietzsche and Freud were also to point to the 'liberating' function of wit in Sterne's novel.

If truth was for Locke the 'marking down in words the agreement or disagreement of words as it is', then the self-critical reflection on the communicability of words in *Tristram Shandy* is also a critical reflection on the communicability of truth. *Tristram Shandy* hence also foregrounds the implicit paradox in Cervantes (which we have compared to Epimenides' Cretan liar paradox), that the criticism of fiction from within fiction not only leads to the author's self-critical reflection on the truth of his own work (implied perhaps by Tristram's statement that 'try as he may' he can never catch up with his own self), but to a criticism of the 'objectively-given' rules governing other forms of linguistic communication, which are (as suggested in 4.1) used by the author of the fiction in a self-consciously subjective manner.

As a means to the criticism of both 'objectively-given' rules for discourse and of the 'truth' of other fictions, parody has functioned as a meta-critique to other texts. But in also putting into doubt its ability to analyse its own activity as meta-criticism modern meta-fictional parody has also, as suggested earlier, offered a criticism to Friedrich Schlegel's concept of irony as a higher form of reflexion, showing the limits of this reflexion in reflecting on itself. Though parody is still used as a meta-critique of other texts, its reflexive function is not necessarily seen as raising it to a 'higher' level of reflexion in which the self is 'liberated' from the world, as in Schlegel's Idealist view. In the worlds of Magritte and Cannetti, for example, it has been seen that the result may be the very opposite – the imprisonment of the self in his artificially created world. Hence Foucault's analysis of *Don Quixote* as representative of a crisis of reflection must be taken further to see it (the *Quixote*), too as the subject of criticism in the modernist episteme.

Parody has perhaps continued to serve the moderns in the self-criticism by which it is also criticised, because, as Viktor Sklovskij wrote of *Tristram Shandy*, that which was typical of it was its 'laying-bare of the devices of writing'. This, for the Russian Formalists, was also to be seen as characteristic of parody in general. Tynjanov in his essay on Dostoevsky and Gogol, and the theory of parody (of 1921),[24] described parody as the 'mechanisation' of the device:

> The essence of parody lies in its mechanisation of a certain device, where this mechanisation is naturally only to be noticed when the device which it 'mechanises' is known. In this way parody fulfils a double task: 1) the mechanisation of a certain device and 2) the organisation of new material, to which the old, mechanised device also belongs.

Here Tynjanov also indicated how, in his view, the 'laying-bare' of the device, or its mechanisation (by, for example, repetition, juxtaposition, punning, etc.) could lead to an older work being both transformed and made a part of the next text, as part of the material organised into the new text, in the development of which it has already played a part.

This is important for understanding Tynjanov's use of the word 'break' in speaking of the relationship of a parody to its literary tradition at the beginning of his essay, where he wrote: '. . . There is no continuation of a straight line, rather it concerns a breaking away . . . a battle.' The 'battle' of a parody text with its tradition leads to a break which, as the rest of Tynjanov's discussion of Dostoevsky and Gogol shows, preserved the target of parody within the parody itself, as a part of a new line of development of the literary work. So, too, at the conclusion of his essay, Tynjanov wrote quite explicitly that the parody exists 'in its dialectical game with the device'.

Tynjanov's view of parody as a 'break' with tradition (which also may break that tradition itself) assumes then a dialectical concept of change (by which means a work may transform its own models) which is typical of the modern episteme though not yet sceptical of the limits of parody. Dostoevsky's transformation of Gogol, Cervantes' transformation of the knightly Romance, and Sterne's refunctioning of the Cervantic novel — though each in its own way representing a different form and degree of transformation — may all be seen as demonstrating the function of parody in dialectically breaking with its past to make it a part of a new tradition. One of Sterne's own legacies to the modern novel was, moreover, his transformation of the form of the literary work into its theme, so that Samuel Beckett could later write of Joyce in the 1920s: 'Here form *is* content, content *is* form . . . His writing is not *about* something; *it is that something itself.*' (And in his address to the French Philosophical Society on 22 February 1969 Foucault took as his text the title of Beckett's 'Who cares who's speaking?' to argue, as Beckett had in speaking of Joyce, that writing today had freed itself from content to talk about itself — that is, to make itself into its own subject. In doing this, however, the individual author has also, in Foucault's argument, receded into the background of the text.) Viktor Sklovskij (for whom *Tristram Shandy* was the 'representative' novel) could also write in the 1920s that the foregrounding of the form of the novel (its reflection in the novel itself) had, with the help of its simultaneous dissolution, transformed it into the content of the novel. This 'simultaneous dissolution' of form and of the idea of form, which characterises the structural discontinuity of the modern text, has, in part at least, been attempted through the parodistic construction of a form which had as its aim its own deconstruction. And it was the story of this process of construction and deconstruction which — paralleling the unfinished story of Tristram's birth in *Tristram Shandy* — introduced a new tradition in literary history which marked the reconstruction and transformation of the tradition of the Cervantic novel.

Hence our introductory comments on the importance given parody as a paradigm of fiction by the Formalists at the beginning of this century, may also be seen as reflecting the modernist episteme as one in which parody becomes both a symptom and a tool of self-reflection, and of the 'Verfremdung' of the self from its past.

4.6 Towards a Sociology of Parody

The individual parody text may not only serve as evidence for a theory of the role of parody in the history of our literary discourse, but — in the sense of Sartre's 'regressive-progressive' method (used in his Flaubert study) — may set both the limits for the definition and

theoreticisation of the general, and suggest a specific meaning for itself
against this context of the general. Just as individual and whole may be
related in the parody text's internalisation of its own prehistory (arche)
and context, through its internalisation of other texts, and through its
evocation of its reader's horizon of expectations and 'pre-reading' knowledge for those texts, a theory of the individual parody text's relationship to its literary history and context must also take the definition of
the individual text as a definition of a meaning-giving moment in the
broader structure of literary history. It is in this way that the meaning
of the individual text can also be defined *vis-à-vis* a context. The
hermeneutic circle of interpretation implied in this mutually defining
relationship between text and context must, however, also be seen as a
'way around' the problem of analytical meta-language, in which the
commentator is able to comment on the discourse of others, but not,
at the same time, on his own commentary. For in the hermeneutical
interpretation subject and object are used to reflect upon each other.

The structure of meta-language, in which meta-comment A comments
on its object B, is, as has been seen, also used more freely in meta-
fictions such as parody, to establish a reciprocal, often ambiguous
reflection between subject and object (AA ↔ AB, where B is embedded
in the medium of A). Hermeneutical methods in which A and B interpret each other have similarly been able to offer an alternative to the
limits of meta-analysis by using the object of analysis to reflect back
on the subject unable to analyse itself. The modernist crisis of reflexion
and debates on the role of the subject in our discourse in modern
structuralist and deconstructionist analysis also reflect upon this awareness of the limits of self-analysis, but as in parody, a hermeneutical
method of interpretation may remain inconclusive and imprecise. What
is gained in interpretative information about the subject may again be
lost in the inconclusive nature of the interpretation's findings. From
within fiction, however, parodists such as Sterne have appeared to
support the challenge to the imagination offered by such an interpretative process, while also, in the manner of higher critics, playing out
the ironic game of the meta-critic who may never 'catch up' with his
self. In this way, moreover, the interpretative circle is kept open and,
as in many meta-fictional parodies, the dialogue between the interpreter
and his subject made dialectical, and the circles of interpretation
spiral-like.

The creative moment in interpretation, in reading, or in criticism,
which Sterne, for example, encourages with the open structure of his
interpretation of his own process of writing, is also open and reflexive,

and it is perhaps not surprising that modern deconstructionist criticism, for example, has tended to see itself as a creative form of inter-pretation, and to have sometimes taken the form of imaginative literature. The 'hermeneutics of silence', also spoken of by Sartre, points again, however, to the archaeological function of interpretation (also, as we have seen, operative in parody) in divining the meaningful silences in the discourse of others as well as in its own speech. The ambiguous function of both political and non-political parody in concealing as well as revealing concealed textual meanings not only serves to comment on the 'agonistic' nature of the process involved in applying the rules of speech in fiction, but to reveal extra-textual controls on language, such as censorship, normative criticism, or the forms of production governing the publication of texts. It is these controls — as well as the relationship of the individual text to its specific context — which will be the subject of the following sociology of parody.

A study of parody as a meta-fictional analysis of the composition and reception of literary texts, and of its role in the transformation of epistemes hence also raises the question of a sociology of parody, of a study that is, of the material conditions, and institutions, affecting its composition and reception. Here, however, theory alone must prove inadequate. While it can be used to point to the areas to be subjected to sociological analysis — such as book production, copyright, censor-ship — it must eventually make way for empirical evidence and a more positivistic study of the relationship between the parody and society. This is not to suggest, however, that a purely positivistic method may tell us all we want to know about the relationship. Rather it completes the study, suggested in dialectical meta-fictional parody itself, of the material and epistemological 'contradictions' involved in the com-position and reception of fiction. Here, too, positivism must become reflexive.

Michail Bachtin's studies of the 'carnivalistic' function of parody in the novels of Rabelais suggested such a reflexive approach to empirical evidence in taking the experience of the street carnival to explain the psychological mechanisms at work in the 'liberating' laughter of narrative parody. As noted earlier, it has also been suggested that the figure of the censor himself (representing the forces of repression from which laughter liberated the onlooker) was present in carnivals, such as in, for example, the role of the Master of the Lord of Misrule festivities. As a metaphor for Revolution, the parodistic games of the carnival represent both the satiric inversion of the world and the masking of its revolutionary purpose; and the internalisation of censor in its activities has also been taken as explaining the legitimation of these activities.

In his *Pathology of Everyday Life* Freud quotes Goethe on Lichtenberg as saying that where Lichtenberg makes a joke a problem lies concealed. So, too, with the parody and irony of works threatened by external censorship, a joke may serve to protect a writer's discussion of a problem under taboo from legislative action. But — in Freud's sense, too — the joke made by a parodist may also conceal a problem from the author himself which has been 'censored' by the author's own processes of repression. The parodist's own ambiguous relationship to the text — as both model and target — is but one source of such 'problems'. Freud's method of reading repressed material — by the symptoms of repression such as displacement and juxtaposition — provides us also with an analogy to the techniques of reading used by the parodist, where these symptoms of repression are themselves used to distort other texts, and sometimes also used to mirror the distorting effect of external censorship on the processes of writing. But the symptoms of repression to be found in the language of the parodist — a writer practised in the art of manipulating language — are often to be found less in specific linguistic examples than in his general attitude to his text and to the activity of writing in general.

It is clear that the parodist may often have been led to conceal critical comment behind metaphor and irony, and be a subject under more threat of repression than other writers, and therefore more susceptible, too, to the practice of self-censorship. The relationship between censorship and parody was one which Michail Bachtin was particularly interested in. And here we also see how the critical discussion of parody may itself conceal an unorthodox and challenging attitude to the canons of literary tradition and literary criticism. For it is clear that for Bachtin the critic's analysis of past examples of parody written under the threat of censorship also offered the opportunity to speak esoterically of contemporaneous cases of repression both of parody and the criticism of parody as offered, for example, by the Formalist school. Bachtin's analysis of the relationship between repression and liberation in the medieval carnival and in modern parody can also be seen as an exercise in the parodistic language of showing 'how' as well as 'that'. For it does not only describe historical cases of parody but uses those examples to provide a mirror to Bachtin's own world, and a clue to the fact that he, like earlier parodists, is using the analysis of his subject-matter to comment indirectly on his society in the absence of the tools of direct criticism frowned upon (together with parodistic laughter) in that time. The self-reference typical of parody is used by Bachtin to relate the medieval practice of restricting parodistic criticism to his own situation. Here parody acts as a model for literary criticism, but in Bachtin's oblique references to the relevance of his descriptions of the censorship of parody to his own world, he also makes of it a metaphor – restricting his own social criticism to a covert level of reference. Thus, in speaking of parody, Bachtin takes as his target the censorship which had for centuries led writers to hide behind what another Russian Formalist, Tynjanov, has called the 'word-mask' of parody, while also, like those parodists themselves, bowing to the pressures of censorship in speaking only obliquely of contemporary manifestations of both parody and censorship.

A direct sociological study of censorship and parody, using or referring to empirical evidence, is, of course, made difficult when the conditions supporting those phenomena continue to exist, and to affect the researchers themselves. In this case, however, the similarity of the meta-language to its subject (parody) may serve a useful purpose in providing a metaphorical 'Aesopian' language for the critic to speak covertly of his own situation.

Bachtin has also argued that both parody and the carnival could serve to subvert concepts of hierarchy – the one in undermining the hierarchy of literary styles maintained in poetics, and the other the social hierarchy of class.

And in his 'Philosophical Dictionary' Voltaire also used the religious folk festival to speak of a form of blasphemy not acceptable to orthodox and upper circles of society, and to point to the censorship applied by theologians in his own time to the 'parodia sacra', to biblical parody and satire. Voltaire's ironic reversal of the Rationalist assumption that the natural, and the naive, represents an underdeveloped state of freedom or, indeed, a lack of freedom, in his praise of folk parody, also attacks the censorship of parody made in the name of Reason. So that here Rationalism is condemned as taking rather than giving freedom.

Parody has been put to work in the cause of subverting established canons – of literary, political, and ideological kinds. It has also been used to 'mask' criticism not able to be voiced openly. Yet it has, moreover, also been put to work in the cause of counter-revolutionary movements to mock subversion. Ironically, Marx's use of parody to parody Young Hegelian parody in *The Holy Family* of 1844/5, entrenched him even further in the style he was attacking because of its counter-argumentative and mirroring functions. And the use of parody to mock the parody used by an opponent for subversive purposes might also be suspected of paradoxically joining in the very game of subversion the conservative parodist would attack. In the political arena such philosophical niceties have, however, more often than not, been silenced for the sake of exploiting the subversive and aggressive qualities of the enemy's parody. Not only do counter-Reformation parodies, for example, attempt to outdo Reformation satires on Pope and Church in their use of caricature, the grotesque, wit and invective, but — by their use of parody — utilise the language of their opponents to make them part of a new debate, and to catch the ear of their audience.

In that these 'counter-parodies' defend established positions, there is, moreover, no question (as there was for Marx in 1845) of breaking with an old epistemological position and style, to establish a new method of criticism to that used by the opponent or target. The function of the 'counter-parody' is to defend other, but older, methods and beliefs.

Hence, though using the parody used by an opponent did not, for example, in the case of counter-Reformation parody, itself defend the older methods of criticism, it did not necessarily lead to the con- tradictions met by Marx when he used parody in a counter- argumentative way to mock the outdated use of parody by his targets, but with the purpose of freeing his style from theirs to find a new critical method. For Marx, a dialectical form of parody was needed — one which would supersede itself in the process of making itself into the antithesis of its desired goal — or a complete break with its method.

There is also a certain confidence in the stability of the past, and in its ability to hold the future at bay, in the laughter of 'counter- parody' and in its use of its opponents' methods to defend its own cause. But the tactical use of counter-parody to insinuate the parodist into the camp of his opponent — and into his audience — must also not be overlooked. The 'masking function' of parody to protect the identity of the parodist is ironically exploited in counter-parody when the mask of the parodist is worn by the counter-revolutionary into the 'herd of wolves' whom he would convert to his own genus. This 'counter-subversive' use of parody might also be seen as an attempt to control subversion by 'internalising' it within the status quo. And its 'legalisation' of parody (as in the medieval carnival) was to function as a control on other 'illegal' subversive uses of parody while also giving the state both the appearance of liberality, and control over the liberating functions of the parodistic laughter used by its opponents for politically subversive aims.

The conservative 'counter-subversive' use of parody may, however, also be seen as paradoxical in that it utilises a 'subversive' method in the cause of eliminating subversion. Yet the question of whether this reinforces or 'subverts' the subversive function of parody relates to a goal of 'methodological propriety' which few satiric parodies (of, for example, the counter-Reformation) had as their aim. In critical revolutionary periods it has been the political rather than the methodological which has determined the propagandist's aims and the counter-parodies of such periods have been satirical rather than meta-fictional and reflexive.

The use of slogans, cliches, and other words specific to the sociolect of a group serve to give entrance to that group, and are often used in an unreflexive way for this purpose. The child's imitation of the modish words of its peer group has some similarity with the use of political slogans for the unreflexive purpose of sharing the identity of a group, and of subsuming the identity of the individual within it. The parodistic meta-fictional use of preformed language, however, does not imitate the language of its model only to gain acceptance from its followers, or readers, but to critically analyse its own relationship to its model and the discourse represented by it, to distinguish itself from its model, and to refunction it as part of a new text-world. Here the subject's subsuming of his individual identity in that of another is reversed, and the identity of the target text critically laid bare before being made a part of the parody text. This analysis may also, as mentioned earlier, serve a tendentious purpose in attributing a 'false' identity to the target in order to caricature him, and can, in both cases, be subversive.

Parody used as a tool against the 'poetaster' had of course long been a means of attacking the deviational in literature. When it is remembered that some definitions of parody have described parody as establishing norms in order to dismantle them again before the eyes of the reader, then the use of parody for the defence of the norms destroyed by other parodists might also be questioned. Here, too, however, a distinction must not only be made between specific and general use of parody (the first being used against a particular target, the second against the normative as such), but between counter-argumentative and dialectical parody. The first, counter-argumentative parody, might be said to be of a less complex kind than the latter in countering one argument, and one kind of parody, with another, while dialectical parody may aim at

producing a new subject, and a new style, from its refunctioning of its
target as a part of its own text, as in meta-fictions such as Cervantes'
Don Quixote, or Sterne's *Tristram Shandy*.

Foucault's analysis, in 'L'ordre du discours' (December 1970), of
the factors controlling our written and spoken discourse, has suggested
a connection between the censorship of discourse and the demand for
a 'will to truth' in literature, interesting also for a sociology of parody.
For the history of the condemnation of parody as politically subversive,
'frivolous', or anti-rational, has reflected these impositions. But, as
the analysis of these controls, of the language manipulated by them,
and of the discourse of discourse itself, parody has presented both
critiques of its censors and, in some cases, led to the strengthening of
such controls. And in its application of analysis to its own discourse,
and as a part of the 'language scepticism' of the twentieth century,
parody has not only played a role in changing texts, but has also
become part of an episteme which has canonised parodistic techniques
such as discontinuity – to itself control discourse, in a new manner.

Leslie Bodi has pointed out, in discussions on parody[25] and on
the literature of the German Democratic Republic,[26] that a sociology
of parody must explain 'extra-literary' as well as literary forms of
receiving texts relating directly to the reading of the written word.
Thus he explains that when copies of Plenzdorf's *Die neuen Leiden des
jungen W* went out of print, the reaction of the reading public, to buy
up copies of Goethe's *Die Leiden des jungen Werthers* (the basic text
'parodied' in Plenzdorf's work), suggested that the 'parodistic' reading
of that work suggested by Plenzdorf's text and play was to be continued independently of his text, in its absence, by the readers themselves. Parody, often used in 'samizdat' writings, thus also becomes a
way of reading texts written without parody which, though often
not transferred into print, could become known to and practised by a
considerable number of readers.

This point about the possibility of a reader making his own parody
of a text in the absence of the published parody, takes to a new conclusion Borges' thesis in his story of 'Pierre Menard, Author of the
Quixote', that we may read a book through our idea of its author, to
realise the text again in a new objectification. It also draws to a new
and ironic conclusion the thesis of phenomenologists that the text is
realised in its interpretation by the reader, pointing again, too, to the
role of the parodist as reader of other texts, whose objectification
of his reading in the parody text serves as a model for other readings,
where other texts based, for example, on belief in their own originality,

may inhibit such 'imitative' readings.

Variations in individual reader reactions would make it of course difficult for a comprehensive sociological study of the reception of parody to be made in an introduction to the subject such as this, but we have tried to suggest various theoretical approaches to the role of the reader in the text which might serve such a task, as well as pointing to the role of the parodist as reader, and to the parody as a means of defining a reading public and its expectations through the books it is expected to have read, or through explicit reader satire and caricature.

Other problems related to the use of parody to avoid censorship, which I have dealt with elsewhere,[27] include the limitation of the parodist to a group of initiates and, of course, to a covert language which may prove incomprehensible to later audiences, especially if the target of the parody (through the effectivity of the parodist's attack or for other reasons) is eliminated from the memory of the reading public.

In Chapter 12 of his *Ideen. Das Buch le Grand*, Heine wrote a parody of the censor which speaks the universal language of silence. Heine's parody consists, that is, in the 'imitation' and ironic concretisation of the silences caused by the censor in the work of his 'victim'. In the sense that parody was used as a covert means of criticising censorship, or of escaping its restrictions on the satire of other targets, it, too, could be seen as a text built on a sub-text of 'silences', and Heine's parody can also be seen as ironically self-referential:

Die deutschen Zensoren   —   —   —   —   —
—   —   —   —   —   —   —   —   —   —
—   —   —   —   —   —   —   —   —   —
—   —   —   —   —   Dummköpfe   —   —
—   —   —   —   —   —   —   —   —   —
—   —   —   —   —   —   —   —   —   —

Here too, as with other cases of parody, the reader is asked to fill in the missing words, and here the verb 'are', between the remaining words 'The German censors' (who are ironically given to be above censorship) and 'blockheads', suggests itself as the simplest and most obvious word needed to complete the sentence. Not only is the reader made party to the writer's satire of the censor by filling the missing word, he is also asked, as in Sterne's *Tristram Shandy*, to use both his imagination and his sense of style to complete the sentence, and to see himself then as superior to the censors who would, in the sense of Enlightenment

justifications of censorship used in the early nineteenth century in
Prussia, control him under the pretence of knowing better, and of
acting in his own good in the protection of the Reason their good
sense was given to represent. And while Heine's parody literally forces
the reader to read between (or behind) the given lines which stand there
emptied of words, it also demonstrates how, by contrast, the censor
has not given depth to the texts he 'protects' but reduced them to a
satire against himself.

When Reiner Kunze (DDR) republishes this attack by Heine on the
German censors in his piece 'Unzensiertes über die Zensur, (in
Geständnisse, W. Gössmann (ed.), Düsseldorf, 1972), Heine's piece is
again given the chance to become relevant to contemporary reality.
And Kunze also uses Heine to discuss the unpredictable character of
censorship then and now — where vagueness in its edicts allowed
writers to sometimes publish criticism of censorship itself. Often, however, this vagueness also allowed the censor to catch out his best
critics by giving them the chance to reveal themselves to him. While
Heine wished to preserve this subtle game, in order to utilise it as far
as he could to print criticism of the censors, others (such as Marx in
1843 and the 'Tendenzdichter' of the same time) openly challenged
the censor. For Marx in 1843, as editor of the *Rheinische Zeitung*, the
use of this tactic seems to have been based not only in the desire to see
the censor reveal his hand against more open opposition from his
critics but in a Young Hegelian belief in the dialectical supersession of
censorship which would eventuate from the confrontation of it with
its contradiction. In Kunze's 'Unzensiertes über die Zensur' the irony
of the continuation of censorship within some forms of Marxism is also
expressed through the Aesopian language of irony. His montage of
Heine's 'Die deutschen Zensoren . . . Dummköpfe' is followed by the
ironic note — 'Here Heine has been unfaithful to his maxim to write
"not just for one country but for the world" — said my Slavonic
colleague N.N.' Should Heine have then written 'censors . . . are
blockheads'? This note precedes another ironic refunctioning of
Heine's works for Kunze's own time. And here the reader of Heine
must read beyond the words in front of him to the words concealed
beneath them. For without comment on its context, Kunze then takes
a late passage from Heine — criticising (from the point of view of the
poet) the communists of his time — to speak further of Heine's criticism
of censorship. Heine had written in 1855 that poetry might suffer in
the new communist society, and (with irony), so that the old women
would use the pages of his *Buch der Lieder* as paper bags for their

tobacco. Kunze writes (referring explicitly only to the latter image) that this would be too dangerous – 'for imagine how a poem of Heine's against the censor would confuse those "good old women".' Rather Heine *inside* the bags, finely cut:

Eher Heine *in* Tüten, fein abgewogen
Und der Name hebt das Ansehen des Ladens.

Though both such a use of parody and the censored text might be described as a type of codex palimpsestus, a written-over text, it is only in the parody that the written-over text is also intended to shine through and to create the ambiguity which doubles the possible meanings of the text, rather than to reduce them as in the censored work. Heine's parody of the German censors shows censorship not only to have aimed at this reduction of the text, but unwittingly to have thereby created an ambiguity which reverses its purpose, turns the satire back onto itself, and depicts it as a world upside down in which its attempts to protect Reason lead to the absurd.

Heine's parody of the language of censorship in fact follows the repetition of the 'Napoleonic' motto of the book: 'Du sublime au ridicule il n'y a qu'un pas, Madame!' Its 'Shandean' appearance and association of apparently disconnected ideas is, however, in itself 'sublime'. Also in the style of *Tristram Shandy*, however, a chapter then follows on the parodistic production and consumption of quotations. These 'Zitate' are spoken of as useful, three-dimensional, even edible commodities, necessary for many authors to keep themselves alive. This also becomes part of an ironic satire on plagiarism, from which Heine (who had been accused of it himself, and who attacked the charge elsewhere) both dissociates himself and admits to understanding. So he writes in Chapter 12 of the *Ideen*:

Ausserdem kenne ich den Kunstgriff grosser Geister, die es verstehen, die Korinthen aus den Semmeln, und die Zitate aus den Kollegienheften herauszupicken . . . [Moreover, I know the trick of great minds, who understand how to pick the currants out of buns and quotations from learned journals . . .]

Here Heine not only exaggerates, with self-irony, the greatness of minds who understand how to borrow quotations, but reductively compares this activity to that of picking currants out of buns – not, in itself, for Heine a stupid action, for it also serves to denigrate the 'buns' from which the tastier quotations are picked. Heine's understanding of these 'great minds' cannot in itself be great by virtue of its empathy with them, but can be so by virtue of its higher reflexion on them, and on itself, as well as in its use of irony for this purpose. For it is through this use of irony that the parodist Heine distinguishes himself from the other borrowers whom he mocks.

Heine's critics amongst his contemporaries saw, however, his achievement in a more negative light. For them Heine's reflexive satire was yet another example of his combination of egoism and superficiality. The Young Hegelian Arnold Ruge's largely positive essay on Heine[28] of 1838 gave an account of the function of wit in the process of bringing the self to consciousness which, for all of Ruge's criticism of the Romantics in his Halle Yearbooks from the same year, at first appears to echo theories of Romantic irony such as those of Friedrich Schlegel's:

> Es ist der Begriff des Witzes, dass er überall das Selbstbewusstsein der Person geltend macht und den unbefangenen, den unmittelbaren Zustand der Person aufhebt, welches dadurch geschieht, dass die harmlose und unbewusste Gestalt plötzlich, so wie sie ist, mitten in das Licht des Selbstbewusstseins herein versetzt wird.[29]

From this description of wit as the supersession of naivete in its 'foregrounding' of the self in the consciousness of the subject, Ruge then went on, however, to turn this process of self-reflexion into an attack on Heine's 'coquettish' use of wit to put his ego on show – to make his self 'interesting':

> Die Heine'sche Witzpoesie ist die coquette Poesie, und ihr Princip die Gefallsucht des Subjects, welches auf Kosten der Substanz sich interessant machen will.[30]

Here Ruge's Young-Hegelian emphasis on the priority of the criticism of reality attacks both the Fichtean concentration on the subject and what he sees to be Heine's further devaluation of irony into narcissism. Other Young Hegelians, such as Bruno Bauer and Karl Marx, had also learnt much from Heine's use of irony as a cover for political criticism. But Ruge's accusation of superficiality and egoism, though argued as a variation on the Romantic theory of irony as a 'Potenzierung' of the self in self-reflexion, is echoed in many of the descriptions of Heine's parody and irony as 'frivolous'. Sterne too had been accused of

'frivolity', and the self-reflexive value of his parodistic games ignored
by some of his contemporaries. Later, in the twentieth century,
Rebecca West offered a similar charge against Joyce's *Ulysses* in calling
it a work of 'narcissism, a compulsion to make a self-image with an eye
to the approval of others'. But if narcissism may be defined as an
obsession with the mirroring of the self, as well as a failure to relate to
other selves, parody — as it is to be found in Sterne, Heine, Joyce,
and others — cannot be accused of being, in any technical sense at least,
narcissistic. For in reflecting the author through other texts, as well as
self-critically through his own, and in differentiating style while making
self-reflexion a means to self-criticism as well as to satire against the
unreflective work, parody may present an attack on the naive obsession
with style as a mirror to either the external or internal world of the
author, while self-critically digging its own archaeology.

Heine uses both irony and satire together in many of his works, to
offer clearly 'outward-going' attacks on the censor, whose control had
made irony into a 'franca lingua' of the Young Germany movement.
But the use of irony in political literature raises the question as to
how irony and parody (or other such 'Aesopian languages') may both
help an author to express publically banned opinions and to escape
censorship, if the use of them also entails concealing his meaning from
his general reader. Several explanations of this problem may be given —
some of which may seem contradictory when not related to their
specific contexts. Two such apparently contradictory explanations
are, for example, that the censor (1) would be less able to understand
irony than the majority of the author's readers, and (2) that he would —
in thinking himself more clever than both the author and his readers —
consider his understanding of the irony exceptional, and allow it to be
printed because of the difficulties in interpretation it would make for
other readers. In actual fact other considerations — such as whether
the ironist or parodist had used specifically banned terms — would have
been decisive, but one must also distinguish, with the censor, between
the public's attraction to the humour of the parody, and their ability
to understand its subversion.

Other points made in the reports of the nineteenth-century censors
and secret police about parody and irony which may seem contradictory are (1) that the comic element in ironic literature made it
more popular than other forms of critical writing, and (2) that directly
'pathetic', serious criticism of authority was more dangerous than
criticism made by way of more 'light-hearted', 'less serious' literary
forms. Often these attitudes are specific to the individual censors

involved, as well as to the directions given him. Again these directions were often concerned with listing words — such as, in nineteenth-century Restoration Europe, 'tyranny' and 'la liberte' — and it was especially for this reason that authors chose to use irony and metaphor to speak indirectly of certain banned subjects.

But although the use of parody to smuggle ideas past the censor or other unsympathetic readers was often regarded by Heine and other Young Germans as a limitation on their style, it could also give them the freedom of using poetic metaphor to describe their political realities, and to indulge in poetry while doing so, where otherwise the prose of political reportage held sway. Thus Heine could call the freedom given the dancers in the masked ball by their masks, the 'most beautiful' of all freedoms:

> Und Mensch ist man erst recht auf dem Maskenballe, wo die
> wächserne Larve unsere gewöhnliche Fleischlarve bedeckt, wo
> das schlichte Du die urgesellschaftliche Vertraulichkeit herstellt,
> wo ein alle Ansprüche verhüllender Domino die schönste
> Gleichheit hervorbringt, und wo die schönste Freiheit herrscht —
> Maskenfreiheit.[31]

And yet an antithetical argument to that suggested above can also be given here.

For Heine's substitution of 'mask' for 'Mensch' (or 'human being') in the word 'Maskenfreiheit' creates a neologism which, by both its newness and its echo of the word for human freedom, 'Menschen-freiheit', only underlines more his concern for an open, unmasked realisation of the Bill of Human Rights of 1789. A closer look at the above passage will then show the call of 1789 for 'fraternité, égalité, and liberté' to lie 'masked' under names such as 'urgesellschaftliche Vertraulichkeit', and, more openly, 'Gleichheit' and 'Freiheit'. But only when extracted from the text and strung together again[32] do they make the slogan which refers us back to the Bill of Human Rights, and to the demand for freedom of speech which would mean the end of the masking of Liberty and, hence, of the need for 'Maskenfreiheit' — the freedom given by the mask. The esoteric reference to the Bill of Human Rights in this passage may draw our attention to the clause for freedom of speech (threatened by the 'Carlsbad decrees' when Heine wrote this passage) by the very fact that this reference is made covertly within a discussion of the freedom given by masking. The difference between the 'Maskenfreiheit' given in the carnival and the necessity to wear masks under censorship (including the 'word-masks' provided by the parodistic use of other texts) can now, moreover, be seen to exist in the fact that the former ('Maskenfreiheit') gives the wearer of the mask the freedom of anonymity in an exceptional situation reversing the normal situation where open, unmasked faces are the rule, while censorship, on the other hand, enforces a continuous masking of the individual from which there is even little temporary release. Hence the concept of 'Maskenfreiheit' may also imply the ideal of a situation where freedom is the rule and masking the exception — a situation, that is, which inverts that of a society of writers oppressed by censorship, in which masking is the rule and freedom the exception. Here, too, parody — the genre most favoured in carnival — represented both 'Maskenfreiheit' and the absence of those human liberties including the freedom from censorship, which it was being used to defend.

In his essay 'Critique et vérité' (Paris, 1966) Roland Barthes speaks of how criticism as a form of meta-language has come under suspicion: the infinite possibilities of comment offered by meta-language, its liberation from the verification normally associated with object-languages or languages purporting to represent the world of things, have all made it, in Barthes' view, a more dangerous form of discourse than others. For such reasons, too, parody has also come under suspicion as a subversive form of meta-criticism which, like the passage from Heine looked at above, confuses the normal processes of interpretation by offering more than one message at once, and a self-reflexive, ironic reading of its text at the same time.

When meta-language also has the function of undermining rather than perpetuating authorities (whether institutional or literary) then its 'subversive function' also becomes potentially parodic. As meta-fiction the parody has not been given a directly performative function as propaganda, yet it has been suspected of being subversive of representation, and of other familiar, controllable forms of discourse. The charge of 'frivolity' made against Heine by Biedermeier, and more radical critics amongst his contemporaries, might also be seen as being symptomatic of this fear of subversion from a language which appears not to be subject to the rules of normal speech, and which may demand from the reader a use of both intellect and imagination, in the 'demasking' of its codes. For in using the work of another as a word-mask for its own message, parody has been a particularly subversive form of criticism, threatening to other forms of criticism, and for this reason too, perhaps, at times one of the most ignored forms of

literary criticism. Ironically, parody – the art of using silence, as well
as meta-linguistic and metaphoric comments, for the covert criticism
of its targets – has thus itself often been silenced in the canon of
literary criticism. Described, as has been seen, as a negative song sung
'in opposition' to others, or as 'burlesque', parody has been denied the
attention it might otherwise have been afforded by its role in literary
history, while reasons for this, such as censorship, have also been
silenced. For censorship – an institution which has forced silence on
writers – has often also used silence to protect itself: decrees announcing
it in the nineteenth century in Prussia, for example, rarely named it as
censorship, and it has otherwise gone under such names as the
protector of public morality, good taste, or the upholder of truth –
names which it could represent or distort. All these forms of silences
might be relevant to a reading of parody, but this will depend on the
character and specific controls present in the age in which a work is
produced and received.

   One other subject for a sociology of parody which can at least be
suggested here, has to do with the changing laws of copyright which
affected concepts of originality and, subsequently, the evaluation of
parodistic imitation. In eighteenth-century Prussia, for example,
publishers and authors who had complained of lack of protection
from plagiarism and piracy, eventually, on 18 December 1773,
obtained the 'Saxon Mandate' protecting the unauthorised reprinting
of texts. Coming at approximately the same time as Gottsched's
condemnation of parody and satire, this ruling led, however, to a
further restriction of parody in Germany. This copyright law both
reflected and helped support the change in attitude from the 'Baroque'
belief in literature as the common property of authors to the belief
(supported by Romantic concepts of the individual genius – such as
that shared by the writers of Germany's 'Storm and Stress' in the
1770s) of literature as the property of the individual author. Previously
parody had not been, as it was now to be, faced by the threat of
being condemned under law as plagiarism. But yet another effect of
the copyright laws was that now censorship was justified by the State
not only as a form of protection of the individual, but, in the
Enlightenment State, as the State's protection of literature as one of
its personal commodities. The responsibility of the writer under law
was now twofold.

   In discussing the relationship between copyright, plagiarism and
parody, Ernst Hefti[33] has pointed to the difficulty of defining parody
to serve the law when not only the forms of parody may change, but

the context of a parody definition affect a change in the description
of the term. But this is of course not the only problem which exists in
evaluating whether a parody has broken a law of copyright or not. A
law of copyright may be phrased to define the limits by which a work
may be quoted, in order to protect authors and publishers, but the
question of defamation which is also often raised when a parody is
concerned raises other legal issues sometimes not covered by the copyright law. And when parody has been used not in order to attack the
text it refunctions but, for example, another author who has used the
text, then the position of the parodist before the law may be ambiguous
on at least two counts — relating to the literary text imitated and the
person satirised (or 'defamed') through it. The latter has occasionally
given rise to separate cases of libel, but in that the parody of the text
in question may have been used as a mask to protect the author from
this charge, he may rather admit only to its parodistic character, in a
similar manner to William Hone in his trials for blasphemy at the
beginning of the nineteenth century. Whether the use of parody to
satirise its use by another writer, or 'poetaster' necessarily also breaks
a law of copyright or brings that work into disrepute, is often also a
question which can only be evaluated with reference to the effect of
the parody on the situation of the other book, its popularity and sales,
at that time.

   In discussing the various forms of redress to the law possessed by
authors and publishers against the parody of their work, Hefti implicitly raises the question of how restricted parodists have felt in
parodying contemporary works to which laws of copyright protecting
them from parody applied. Even the lack of clarity in the laws which
Hefti discusses (of the Federal Republic of Germany, Italy, France,
Switzerland and the United States of America) may be seen as an
inhibiting factor, though this is a problematic point. In Germany Hefti
finds little mention of parody in discussions of the Law of Copyright,
but points out[34] that such cases could come either before the criminal
courts or the copyright tribunal. In general, cases concerning parody
have had to decide whether it was a plagiaristic imitation, a 'Bearbeitung'
dependent on the model text, or a 'freie Benutzung' of the other text,
where some 'originality' on the part of the parodist can be proven.
Here originality again appears as a criterion for determining breakage
of copyright law, and lack of originality as a charge against the parodist.

   Discussions over the liability of parodists to be charged under laws
of copyright have also implied the question of whether the parodist
too was to be protected by copyright, and indicates the existence of

yet another threat to the parodist from the law, that his own work, as a
form of 'plagiarism', might not itself be protected from literary piracy.

Hefti pleads for a more exact stylistic definition of parody, but no
matter how clearly a parody may be so defined, if the ability of the law
to exclude it from protection, or to charge it as breaking copyright, is
not also clearly defined and limited, then such a definition will serve
little. In law, too, such a definition may only serve as a guideline for
those making judgement. If, however, such a definition were to be
set for judging contemporary cases then it might also prove counter-
productive in that the legal definition, directed towards explaining
the position of parody *vis-à-vis* copyright law, could not encompass
all the variations found within literary practice, nor keep up with
changes in usage within the literary world.

And while a concept of originality may continue to be used in distinguishing parody from plagiarism, it may in fact be financial
questions, such as the effect of the parody on the sale of the original,
which are of central concern to the plaintiff of a copyright suit. A
purely stylistic definition of parody — or one based on determining
the level of originality in the work — would be irrelevant to this
question. Concepts such as 'originality' are, of course, themselves as
much in need of definition as parody, and particularly if they are to
be used in courts of law. As Hefti points out, it is also possible to
argue on the financial issues involved from several different points
of view.[35] For example, a parody might be said to either decrease or
increase the sales of the original — by either replacing it on a market
or by increasing its notoriety,[36] by telling more readers about the
original (through giving it a 'new edition'), or by making it clear to
the reader that a successful reading of the parody may be dependent
on the reader knowing the original. There are, in fact, as many
possibilities here as there have been parodies, and to restrict them to
one exclusive definition would appear to be more dangerous for the
parodist than even vagueness.

In that the parody may force the reader to go back to the text
referred to by the parodist, to the institutions limiting the form parody
or direct satire could then take, and to the readers whose expectations
are defined in the parodist's quotation of his target text, it appears to
demand an empirical as well as a theoretical study of its sociological,
literary-historical and, in some cases, political context. In making both
a literary work and the expectations of its readers a part of its own
text, the parody work comes to a new generation of readers with
demands for historical awareness as well as literary understanding, so

that more is required than a mere definition to evaluate the relationship of a parody to its target. Meta-fictional parody thus not only raises the need for a theoretical understanding of its critically self-reflective functions in criticising literary works and in transforming literary traditions, but focuses the attention of the reader on the role played by extra-literary material and epistemological forces in the composition and reception of the text. And here too the parody may suggest a contradiction to — rather than an identity with — its context.

Notes

1. See Siegfried J. Schmidt, *Texttheorie* (München, 1973), on the preconditions of communications acts, especially p. 44, 4.1.1.(b): 'Jeder naturliche Sprecher vollzieht seine Sprechakte im Rahmen von Kommunikationssituationen, bezieht sich auf diese, modifiziert sie und bringt neue hervor.'
2. John Searle, 'The Logical Status of Fictional Discourse', in *New Literary History*, vol. 6, Winter 1975, no. 2, p. 325. Stanley E. Fish has also criticised the application of Austin's and Searle's speech-act theories to literary texts, in 'How to do things with Austin and Searle: Speech-act Theory and Literary Criticism', in *Modern Language Notes*, 91, no. 5 (1976), pp. 983–1025.
3. See Siegfried J. Schmidt, *Literaturwissenschaft als argumentierende Wissenschaft*, Section 5.6.3.3.3.
4. See Searle, *Speech Acts* (Cambridge, 1969), Ch. 3.
5. H.R. Jauss, *Literaturgeschichte als Provokation der Literaturwissenschaft* (Konstanz, 1967), p. 33. Jauss has also spoken of this function of parody in his contributions to the symposium on 'Das Komische', published 1976, München, ed. Preisendanz and Warning.
6. Quintilian, *Institutio Oratoria*, transl. H.E. Butler (Harvard, 1960), p. 485.
7. *Der Akt des Lesens* (München, 1976).
8. James E. Swearingen, *Reflexivity in 'Tristram Shandy'* (Yale, 1977).
9. Ibid., pp. 242ff. Another function of comedy in *Tristram Shandy* is, as Sterne writes (4, 32), and Swearingen notes, its function in 'healing' the spirit. Though Swearingen claims Sterne's evaluation of the healing powers of wit deviates from the beliefs held by Locke, it was not itself without effect on philosophical thinking in the late eighteenth century. Kant, writing in Prussia in the 1790s, where Gottsched's denunciation of satire had held sway, attributed a cleansing role to wit (and its comic forms) in the exchange or renewal of intellectual concepts. In his *Anthropologie*, for example, Kant also praised the parodies of Fielding, connecting thus the Cervantic traditions (to which *Tristram Shandy* was also seen to belong), to this concept of wit.
10. Swearingen, *Reflexivity*, p. 194.
11. Ibid., p. 253.
12. First published Paris 1972 from a paper given in August 1971, and translated in *Glyph* I, 1977, pp. 172ff, with a reply by John Searle 'Reiterating the Differences: A Reply to Derrida', pp. 198ff.
13. *Glyph*, p. 179.
14. Joyce, *Our Exagminations*, p. 3.
15. See also Rose, *Reading the Young Marx and Engels*, Part 2.
16. Michel Foucault, *Les Mots et les Choses* (Paris, 1966), end of Ch. 1.
17. Jurij M. Lotman, *Probleme der Kinoästhetik. Einführung in die Semiotik*

des Films (1973), transl. Chr. Böhler-Auras (Fr. am Main, 1977), p. 94: Auf der linken Seite steht ein Künstler, der gerade ein Bild malt. Von der Leinwand vor ihm sehen wir nur die Rückseite. Aber der dargestellte Maler ist ja Velasquez selbst. Was wir vor uns sehen, ein Bild von Velasquez, wird uns auf diese Weise noch einmal von der Rückseite her gezeigt. Die Einbeziehung des Künstlers ins Gemälde, die Einfügung des von ihm gemalten Bildes in die abgebildete Wirklichkeit kombiniert ebenso wie die Filme '8½' oder 'Alles zu verkaufen' eine genuin realistische Darstellung mit dem deutlichen Hinweis, dass es sich ja um eine *Abbildung*, d.h. *um eine Konventionalität* handelt.

18. I have discussed this in detail in an article, 'Die strukturelle Einheit von Heines *Rabbi von Bacherach*', in *Heine Jahrbuch 1976* (Düsseldorf, 1976).

19. Heine, 'Einleitung zum *Don Quichotte*', 1837, in *Sämtliche Werke*, Ernst Elster ed. (Leipzig, 1893), vol. 7, p. 313.

20. James E. Swearingen has also suggested similarities between Don Quixote and Tristram Shandy in *Reflexivity in 'Tristram Shandy'*, but has not explicitly dealt with them in terms of the reader and the author.

21. Swearingen, *Reflexivity*, p. 14.

22. Ibid., pp. 14–15.

23. Ibid., p. 25.

24. Dostoevskij und Gogol: 'Zur Theorie der Parodie', in *Russischer Formalismus*, texts exited by Jurij Striedter (München, 1971), pp. 300–71.

25. Paper given in the Seminar on Parody, Humanities Research Centre, Canberra, July 1976.

26. Paper given in the Seminar on Literature of The German Democratic Republic, University of New South Wales, April 1977.

27. Rose, *Reading the Young Marx and Engels*.

28. Arnold Ruge, reprinted in *Heine in Deutschland, Dokumente seiner Rezeption, 1834–1956*, Karl Theo Kleinknecht (ed.) (Tübingen, 1976).

29. Ibid., p. 27. Later, in 1841, another 'Hegelian', Søren Kierkegaard, was to write his new defence of irony.

30. Ibid., p. 39.

31. Second 'Brief aus Berlin' (1822).

32. Heine used a similar technique in his 'Weberlied' of 1844 to refer with biting satire to the misuse of the army in quelling the weavers' revolts of 1842, by weaving the oath taken by the army – for God, King and country – into the weaver's complaint, that help for his cause had come from none of these sources.

33. Ernst Hefti, *Die Parodie im Urheberrecht* (Berlin, 1977).

34. Ibid. p. 4.

35. Ibid., pp. 57ff.

36. Ibid., p. 59.

CONCLUSION

It has not been our purpose to give an exhaustive account of the many different definitions of parody devised over the centuries, but to outline the possible forms and functions taken by meta-fictional parody, and to point to its role both in transforming literary history, and in attacking the epistemological presuppositions and expectations of the readers of certain ages for specific texts, for specific theories of the text, and for a specific relationship between author, reader, and the institutions controlling both. The 'crisis of representation' discussed through parody in the works of modern authors such as Borges and Canetti (and many others not mentioned), has extended the critique of the relationship between fiction and world made in parodies such as *Don Quixote*. In evoking the expectations of an audience for the imitation of a certain work only to 'disappoint' or shock the reader with another text, parody has also enabled the author to attack reader expectations for imitative or representational works. And through such parody, criticism of representational art has hence often been related to the social historical context of the reader's world.

The self-critical reflexivity with which modern parodists have also submitted their meta-fiction to analysis has not only made meta-fictional parody characteristic of the modernist episteme, but has contributed to the identity given this episteme by Formalists and Structuralists who have based theories of the text on examples of parody. So parody, once considered anti-normative, and hence also anti-generic, now represents the discontinuity characteristic of modernism and a 'poetics of contradiction' which must ironically, also resist its own canonisation as normative.

Though once excluded from the forms of literature privileged in poetics and literary history, parody has, ironically perhaps, through theories such as those offered by the Russian Formalists, come itself to control norms of literary criticism, and to canonise concepts such as intertextuality and discontinuity as characteristic of modern fiction. Here parody has served not only to depict norms of previous poetics (such as mimesis) as inverted, but to turn these older poetics upside down, to stand them, in the parodist's view, on their feet. Here another irony in the history of defining parody — the denigration of parody as plagiarism or as 'mere imitation' of other works — is made

185

clear with the emergence of parody as a critique of mimesis, and of the assumption, that identity with its object is an aim, and possibility, of artistic representation.

Parody has been used to criticise both naive belief in the 'reality' of fiction (as in Cervantes' *Don Quixote*) and the privileging of artistic illusion made in Aristotelian Poetics (as, for example, criticised in Brecht's theory of epic theatre).[1] But parody has also used both mimesis and the illusion of realism to dialectically establish its own 'Poetics of Contradiction', a poetics built on the supersession of imitation in art and fiction by means of which the illusion of reality given in fiction is used to analyse the peculiarities of the fictional world itself. This self-consciousness in parody has also been used to criticise the unreflexive use of illusion in propaganda as well as in fiction proper, to offer new insights into the communication of discourse, or to create new texts from old.

In such parody the anthropological function attributed to art is grounded less in the 'Aristotelian' belief that imitation of the human world could (as in the cathartic moment in tragedy) create a liberating effect in the audience identifying with it (criticised by Brecht), than in the thesis (Freud, Bachtin), that the supersession of imitation in parody could liberate censored or sublimated beliefs in its audience through criticism and laughter. Kant's attribution of a creative liberating effect to parody in correcting prejudices created by illusionistic realistic literature, or the self-reflexive use of parody in *Tristram Shandy*, are symptomatic of an earlier criticism of illusionism in art which parodies such as *Don Quixote* had offered. But the criticism of illusionistic art in modern meta-fictional parody also represents the development of a poetics of contradiction in which identity between the sign, its object, and meaning is put into doubt, and the meta-language used in parody to criticise other works itself shown to be unable to describe its own activity.

From being regarded as a mirror to other texts, as, for example, in definitions of the Ancient form of the para-ode as a song sung in imitation of the Homeric rhapsodes, or as a chorus commenting on other choruses in the drama, or from its definition as 'simulatio' in Rhetorics, parody has progressed (by its own ability to transform dialectically the tradition from which it itself comes) to become a way to an 'archaeology of the text' to a self-reflexive mirror to discourse, to a critique of itself, and so, too, to an analysis (ironically made from within fiction itself) of concepts of reflection and representation restricting parody (and literature as such), to the role of reflecting an external world of objects. But in progressing further than the Cervantic criticism of the Romance as deceptive reflection of the object-world, in also submitting itself to criticism, modern meta-fictional parody has presented itself as a method of discourse which both limits the parodist further to the text which he would criticise and free himself from, and which enables him to dialectically transform the history of discourse through the same internalisation of the target of his criticism which binds him to it. The ironic consciousness of the ambiguity of parody as a method of liberation is also expressed in parodies of the dialectic itself in works such as Canetti's *Die Blendung*, or in theoretical critiques of the inadequacies of dialectical method in works such as Adorno's 'Negative Aesthetics'.

Both in its role as a means to the dialectical refunctioning of tradition, and reduced to the agonistic word-games of absurdist fiction, modern parody has served to criticise naive concepts of mimesis in art and fiction. In a broad historical sense, then, parody has played a part in breaking the hold of pre-established theories in the literary canon, and preformed expectations within the reading public implied by the canonisation of those theories and their representative works. The different forms taken by specific parodies have also to be related to the nature of their target — not least because that target itself became integrated in the parody text.

The theories of the Formalists of the 1920s, who saw parody as a basic transforming device in the history of literature, were symptomatic not only of the rejection of a naive, static view of art as the reflection of the world of objects for a dialectical view of parody, but the consciousness of the time of itself as a period of revolutionary upheaval. Here, too, the function of parody in 'showing how' the work of fiction was made, reflected an emphasis on the importance of critical self-reflexion in art as well as a new 'mechanistic age', concerned with the structure of meaning.

Seen in its role as a meta-fictional critique of the production and reception of literary texts, parody raises questions not only of a theoretical literary nature about the processes involved in the writing of fiction but, in focusing too on the role of the reader in the reception of the text, or on the role of authority in the control of both its production and reception, raises questions of a sociological nature which relate the text again to its social context. Some of these questions have been outlined here in an attempt to illustrate the many complex epistemological, heuristic, poetic, political, and social functions parody has had in literary history, to indicate its role as both a critically distorting and self-reflecting mirror to the writing and reception of literary texts, and a means to the supersession of imitation and the concept of representation in discourses of the modern episteme, but also to point to its new role in theory as a difficult self-critical 'norm' of discontinuity. Hence the ancient concept of parody — as a song both beside and opposite its model or target — now also serves to explain the ambiguous relationship of parody (as a form of self-critical meta-criticism) to its own discourse, and its ambivalent functions as both a critique of other fictions and as the means to the development of the fictional world from within which its own meta-fictional critiques are made.

Notes

1. Rainer Warning has investigated the attack made on the Aristotelian legitimation of illusion in fiction given in Sterne's *Tristram Shandy* and Diderot's *Jacques le Fataliste* in *Illusion und Wirklichkeit in Tristram Shandy und Jacques le Fataliste* (München, 1965).

BIBLIOGRAPHY OF WORKS ON PARODY

Bachtin, Michail, *Literatur und Karneval: Zur Romantheorie und Lachkultur* (München, 1969).

Becker, Erik, 'Parodie und Plagiat', in *Plagiat*, Schriftenreihe der Internationalen Gesellschaft für Urheberrecht, vol. 14, 1959.

Beckett and others, *Our Exagmination Round his Factification for Incamination of Work in Progress* (1929) (London, 1972).

The Bodley Head Beerbohm, David Cecil (ed.), (London, 1970).

Bond, Richmond P., *English Burlesque Poetry, 1700–1750* (Cambridge, Mass., 1932).

Booth, Wayne C., *A Rhetoric of Irony* (Chicago, 1974).

Borges, Luis, *Labyrinths*, D.A. Yates and J.E. Irby (eds.), (Harmondsworth, 1976).

Bramble, J.C., *Persius and the Programmatic Satire* (Cambridge, 1974).

Buchheit, V., 'Homerparodie und Literaturkritik in Horazens Satiren 17 und 19', *Gymnasium*, 75 (1968), pp. 519–55.

Cèbe, J-P., *La caricature et la parodie dans le monde romain antique des origines à Juvénal* (Paris, 1966).

Clinton-Baddeley, V.C., *The Burlesque Tradition in the English Theatre After 1660* (London, 1952).

Coffey, Michael, *Roman Satire* (London, 1976).

Courtney, E., 'Parody and Literary Allusion in Menippean Satire', *Philologue* 106 (1962), pp. 86–100.

Davidson, Israel, *Parody in Jewish Literature* (Colombia, 1907).

Davis, J.L., 'Criticism and Parody', in *Thought*, 26 (1951), pp. 180–204.

Delepierre, O., *La parodie chez les Grecs, chez les Romains et chez les Modernes* (London, 1870).

Donaldson, Ian, *The World Upside Down: Comedy from Jonson to Fielding* (Oxford, 1970).

Dover, K.J., *Aristophanic Comedy* (Berkeley and Los Angeles, 1972).

Feinberg, L., *Introduction to Satire* (Iowa, 1967).

Felsteiner, J., *The Lies of Art. Max Beerbohm's Parody and Caricature* (New York, 1972).

Foucault, Michel, *Les Mots et les Choses* (Paris, 1966).

Freud, Sigmund, *Der Witz und seine Beziehung zum Unbewussten*, in *Gesammelte Werke*, vol. 9 (Leipzig, 1928).

Frye, Dean, 'The Question of Shakespearean Parody, in *Essays in*

190 Bibliography of Works on Parody

Criticism, 15 (1965), pp. 22–6.

Gabler, Hans Walter, *Zur Funktion Dramatischer und Literarischer Parodie im elisabethanischen Drama* (München, 1965).

Gilman, Sander L., *The Parodic Sermon in European Perspective* (Wiesbaden, 1974).

—— *Nietzschean Parody: An Introduction into reading Nietzsche* (Bonn, 1976).

Goethe, Joh. Wolfgang von, 'Über die Parodie bei den Alten' (1824), in *Goethes sämmtliche Werke: Jubiläums–Ausgabe* (40 vols., Stuttgart and Berlin, 1902–7), vol. 27, pp. 290–3.

Gottsched, Joh. Chr., *Versuch einer critischen Dichtkunst* (1742), (Darmstadt, 1962).

Grannis, V.B., *Dramatic Parody in Eighteenth Century France* (New York, 1931).

Grellman, H., 'Parodie', in *Reallexikon der deutschen Literaturgeschichte*, vol. 2 (Berlin, 1928), pp. 630–53.

Guglielmino, F., *La parodia nella comedia greca antica* (Catania, 1928).

Hanslik, R., 'Parodie', in *Lexikon der alten Welt* (Zürich und Stuttgart, 1965), pp. 2224–6.

Hefti, Ernst, *Die Parodie im Urheberrecht* (Berlin, 1977).

Hempel, Wido, 'Parodie, Travestie und Pastiche', in *Germanische-Romanische Monatsschrift*, 15 (1965), pp. 150ff.

Highet, Gilbert, *The Anatomy of Satire* (Princeton, 1962).

Holden, William P., *Anti-Puritan Satire 1572–1642* (Yale, 1954).

Hope, E.W., 'The Language of Parody. A study in the diction of Aristophanes', dissertation (Baltimore, 1906).

Horn, W., *Gebet und Gebetsparodie in den Komödien des Aristophanes* (Nuremburg, 1970).

Householder, Fred W. Jr., 'Parodia', in *Journal of Classical Philology*, 39 (1944), pp. 1–9.

Iser, Wolfgang, *Der implizierte Leser* (München, 1972).

—— *Der Akt des Lesens* (München, 1977).

Jack, Ian, *Augustan Satire* (Oxford, 1952).

Jacobs, Henry E. and Johnson, Claudia D., *An Annotated Bibliography of Shakespearean Burlesque, Parody and Travesty* (New York, 1975).

Joyce, James, *Ulysses* (London, 1947).

Jump, John D., *Burlesque* (London, 1972).

Karrer, Wolfgang, *Parodie, Travestie, Pastiche* (München, 1977).

Kierkegaard, Søren, *Über den Begriff der Ironie* (Düsseldorf/Köln, 1961).

Kiremidjian, G.D., 'The Aesthetics of Parody', in *Journal of Aesthetics and Art Criticism*, 28 (1969), pp. 231–42.

Kitchin, George, *A Survey of Burlesque and Parody in English* (1931), (New York, 1967).

Koller, Hermann, 'Die Parodie', *Glotta*, 35 (1956), pp. 17–32.

Knoche, Ulrich, *Roman Satire* (1949), transl. E.S. Ramage (Indiana, 1976).

Kormornicka, R., 'Quelques remarques sur la parodie dans les comedies d'Aristophane', in *Quaderni Urbinati di cultura classica*, 3 (1967), pp. 51–74.

Kranz, W., 'Paratragödie', in *Realencyclopädie der classischen Altertumswissenschaft*, 18, 4 (1949), pp. 1410–12.

Kreissmann, B., *Pamela-Shamela*. A study of the criticisms, burlesques, parodies and adaptations of Richardson's 'Pamela', University of Nebraska, 1960 (University of Nebraska Studies, N.S.22).

Kuhn, Hans, 'Was parodiert die Parodie?', in *Neue Rundschau*, 85, 4 (1974), pp. 600ff.

Kurak, A., 'Imitation, Burlesque Poetry and Parody. A study of some Augustan critical distinctions', DISS. (Minneapolis, 1963).

Lausberg, *Handbuch der literarischen Rhetorik*, vol. 1 (München, 1960), p. 929

Lee, G., *Allusion, Parody and Imitation* (Hull, 1971).

Lehmann, Paul, *Die Parodie im Mittelalter*, 2nd edn. (Stuttgart, 1963).

Lelièvre, F.J., 'The Basis of Ancient Parody', in *Greece and Rome*, Ser. 2, I (1954), pp. 66–81.

—— 'Parody in Juvenal and T.S. Elliot', in *Classical Philology*, 53 (1958), pp. 22–5.

Liede, Alfred, 'Parodie', in *Reallexikon der deutschen literaturgeschichte*, vol. 3 (Berlin, 1966).

Lotman, Jurij M., *Probleme der Kinoästhetik, Einführung in die Semiotik des Films* (Frankfurt am Main, 1977).

Lowrey, Burling, *Parody* (New York, 1960).

MacDonald, Dwight (ed.), *Parodies, An Anthology from Chaucer to Beerbohm and After* (London, 1960).

Markiewicz, Henryk, 'On the definitions of Literary Parody', in *To Honor Roman Jakobson* (The Hague, 1966), pp. 1264–72.

Marks, A.W., 'The Parody of liturgical and Biblical texts in Germany in the sixteenth and seventeenth centuries', dissertation (Cambridge, 1969).

Martin, Arthur Shadwell, *On Parody* (New York, 1896).

Mercier, Vivien, *The Irish Comic Tradition* (Oxford, 1969).

Meyer, Herman, *Das Zitat in der Erzählkunst* (Stuttgart, 1961).

Milly, Jean, *Les Pastiches de Proust, edition critique et commentée* (Paris, 1970).

Mitsdörffer, W., 'Die Parodie euripideischer Szenen bei Aristophanes', thesis (Berlin, 1943).

Muecke, Douglas, C., *The Compass of Irony* (London, 1969).

Murray, A.T., *On Parody and Paratragoedia in Aristophanes* (Berlin, 1891).

Neumann, Robert, 'Zur Ästhetik der Parodie', in *Die Parodien* (München, 1962), pp. 551–63.

Neuschäfer, Hans-Jörg, *Der Sinn der Parodie im Don Quijote* (Heidelberg, 1963).

Novak, M.E., 'Defoe's Shortest Way with the Dissenters: Hoax, Parody, Paradox, Fiction, Irony and Satire', in *Modern Language Quarterly*, 27 (1966), pp. 402–17.

Olwa, C., 'La parodie e la critica letteraria nella commedia post-aristofanea', in *Dioniso*, 42 (1968), pp. 25–92.

Pöhlmann, Egert, 'Parodia', in *Glotta*, 50 (1972), pp. 144–56.

Pollard, Arthur, *Satire* (London, 1970).

Poirier, 'The Politics of Self-Parody', in *Partisan Review*, 35 (1968), pp. 339–53.

Preisendanz, Wolfgang, *Über den Witz* (Konstanz, 1970).

Preisendanz, W. and Warning, R. (eds.), *Das Komische* (München, 1976).

Preminger, A.S., 'Parody', in *Encyclopaedia of Poetry and Poetics* (Princeton, 1965).

Pryor, A.D., 'Juvenal's false consolation', *AUMLA*, 18 (November, 1962), pp. 167–80.

Quintilian, *Institutio Oratoria*, transl. H.E. Butler (Harvard, 1960).

Rau, Peter, *Paratragödia. Untersuchungen einer komischen Form des Aristophanes* (München, 1967).

Renwick, W.L., *Introduction to W.E. Aytoun's Stories and Verse* (Edinburgh, 1964).

Riewald, J.G., 'Parody as Criticism', *Neophilologus*, 50 (1966), pp. 125–48.

Riha, Karl, *Cross-Reading and Cross-Talking* (Stuttgart, 1971).

Roberts, David, *Kopf und Welt* (München, 1975).

Röhrich, Lutz, *Gebärde-Metaphor-Parodie* (Düsseldorf, 1967).

Rose, Margaret, *Die Parodie. Eine Funktion der biblischen Sprache in Heines Lyrik* (Meisenheim/Glan, 1976).

—— *Reading the Young Marx and Engels. Poetry, Parody and the Censor* (London, 1978).

Ross, D.O., Jr. 'The "Celux" and "Moretum" as Post-Augustan Literary

Parodies', in *Harvard Studies in Classical Philology*, 79 (1975),
pp. 235–63.
Rotermund, Erwin, *Die Parodie in der modernen deutschen Lyrik*
(München, 1963).
—— *Gegengesänge* (München, 1964).
Saint-Denis, E. de, 'La parodie dans la littérature latine de Plaute à
Sénèque, in *L'information littéraire*, 17 (1965), pp. 64–75.
Schiassi, G., 'Parodia e travestimentio mitico nella commedia attica
di mezzo', in *Rendiconti del Instituto Lombardo*, 88 (1955),
pp. 99–120.
Schiffer, E., 'Parody in the Late Work of Thomas Mann', Diss. (Masch.)
(Cambridge, Mass., 1962).
Schlesinger, A.C., 'Indications of Parody in Aristophanes', in
Transactions of the American Philological Association, 67 (1936),
pp. 296–314.
—— 'Identification of Parodies in Aristophanes', in *American Journal
of Philology*, 58 (1937), pp. 294–305.
Schröter, R., 'Horazens Satire I, 7 und die antike Eposparodie', in
Poetica, I (1967), pp. 8–23.
Sedgwick, W.B., 'Parody in Plautus', in *Classical Quarterly*, 21 (1927),
pp. 88–9.
Sera, Manfred, *Utopie und Parodie bei Musil, Broch und Th. Mann*,
(Bonn, 1969).
Shepperson, A.B., *The Novel in Motley* (1936), (New York, 1967).
Shlonsky, Tuvia, 'Literary parody: Remarks on its Method and
Function', in *Proceedings of the 4th Congress of the International
Comparative Association*, F. Jost (ed.), 2 vols. (The Hague, 1966),
2, pp. 797–801.
Smith, Dane Farnsworth, *Plays About the Theatre From 'The Rehearsal'
in 1671 to the Licensing Act in 1737; or, the Self-Conscious Stage
and its Burlesque and Satirical Reflections in the Age of Criticism*
(Oxford, 1936).
Smuda, Manfred, *Becketts Prosa als Metasprache* (München, 1970).
Strohschneider-Kohrs, Ingrid, *Romantische Ironie in Theorie und
Gestaltung* (Tübingen, 1960).
Sühnel, Rudolf, 'Satire, Parodie', in *Literatur (Das Fischer Lexicon)*
W.H. Friedrich and W. Killy (eds.), (Frankfurt am Main, 1965).
Swearingen, James E., *Reflexivity in 'Tristram Shandy', An Essay in
Phenomenological Criticism* (Yale, 1977).
Tynjanov, Jurij, 'Dostoevskij und Gogol: Zur Theorie der Parodie', in
Russischer Formalismus, Jurij Striedter (ed.) (München, 1971).

194   *Bibliography of Works on Parody*

van de Sande Bakhuyzen, W.H., *De parodia in comoediis Aristophanis* (Utrecht, 1877).

Verweyen, Theodor, *Theorie der Parodie. Am Beispiel Peter Rühmkorfs* (München, 1973).

Verweyen, Theodor and Gunther Witting, *Die Parodie in der neueren deutschen Literatur. Eine systematische Einführung* (Darmstadt, 1978).

Warning, Rainer, *Illusion und Wirklichkeit in Tristram Shandy und Jacques le Fataliste* (München, 1965).

Weinbrot, H.D., 'Parody as Imitation in the eighteenth century', in *American Notes and Queries*, 2 (1964), pp. 133–4.

—— 'Translation and Parody: Towards a Genealogy of the Augustan Imitation', in *English Literary History*, 33 (1966), pp. 434–45.

Weisstein, Ulrich, 'Parody, Travesty and Burlesque: Imitation with a Vengeance', in *Proceedings of the 4th Congress of the International Comparative Literature Association*, F. Jost (ed.), 2 vols. (The Hague, 1966), pp. 902–11.

Whitman, Cedric H., *Aristophanes and the Comic Hero* (Mass., 1964).

Wild, F., *Die Batrachomyomachia in England*, thesis (Vienna, 1918).

Worcester, David, *The Art of Satire* (1940), (New York, 1969).

INDEX

Abrams, M.H. 66
Addison, Joseph, 39
Adorno, Theodor W. 103, 145,
    149ff., 155ff., 187
Aeschylus 19¹
Aesopian language 117, 169, 174,
    177
Albertsen, L. 43, 54 n.11
alienation 100, 103, 130, 165
archaeology of texts 13, 14, 77, 83,
    94, 127, 128, 129f., 135ff., 151,
    154, 159ff., 166, 167, 177, 186
Aristophanes 17, 18–19, 20, 24, 33,
    35
Aristotle 18, 19, 35 n.2, 186
Athenäus 18
Attic comedy 19
Aytoun, W.E. 49, 55 n.18

Bachtin, Michail 32, 101, 149,
    167ff., 186
Barthes, Roland 62, 105 n.5, 179
Beckett, Samuel 62ff., 90, 127, 129,
    130, 131, 135, 144, 153, 165
Beerbohm, Max 77ff.
Bernhard, Thomas 155
blasphemy 30f., 32, 169
Bloom, Harold 104
Blumauer, Aloys 75
Bodi, Leslie 172
Booth, Wayne C. 88ff., 106 n.25
Borges, Luis 34, 37 n.31, 65, 68,
    98ff., 115, 129, 130f., 133,
    135, 154, 155, 172, 185
Brecht, Bertolt 36 n.12, 186
Burlesque 17, 18, 39–41, 47, 180

Canetti, Elias 80, 99f., 164, 185,
    187
carnival 31, 167f., 178f.
censorship 13, 22, 31f., 33, 54 n.6,
    59, 108, 110, 116f., 129, 134,
    167ff.
cento 18, 45
Cervantes, Miguel de 13, 17, 21, 29,
    34, 35, 52, 59, 62, 65, 67ff.,
    86ff., 98, 99, 115, 120f., 126,
    128, 130ff., 155

Chaucer 97f.
comic effect 19, 20, 23, 35, 41, 59,
    69, 95
Condillac, Etienne 124
copyright 32, 59, 151, 180ff.
counter-argument 169ff.
counterfeit 21, 43
counter-Reformation 170f.
Cretan liar paradox 86ff., 130, 133,
    163
cross-reading 49f., 123, 140, 160

Dällenbach, Lucien 105 n.8
deconstruction 30, 44, 102, 104f.,
    124, 127, 140, 146, 165, 166,
    167
Derrida, Jacques 102, 124–8, 129
discontinuity 13, 14, 101, 128ff.,
    153f., 165, 185, 188
Donaldson, Ian 54 n.4
Dryden, John 18
Duchamp, Marcel 63, 84

Eagleton, Terry 102, 106 n.35
Engels, Friedrich 48f., 55 n.17
Erasmus 53
Euripides 18, 19, 33

fiction: definition of 113
Fielding, Henry 23, 40, 54 n.6, 69,
    75, 105 n.14, 135
Fish, Stanley E. 183 n.2
Formalists 13, 14, 45, 50, 59, 101,
    128, 130, 149, 153f., 164f., 185,
    187
Foucault, Michel 13, 57, 59, 87,
    128–57, 164, 165; works:
    Archaeology of Knowledge 128f.,
    134, 155; conversation with M.
    Fontana 129; conversation with
    Paolo Caruso 129; *Les Mots et
    les Choses* 13, 57, 90, 128ff.;
    'Nietzsche, Genealogy, and
    History' 135f.; 'The Order of
    Discourse' 172
Frege, G. 112
Freud, Sigmund 31f., 93f., 163, 168,
    186

195